Beliefs

ART BRUT
The collection

Beliefs

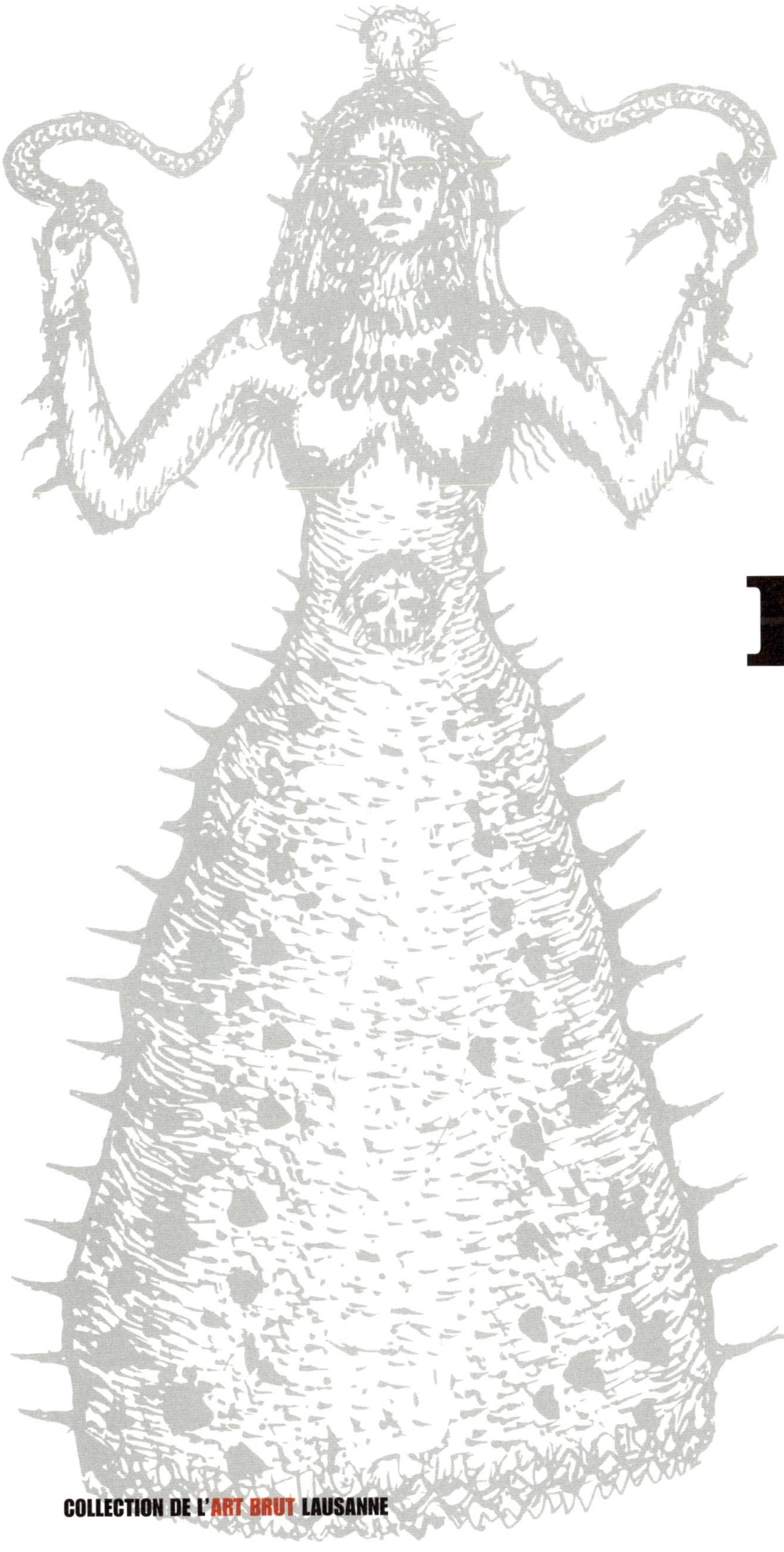

COLLECTION DE L'ART BRUT LAUSANNE

CONTINENTS

Contents

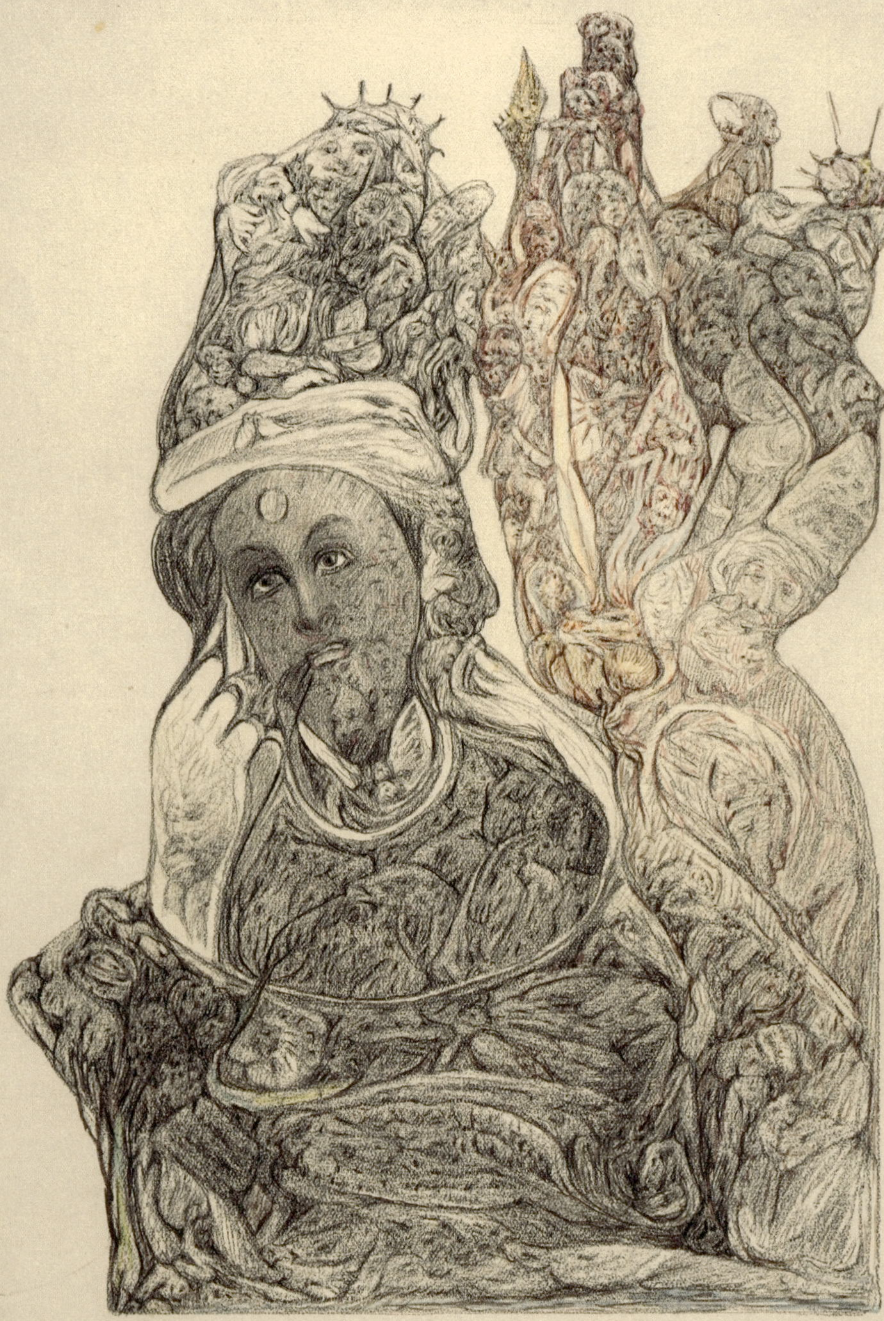

JIDÁŠ ISKARIOTSKÝ

Sedlák
31/XII 24.

Preface

F. Sedlak
Judas Iskariote, 1924
pencil on paper
32 x 22 cm
ni-3997

Centred on the theme of beliefs, this fifth Art Brut biennial draws together a selection of artists whose works, all from our collection, are associated with this topic. Although the term 'belief' is often confined to the sphere of religion, it is used here in a much broader sense. While there are plenty of references to religion, the beliefs in question are often of a personal nature and involve highly idiosyncratic private mythologies.

This theme entails setting aside all judgmental attitudes and accepting forms of belief that lie outside what might be considered 'normal'. These beliefs enable, or have enabled, the artists represented in the exhibition to find meaning in their life and face the difficulties or tragedies that have left their mark on them, such as sickness, confinement, the loss of a loved one, a sudden change in surroundings, social isolation, and destitution.

Whatever the nature of these beliefs, they are all legitimate, because they exist in the eyes of those who created them. Besides, they fulfil an essential function: they enable human beings to transcend their limitations and to exist beyond the physical constraints of their body. For, in the 'Cartesian' Western world, where materialism and capitalism reign unchecked, believing in a spirit, a god, or the power of a lucky charm appears to be necessary for some of us. Organised by Anic Zanzi, curator at the Art Brut Collection, the exhibition therefore presents a multitude of beliefs expressed in a number of works. These are divided into three categories: those that concern religious beliefs, those associated with spiritualism, and those involving private mythologies.

A room on the ground floor is dedicated to artists whose works — sculptures, drawings, paintings, and bas-reliefs — refer to various religions, such as the small drawings by Simone Marye, depicting both Buddha and the Christian God; the paintings of Giovanni Battista Podestà, in which Good confronts Evil according to the precepts of Roman Catholicism; or the Baroque headwear of Palmerino Sorgente, who considers himself to be the 'Pope of popes' and portrays himself as Christ on the cross. This category also includes paintings of saints and Jesus, as well illustrations of episodes from the Bible relating to the Evangelists or Christ's childhood, as in Theo's coloured-pencil or felt-tip pen drawings. The Virgin Mary is also represented in this section, especially in the extraordinary series of 'Virgins – Mother-Goddesses' by Philippe Ducollet-Michaëlef, whose works were acquired for the collection in 2020 and are being exhibited here for the first time. Although these religious themes of course recur throughout the history of art, what makes these Art Brut artists so astonishing and captivating is the way they approach these subjects from their own distinctive angle, providing a totally unique reinterpretation. Charles

Boussion thus draws numerous versions of the Virgin and Child in which the traits are those of his wife or daughter, while Jill Galliéni devotes all her work to St Rita, to whom she prays by adding little writing-like scrawls whose true meaning remains secret.

The exhibition also devotes a room to the work of artists who share their lives with a host of spirits, which they proceed to draw: the approach taken by Ataa Oko, from Ghana; Guyodo, who lives in Haiti; and Noviadi Angkasapura, who lives in Indonesia. Others claim their hands are actually guided by spirits with whom they are in constant close contact. These are all commonly gathered together under the label 'spiritualists'. This category encompasses the paintings of Augustin Lesage, Victor Simon, and Fleury-Joseph Crépin, as well as the drawings of Fernand Desmoulin, Raphaël Lonné, Laure Pigeon, Jane Ruffié, F. Sedlak, Jeanne Tripier, and Henriette Zéphir — all works that are in truth very different but share the feature of having been produced under the influence of spirits. However, it should be said that these self-taught artists often resort to this explanation out of modesty, or the fear of being seen as charlatans.

The last section groups together artists who developed their own mythology, such as Adolf Wölfli, Marc Moret, August Walla, Michel Nedjar, and Antonio Dalla Valle, whose works have a cosmogonic or mystical dimension that protects and transcends them. The anthropologist and ethnologist Emmanuel Grimaud develops this theme in particular in his essay, in which he explains how the very concept of belief is too narrow to encompass all the artistic practices concerned, imbued as they are with invisible forces that draw the artists out of themselves.

So, let us cut ourselves free of preconceptions and be carried into the worlds of these magical, ethereal works.

Sarah Lombardi
DIRECTOR OF THE COLLECTION DE L'ART BRUT, LAUSANNE

Minnie Evans
untitled, 1943
graphite and coloured pencil on paper
20.5 x 14 cm
cab-3495

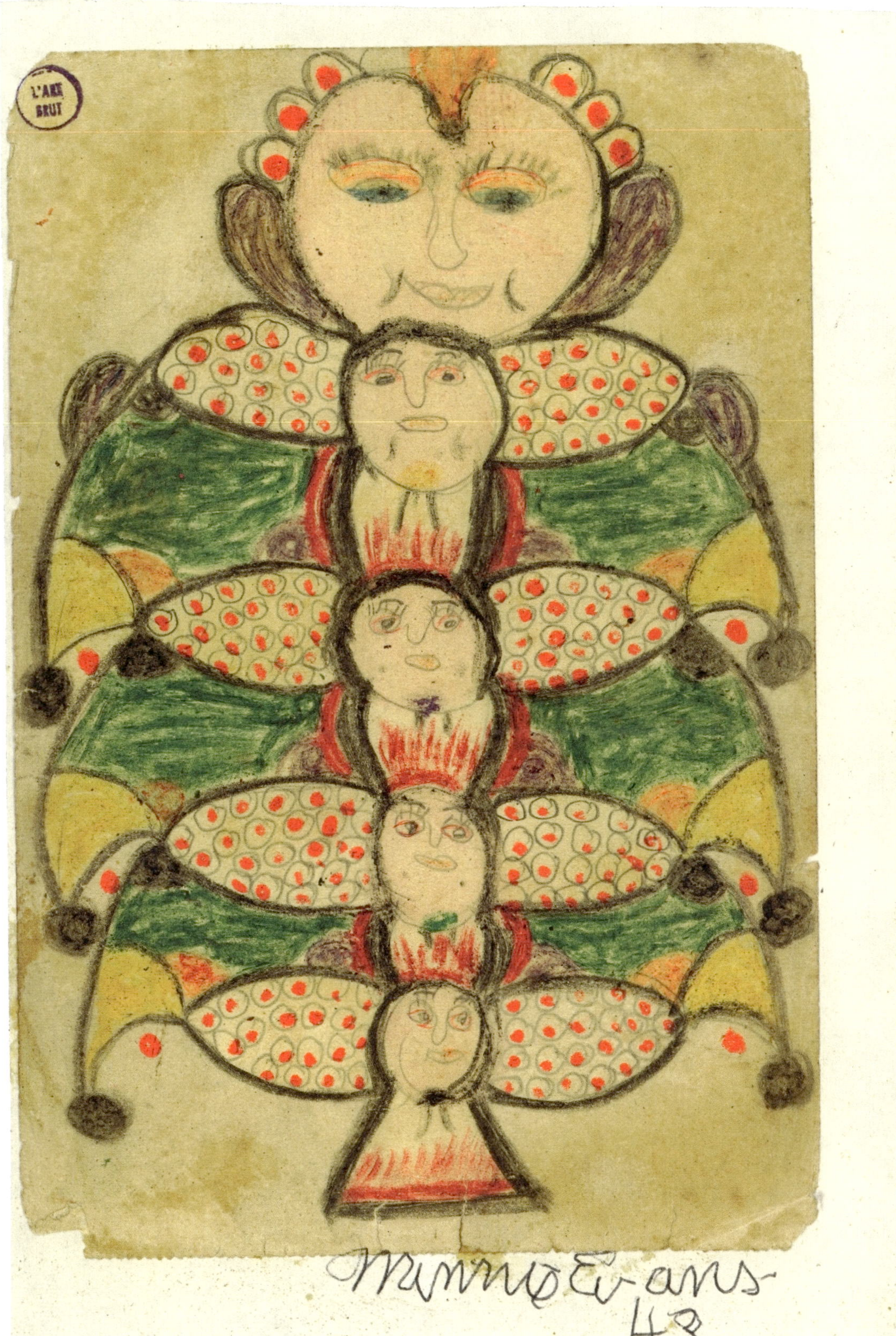
L'ART BRUT
Minnie Evans
43

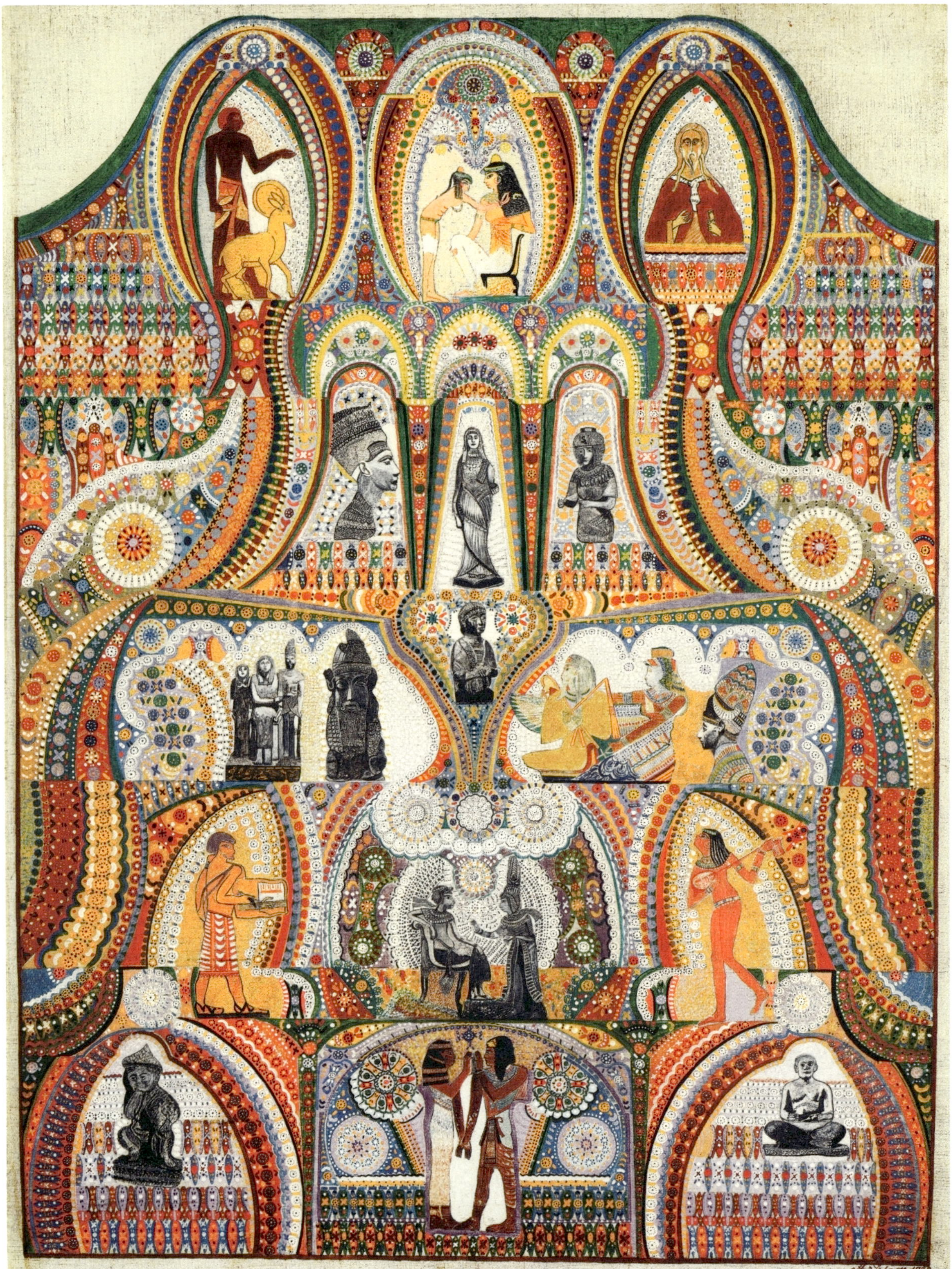
A. Lesage 1938

Connecting with the World

Augustin Lesage
untitled, 1938
oil on canvas
133 x 104 cm
cab-8563

The works gathered for the first three Art Brut biennials — *Vehicles, Architectures*, and *Bodies* — enjoyed what seemed to be a clearly shared iconography and straightforward connection with their respective themes. Selecting the works for this fifth edition, dedicated to *Beliefs*, following on from the previous edition, *Theatres*, has proved more complex. For what is the best way to approach the concept of belief in the field of Art Brut? It can be defined as a not entirely rational faith in a thesis or hypothesis, especially as regards religion, philosophy, and politics. Rejecting all doubt, the certainty it professes is often partly based on a personal, intimate conviction. On the strength of this definition, one wonders which Art Brut artists would not be included in the exhibition, for few have failed to ponder their relationship with the world, seek answers to the basic problems of life, or reflect on the origin of the universe or the meaning of life. Do these matters not lie at the very heart of the process of artistic creation? Are not art and the sacred, art and spirituality, intrinsically linked? As Michel Thévoz points out, up until the Middle Ages 'art did not exist as a specific activity; it was inseparable from magic, mythology, religion, therapy, and everyday pursuits'.[1] And today, 'even assuming the image has been totally desacralised, shouldn't we also admit that this liberation brings with it a loss? Detaching figurative creation from its original magical, ritual, religious, moral, and therapeutic functions also means cutting it off from the wellsprings of its inspiration and dissociating it from the community and social activities in general'.[2] In Art Brut, these functions are incontrovertible and apply in the first instance to the artists themselves. The works cannot be divorced from their creators; they originate in the intrinsic nature of the artists, in their experiences, in their very existence. They are inevitably, in one way or another, transcendent, imbued with a certain spirituality and nourished by beliefs. It isn't in their metaphysical musings that these artists differ so much as in the unique means they invent to come to terms with them; the procedures they adopt to subdue the unknown is what distinguishes them. Seeking explanations regarding the very foundations of existence, life, and death — or, even more 'humbly', their own personal fate — these Art Brut artists, for the most part at loggerheads with society, dropouts and misfits, cannot in principle find any answers in conventional dogmas and standard touchstones, or if they do, they make them their own and reinterpret them. In most cases, they conceive and develop completely personal beliefs. They invent weird theories and build original systems of thought that enable them to step outside what are for the most part gruelling lives.

[1] Michel Thévoz, 'L'archaïsme contestataire', in *Podestà*, Lausanne, Collection de l'Art Brut, Lausanne, 2003.
[2] Ibid.

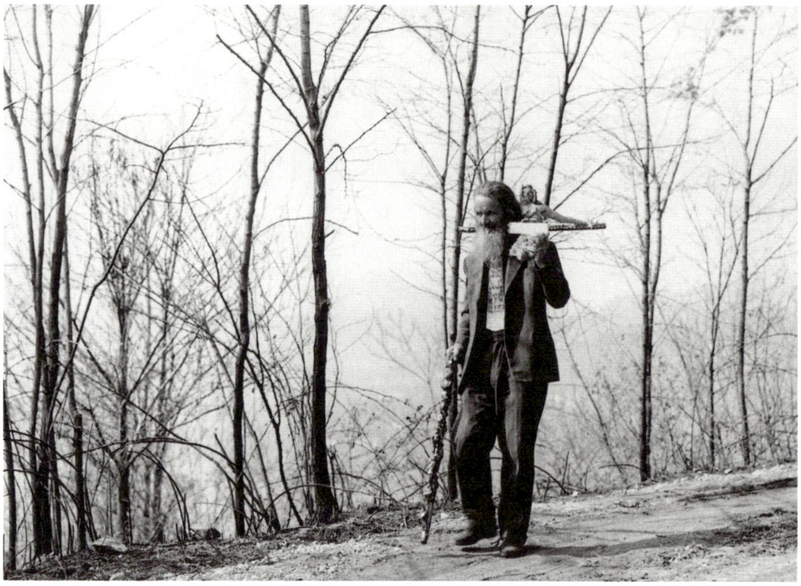

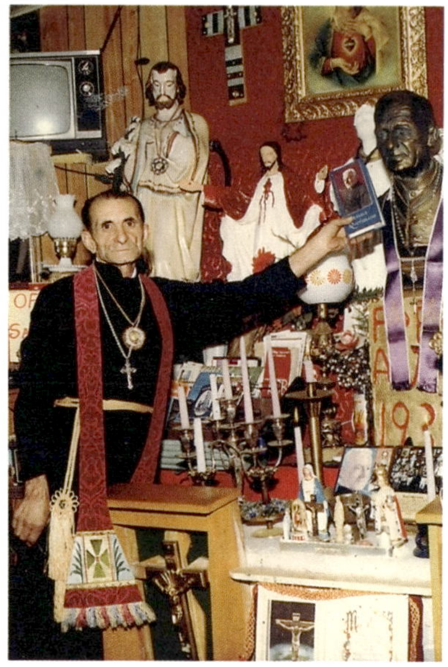

As a matter of principle, all the works chosen for the biennials come from the Art Brut Collection in Lausanne, which by 2021 included seventy thousand works by one thousand artists. In view of this wealth of material, bordering on exhaustiveness, it was necessary to proceed by a process of elimination. It therefore seems only fair to be explicit about the options taken and the approaches followed, bearing in mind that subjective preference is an inevitable part of choice. A total of around three hundred drawings, paintings, assemblages, sculptures, writings, and embroideries by forty-three artists offer a representative selection of the broad range of possible works. The exhibition is designed to suggest associations, inviting the worlds of the various artists to play off each other, even though their inner lives are totally unique. The three main categories group the works into those that have clear links to religion, those featuring spirits, and a large number that express personal mythologies.

Giovanni Battista Podestà carrying the cross he made, April 1968

Palmerino Sorgente in his shop in rue Notre-Dame in Montreal, c. 1980, Quebec (Canada)

Palmerino Sorgente on a leg of his Way of the Cross, c. 1980, Quebec (Canada)

Giovanni Battista Podestà
La Croix, n.d.
mixed media
210 x 70 cm

Religious references and rituals

'It's not me who's the boss, it's him, Christ; he's yours, he's everything's.'
Palmerino Sorgente

While a number of Art Brut artists live on the margins of society, they are nonetheless profoundly influenced by religion, since it plays an important part in their education and in their everyday lives, as well as pervading their imaginations. Most come from countries with deeply entrenched Judaeo-Christian principles, where social life is organised according to shared values that rest on religious foundations, among others.

From the many works with a religious content or that are linked to rituals, we have chosen to present those of Elijah, Palmerino Sorgente, Giovanni Battista Podestà, and Philippe Ducollet-Michaëlef.

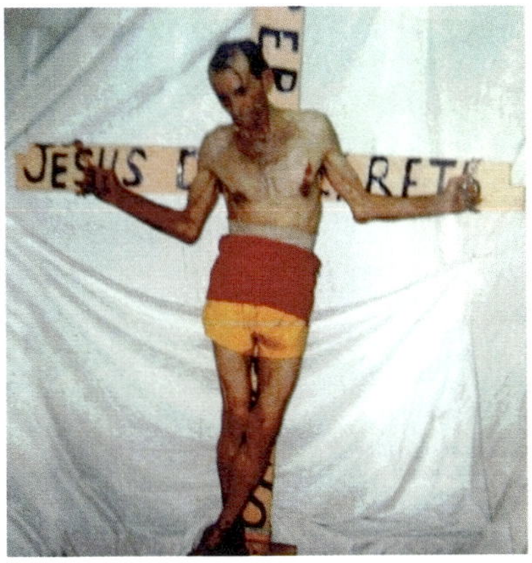

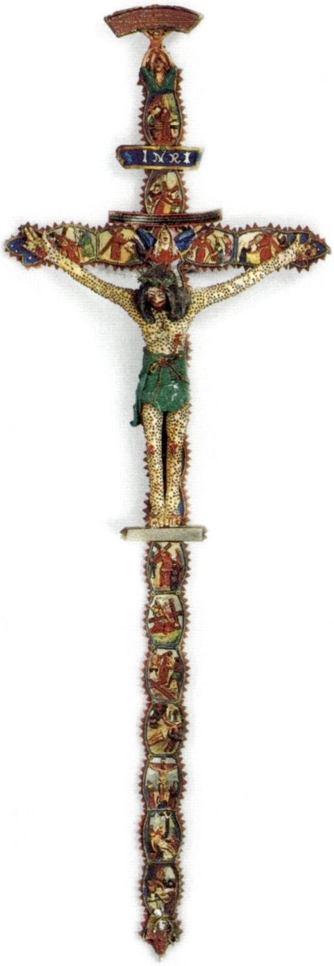

The work of Elijah,[3] who has used this name since she was ordained a priest, is intimately connected to her religious observance. She claims she was saved by divine intervention when she fell seriously ill, and although she was brought up in a Christian family, she only acknowledged Christ when he appeared before her and she was 'reborn'. This event led her to devote herself entirely to her new vocation, building her own chapel where she could worship every Sunday and look after the sick. This Jamaican woman says her art is inspired by God. It is this inspiration that prompts her to cover the walls of her house with angels, saints, and prophets, and to fill her paintings with Biblical themes, the pictures then assuming a protective function. While the subjects are religious, they are mingled with symbols that belong to other beliefs common in Jamaica, something revealed in her fondness for green, yellow (gold), and red — colours typical of the Rastafari movement — which in her painting *The Crusifyxsion of Jesus Christ*, for example (see pp. 66–67), are used in the stripes on the loincloths of the crucified figures and on their crosses. Elijah incorporates rituals belonging to African animism by adding little altars within her consecrated space, on which she places offerings. Just like the other Art Brut artists, she turns her work into an opportunity to blend different religions and eschews any kind of fundamentalism.

Palmerino Sorgente and Giovanni Battista Podestà, two Italian Catholics, also combine art with devotional practices, even going so far as to identify themselves with Christ. The former, based in Montreal, wore a cassock and proclaimed himself 'Pope Palmerino, the servant of Jesus', while the latter delivered sweeping moralising sermons on the banks of Lake Superior. One announced a message of peace, the other, in the grip of a Manichaean view of life, felt compelled to denounce corruption in society and to appeal for redemption. With his hair reaching down to his shoulders, his long beard and Christ-like face, Giovanni Battista Podestà trod his own Way of the Cross in which he carried a cross he carved himself. Palmerino Sorgente commemorated the ordeal of the crucifixion in his own way by wearing a crown of thorns and binding himself to a wooden cross. Their works are basically made using plain and sometimes recovered materials whose colours and brightness make for a stunning impact: sequins, shards of mirrors, red and gold ribbons, tassels and pearls, as well as metallic paper imitating the gold, silver, precious stones, and shimmer of the sculptures and objects of worship that decorate churches, especially in Italy.

In contrast, Philippe Ducollet-Michaëlef, whose oeuvre consists of forty-six sheets containing one hundred and ninety-four drawings of the Virgin, makes no mention of his faith or of any religious practices. In his multiple variations on the theme, he reinterprets the subject of an ancient deity, *The Snake Goddess*, combining her with the Virgin Mary. The motif is handled in groups and repetitively: each figure is distinguished by innumerable variations in the details: a contrasting accessory, an ornament treated differently. Philippe Ducollet-Michaëlef uses elements he finds in Christian iconography, mythology, or sorcery. Crosses are drawn on the bodies of the women-goddesses, on their necks or foreheads, worn as necklaces, or held between their joined hands. Rosaries are placed next to candles, crescent moons appear side by

[3] Sometimes referred to as 'Eli Jah' or 'Eli-Jah'.

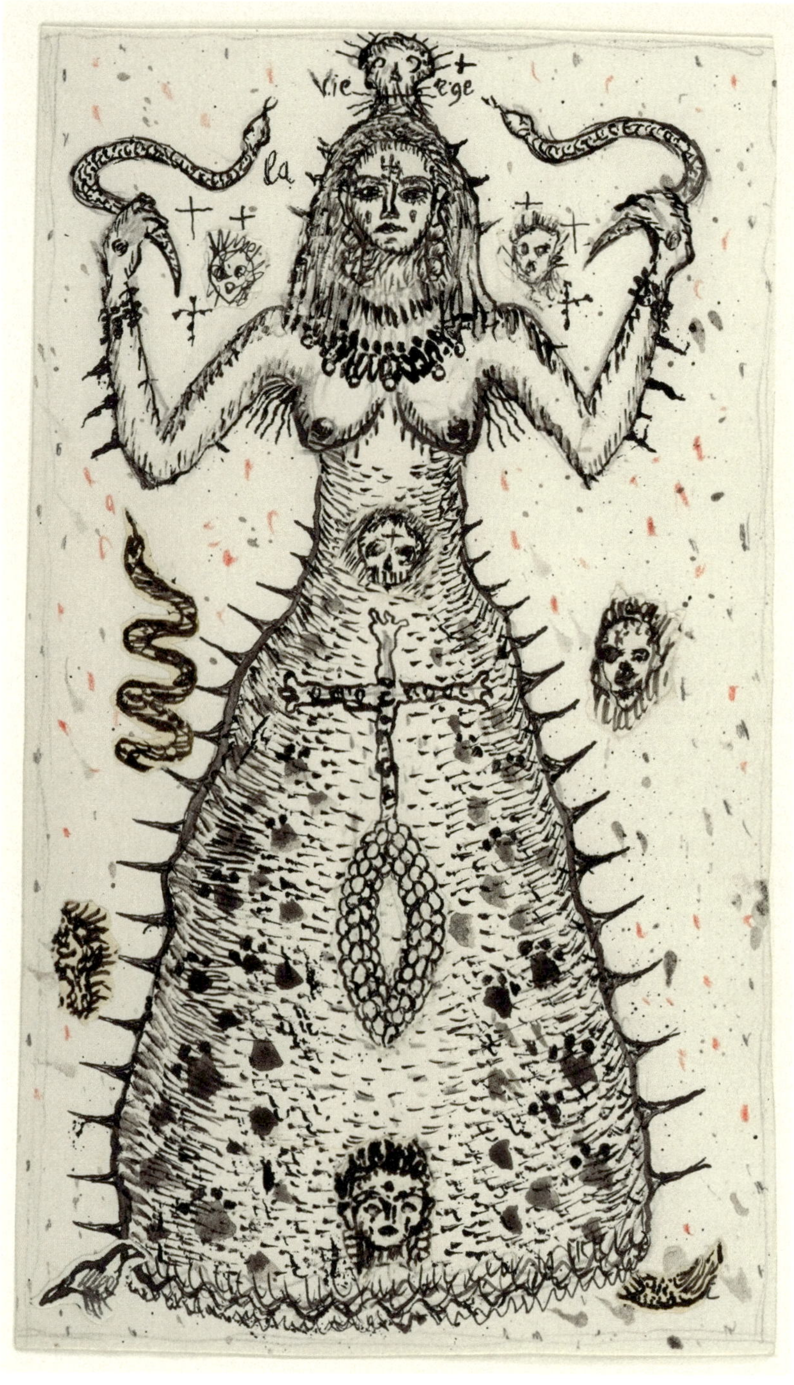

Philippe Ducollet-Michaëlef
Déesse – Mère, vierges saintes, vierges «hindoues» (detail),
between 2006 and 2020
India ink, graphite, coloured pencil, and felt-tip pen on paper
42 x 29.7 cm
ni-10313

side with hearts, and knives are depicted together with severed heads. Here and there can be seen plant motifs, while birds and snakes are dotted throughout, as are revolvers, coffins, stigmata on the hands, and sometimes scenes of crucifixion or hangings. The list is completed by the ubiquitous presence of vulvas and penises applied all over the bodies as decoration, although rarely meeting. Ducollet-Michaëlef borrows religious symbols and mingles sacred and profane in compositions to which he attributes therapeutic, apotropaic properties. Whether examples of religious devotion, reinterpretations of formal motifs, or works of redemption, they all share an interaction with the divine that reveals a fascination with the sacred.

One day they became artists

Attributing responsibility for one's creation to an outside entity, to the hereafter, looks like an astute means of escape or sometimes a skilful evasion: 'For some artists, who are obviously not among those who have acquired social legitimacy, the religious impulse can, along with spiritualism, act as a more or less conscious alibi for inventiveness that breaks free of cultural norms. An artist who is a believer thus brings God into the matter so as to conveniently unload onto Him the stressful responsibility for creating something *ex nihilo*.'[4] Some artists go so far as to devolve this responsibility to the dead. Their guided hand carries out what the spirits dictate, and they respond to voices that urge them to draw, paint, embroider, or write. They generally attend séances where they are inducted into spiritualism, the mediumistic doctrine or practice that became popular in Europe and the United States around the turn of the twentieth century, developed as a series of rituals for communicating with the dead. Are the voices they hear, as in the case of Augustin Lesage, who one day heard, 'You will be a painter one day', in a mine, the voices of the deceased, or rather, as many writings on the question suggest, their own? Madge Gill claimed her work was executed under the guidance of a spirit named 'Myrninerest'.[5] What better way to protect oneself than to palm off responsibility for one's work onto a dead person, a dead person who would automatically be respectable, just as ancestors are in numerous cultures, and beyond any criticism?
Jean Dubuffet took a serious interest in spirit works and began from 1945 to build his own collection of creations by Madge Gill, Laure Pigeon, Jeanne Tripier, Augustin Lesage, Fleury-Joseph Crépin, and Raphaël Lonné. Several of these were already well known in their artists' lifetimes and have since appeared in various exhibitions and publications as the work of spirit artists. Although not all see themselves as belonging together, they are nevertheless viewed as being part of this trend, forming a distinct group, which is something exceptional in the field of Art Brut since each artist stands out precisely on account of his or her originality and freedom, quite independently of any movement. Without wishing to dwell too much on the question of gender, it is nevertheless worth pointing out that as many women as men feel they are the 'recipients' of messages from the hereafter, obey commands, and claim not to be in control of their own work. Men tend to be members of spiritualist clubs, exhibit and sell their paintings, publish their works, and take part in congresses, while women are more likely to work at home, in private. Madge Gill always refused to sell her works on the grounds that they belonged to her guiding spirit. Henriette Zéphir, who never regarded herself as nor claimed to be an 'artist', thought she wasn't the owner of her drawings and didn't think she was free to do what she wanted with them. As for Laure Pigeon, her

[4] Michel Thévoz, *Art Brut, psychose et médiumnité*, Paris, Éditions de la Différence, 1999.
[5] i.e. My inner rest.

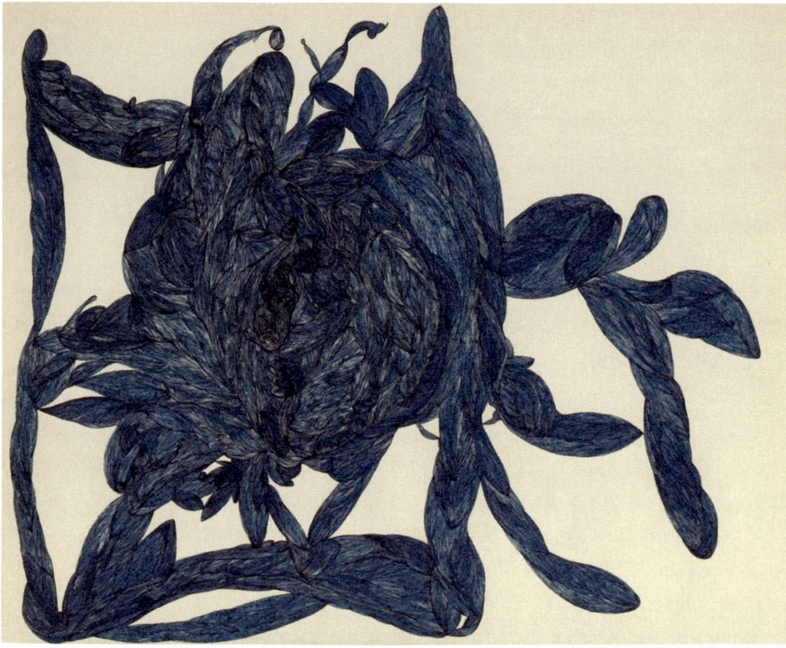

Laure Pigeon
1954, 1954
ink on paper
49 x 64 cm
cab-1767

compositions were only discovered after her death. While also considering themselves no less estranged from their creations, men would seem to be more inclined to present them in public and to talk about them. There also appears to be a distinct difference between the works of men and women as far as style is concerned. The paintings of Augustin Lesage, Fleury-Joseph Crépin, Victor Simon, and Joseph Moindre, in which architectural motifs predominate, are often constructed geometrically, placing an emphasis on symmetry. Close observation of the abundant ornamentation reveals the influence of and references to Christian, Hindu, Oriental, and ancient Egyptian traditions. In contrast, the works of Laure Pigeon, Jeanne Tripier, Jeanne Ruffié, and Madge Gill, curvilinear and almost plant-like as they are, seem more coherent. The hand appears freer, the line more supple, and the compositions are built up of forms that blend into one another at random. Madge Gill's anarchical embroideries recall psychedelic avant-garde works; the pages of Jeanne Tripier's notebooks are filled with abstract blotches that make the invisible visible; Laure's knotted, coiled-up needlework drawings bring to mind the structures of a spider. Is it that women have a greater ability to let themselves go so as to embrace the vibrations they receive from beyond? Are they more susceptible to 'the mental regression or the weakening of the self that provides the conditions for giving free rein to primordial energies, groundbreaking phantasms, and unwonted truths'?[6]

Tangible but inaccessible

In order to reconnect to humanity, to satisfy the need to relate to a reality outside oneself, these Art Brut artists find within themselves the resources

[6] Michel Thévoz, 'Le règne des revenants', in *L'Art spirite*, Lausanne, Collection de l'Art Brut, 2005.

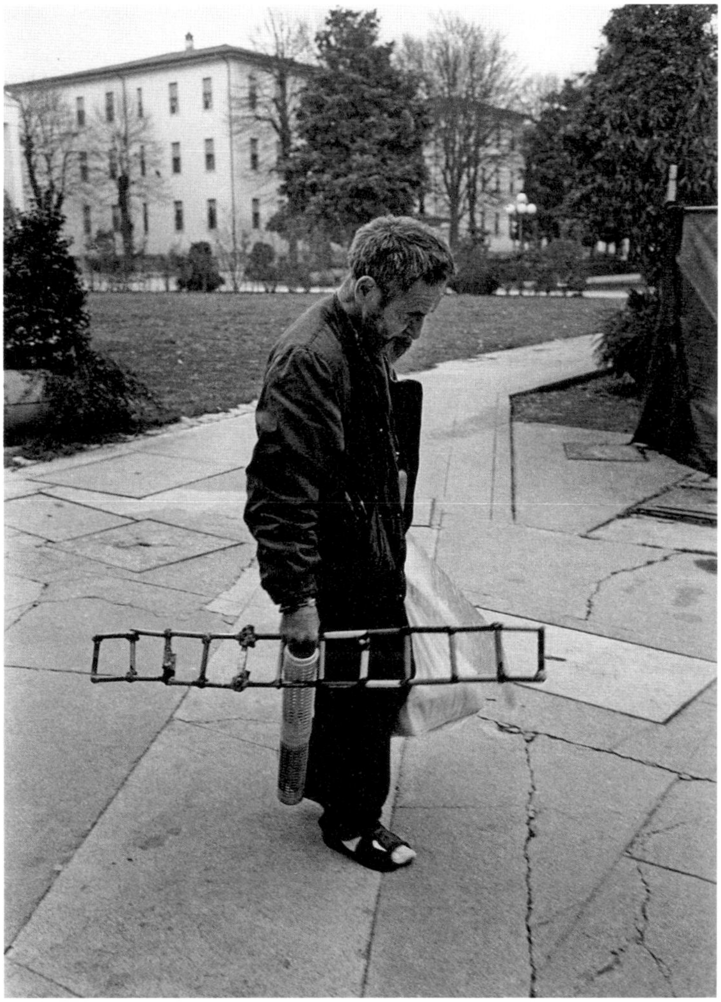

Antonio Dalla Valle, Cremona (Italy), 2005

to make their way off the beaten track and invent entire universes built on personal beliefs, sometimes taking God's place, becoming in their turn demiurges that re-enchant the world. From among all the diverse figures selected who fit this description, we have placed the accent on two artists in particular whose works share the attribute of being aesthetically comparable to works of contemporary art.

When Bianca Tosatti uses the term *Gesamtkunstwerk* (total artwork) in an article on Antonio Dalla Valle,[7] she clearly understands that the artist's work and his life are closely interwoven. The mysterious writings that fill Dalla Valle's notebooks and sheets of paper and the various assemblages he created have a highly personal meaning for him. He cannot drop them until the function he attributes to them has run its course: in his eyes, these objects are imbued with sacredness and instilled with a power he alone understands. A solitary figure, Antonio Dalla Valle spoke with reluctance, communicating only when he had to. He even seems to have taken refuge in his condition as a mental patient so as not to have to offer any explanations about his work or behaviour. When he was asked one day why he wore his shirt back to front, with the buttons on his back, he replied, 'Because I'm mad!' In this way he avoided having to answer the questions of those around him, while at the same time avoiding social norms and conventions. Divorced from the demands of the outside world, he was able to follow his own priorities. Antonio Dalla Valle dedicated himself to his unusual rituals in the institution where he lived, whether in his room, in the workshop he attended, or in the gardens. These practices were not confined to any particular place or moment during the day. Using string and cast-off pieces of cloth torn into strips, he would carefully mark out paths and areas according to precise rationales. They can be regarded as domains where he felt protected against occult forces. The string and strips of cloth in these areas also acted as bonds. When Antonio Dalla Valle sets out series of numbers, letters, and words, he repeats them over and over like an incantation. Geometric shapes, arrows, triangles, and spirals are arranged according to enigmatic diagrams. The words and signs are legible, but their meaning and the way they combine are as incomprehensible as a secret code. Dalla Valle sometimes places his writings at a distance, isolating them and even making them inaccessible, so that the reader faces an extra obstacle. He fits sheets of paper covered with signs

[7] Bianca Tosatti, 'Antonio Dalla Valle', in *L'Art Brut* 22, Lausanne, Collection de l'Art Brut, 2007.

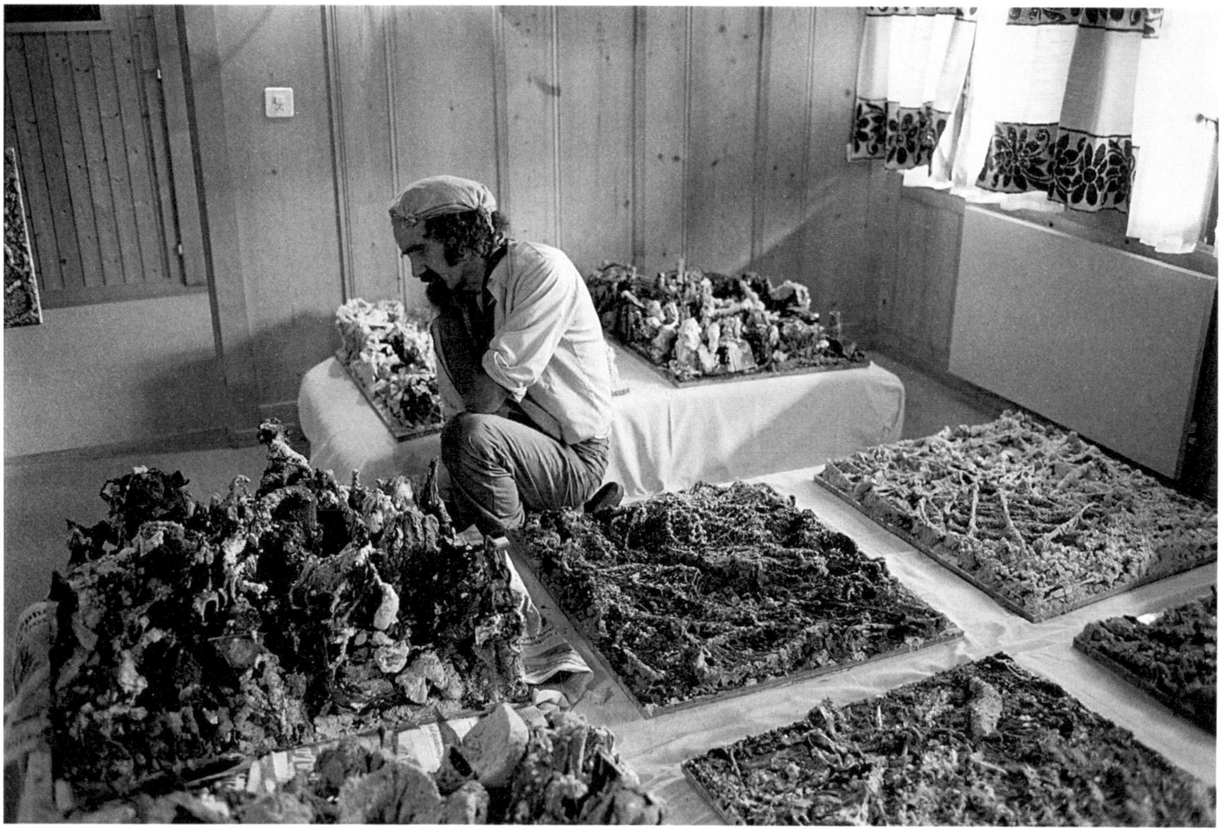

Marc Moret with his collages stored in a room in his farm, 2003

between two plexiglass panes or encloses them in transparent boxes; exercise books are rolled up to create cylinders or are completely wrapped in adhesive tape, turning into solid, sealed blocks. The power associated with the writings can be compared to the potency of magic spells and sacred texts.

His hair half shaved off, hairs burnt, one foot permanently bandaged and several watches on his wrist, Antonio Dalla Valle crowned his striking appearance by also wearing clothes he would cut up and otherwise modify. The tonsure suggests the custom typical of a monk, and his personalised apparel brings to mind the attire suitable for certain functions or the clothes worn at specific ceremonies. Dalla Valle always carried his paraphernalia around with him, ready for use in his magic rituals, notably a collection of objects hanging from his shoulder, including a bag and a kind of totem made of emptied felt-tip pens stuck together so as to form a grille that could block waves of negative energy and capture supernatural forces. Dalla Valle built a whole world in which he could isolate himself and even shut himself away, but where he felt he could safely shelter. All the objects and the works he created are the tangible expression of a complex system painstakingly developed to respond symbolically to the intangible.

The Art Brut Collection acquired a number of pieces by the Swiss artist Marc Moret a few months before his death in 2021. It was hard for Moret to separate himself from the sculpture-reliquaries that had become an essential part of his life. This countryman, who lived like an ascetic and wrote like a poet, claimed to be a practising Christian, although one whose belief was increasingly waning. At first, Moret concentrated on painting, before starting to make collages, as he called them. He produced his paintings and writings in an effort to please, to try to love, he said, while 'the sculptures were an attempt to destroy, although it was never wanton. I needed to do it so as not to live and not to die'.[8] His collages — high-reliefs made from various recovered objects, to which he added sharp pieces of broken glass stuck together with animal (rabbit) glue made by himself — were all made at times when his emotions were fresh, when they made him feel alive.[9] The act of creation and the work's constituents were always associated with a specific person, a relationship. After setting his new work on a wooden stand in a room in the family farmhouse, Marc Moret would stand before it in contemplation. He would perform this ritual daily. When leaving the room he would cross himself and place the sign of the cross on the door, as his father used to do when leaving his heifer in his pasture. These were 'commemorative works', 'personal reliquaries', 'aids in devotion and contemplation', which had healing, propitiatory, as well as redeeming properties. Discussing these high reliefs, Moret once admitted that, 'these collages are myself'.[10] These words echo those of Christian Boltanski, who also died in 2021, for whom death lay at the very heart of his oeuvre: 'The more one works, the more one disappears and the more one turns into one's art. I think it is an artist's deepest wish to become his work.'[11]

Anic Zanzi

CURATOR OF THE COLLECTION DE L'ART BRUT, LAUSANNE

[8] Interview with Mali Genest and Lucienne Peiry, Vuadens, 12 March 2014.
[9] Ibid.
[10] Lucienne Peiry, 'Marc Moret, des reliquaires salvateurs', in *Artension* 168, July-August 2021.
[11] Christian Boltanski, on the occasion of the great retrospective dedicated to him at the Centre Pompidou in Paris, in 2019. https://www.centrepompidou.fr/en/magazine/article/christian-boltanski-a-lepreuve-du-temps

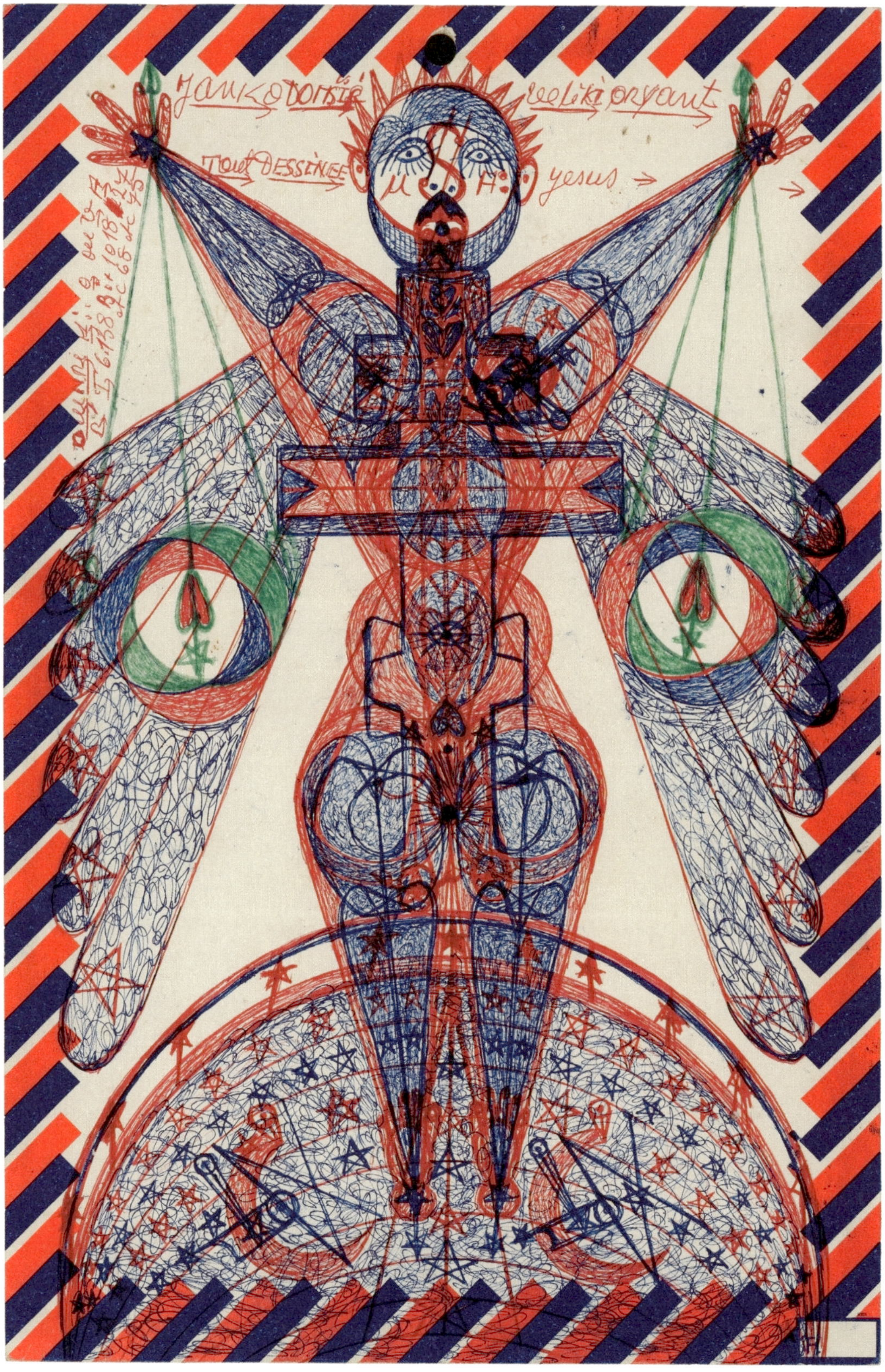
Tout DESSINEE
yesus

Make Your Own Gods

Janko Domsic
Tout dessinée U$A Jésus ..., 1970
ballpoint pen on printed cardboard
42.5 x 28 cm
cab-7596

'We are all sleeping avatars
of God, with amnesia.'
Philip K. Dick, *The Exegesis*

The German philosopher Helmuth Plessner once hypothesised that human beings distinguished themselves from other animals by their remarkable gift for what he termed eccentricity.[1] This should not be taken to mean that humans are by their very nature excessive, but rather that they are capable of stepping outside their bodies, for better or for worse—to be here, but at the same time absent or elsewhere, and present, both within and outside their bodies. The artists brought together in this exhibition are not obliged to step outside their bodies to commune with God or other entities, or to fashion universes with aspects that may be beyond our comprehension. All they need to do is to place themselves in a suitably receptive state. Some create their own gods, others regard themselves as the great watchmaker of the universe, still others invent languages or codes and receive hidden messages. To speak of beliefs with regard to them merely reveals our inability to enter into their worlds. Certain space-times have their own coordinates, others seem more familiar, nebulae peopled by anthropomorphic or zoomorphic creatures, spirits, or deities. But using the term 'belief' is merely a way of admitting the difficulties we face: What takes place when a creative process hinges on something invisible, making it the motor that drives it forward? What happens to a work when the invisible is in charge? It is always someone else's invisible, and one must begin by asking oneself what one's own invisible consists of, since something is only invisible for those unable to see or hear. The invisible of the artists exhibited seems, in contrast, to be saturated with information. The rest of us, blind and oblivious to realities we cannot perceive or messages we don't hear, have no choice other than to consign all this to the realm of 'beliefs'. Whether it is a layer of reality only the artist can apprehend, entities he alone can perceive, we must accept the evidence: powerful generators of creativity are at work in these mechanisms miraculously squeezed into the term 'belief'.

The invisible provides the impetus

Developing beliefs that are feasible and dependable is not an obvious process. 'How is belief fixed?' wondered Charles Sanders Peirce (1877). In our everyday life, we spend our time moving to and fro between doubt and belief,

[1] Helmuth Plessner, *The Levels of Organic Life and the Human*, 'Forms of Living' series (New York: Fordham University Press, 2019).

he noted, with doubt being 'an uneasy and dissatisfied state from which we struggle to free ourselves and pass into the state of belief', which can be described as 'a calm and satisfactory state'.[2] For Peirce, belief was basically nothing other than a mental state, the only fully satisfactory one as it predisposes one to act, nourished by its antagonist, doubt. 'The irritation of doubt is the only immediate motive for the struggle to attain belief. [. . .] With the doubt, therefore, the struggle begins, and with the cessation of doubt it ends.' And there was no doubt in the mind of the American pragmatist philosopher, who believed in science and democracy, that modern science did not stand in opposition to belief. For him, science was the only way to fashion beliefs that could stand the test of scrutiny and could be sustainable and shared. Living is always a sort of gamble, and the idea that life is worth living depends also on belief, as William James himself affirmed one day. In his book *The Will to Believe* (1897), he also introduced a felicitous expression to describe the things that keep us alive, from which we can draw considerable, inexhaustible energy, on condition that they are themselves fully alive, that is, kept at a certain level of activation. He called these beliefs 'live hypotheses', genuine possibilities prompting one to act irrevocably. In contrast, 'dead hypotheses' do not represent true possibilities and do not lead to action. A dead hypothesis is 'an appeal to action that would find no echo in our consciousness'. It is a hypothesis regarding the world and its possibilities that no longer chimes with our subjectivity, whereas a live hypothesis 'resonates', 'disposes to action', and engages us in a profound way. There are obviously no live hypotheses within us that would be so forever, or dead hypotheses that would be so forever. Belief in God or in communism, for example, are 'dead hypotheses' for some, but in others they have a profoundly live aspect. A pragmatic approach. Beliefs live and die, whether they be political, religious, or scientific. But what about those beliefs that lead to creation, of which this exhibition offers a panoply? Do they imply doubt or is it out of the question? And can they be shared or are they rather motors, driving forces that we keep hidden away, nurtured in their indecipherability?

Pirated mysticism

The worst thing to do would be to consign everything to do with belief to the domain of religion or to assume that a proper belief always includes a transcendent aspect or a god. Not all beliefs are religious — it is not unusual to have a cast-iron belief that our pets understand us when we talk to them; but do they really? And there are any number of rituals that need no act of faith or belief in God to exist; they are simply formulas and actions sometimes performed completely unthinkingly. On the other hand, they always include something that is invisible and enigmatic regarding the possible worlds they conjure up, a little something that has to slip past all attempts to understand and leaves those who are denied access in the dark. Of course, the Art Brut artists challenge our relationship to religion in the classic sense of the term, especially as regards Christianity, and it is tempting to look out for anything

[2] 'Doubt is an uneasy and dissatisfied state from which we struggle to free ourselves and pass into the state of belief; while the latter is a calm and satisfactory state which we do not wish to avoid, or to change to a belief in anything else. On the contrary, we cling tenaciously, not merely to believing, but to believing just what we do believe. Thus, both doubt and belief have positive effects upon us, though very different ones. Belief does not make us act at once, but puts us into such a condition that we shall behave in some certain way, when the occasion arises. Doubt has not the least such active effect, but stimulates us to inquiry until it is destroyed.' C. S. Peirce, *The Fixation of Belief*, 1877.

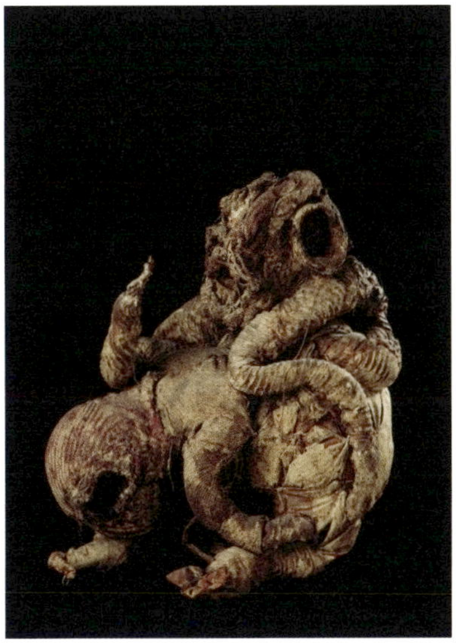

Michel Nedjar
untitled, between 1976 and 1982
assemblage of textiles, needlework, string and miscellaneous materials, all daubed
52 x 31 x 47 cm
cab-5194

suggesting cults, fetishes, or rituals. The religion in question is distorted, reinvented, pirated, exploited, even barbarised, for creative ends. The presence of a god, or gods, spirits or powers, performances designed as rituals, the use of codes, prayers, and esoteric formulas, sometimes repeated obsessively, in which objects are activated by procedures that bear some sort of relation, whether close or distant, to magic, assures us we are in the typical realm of religion, as common sense perceives it. In actual fact, we are essentially and above all in the realm of creation in which the creators are engaged to their very core. The point is that the artists gathered here immediately go to the very heart of the matter, reaching for what enables them to nourish and stimulate their fervid imagination. They have internalised what they find useful to poach in the religious imagination, in the multitude of its mechanisms, so as to achieve a cosmic scale and establish a relationship with the entire universe. They do the same with magical thinking, with its encoding procedures and the principles of concealment that take totally astonishing forms here. They have understood of their own accord, without reading *A General Theory of Magic* (1904), the celebrated article written by the ethnologists Hubert and Mauss, what anthropology took a long time to take on board: that all those who call themselves soothsayers, shamans, priests, and prophets are also to some extent artists, and that from a technical standpoint they are all part of the same category of beings, creators playing with powers. Interacting with what is invisible is something that goes beyond art's capacities, but it is not the exclusive province of religion.

Fetishes, traps, and cosmo-telluric connections

The point is that all creation is in part the formulation, at times stuttering and at others remarkably articulate, of a live hypothesis (in James's sense) that includes an irreducible portion of invisibility. It orientates it as its governing principle as well as enabling it to remain active and fully alive. To wonder what it is that Art Brut artists actually believe in inevitably leads to the question of what invisible entities, which are necessarily plural and diverse, they connect with in order to create, and how it is that these invisible entities have the power, compared with other possible connections, to transport the artists and their creations into a state of unparalleled, sublime engagement. Some allow themselves to be swamped by a plethora of entities, both known and unknown, whether infra- or extra-terrestrial, and the world is thus repopulated through them, while others have found in them their mode of expression, even if it means clothing it in the aura of a secret. One such is Antonio Dalla Valle, about whom no one now can say what the detonator and the objects he placed in plexiglass boxes or wrapped in adhesive tape were for or how they operated. Magical processes? If so, it was magic whose secrets only he knew and whose rules were themselves hidden away under plastic. He was not the only one to go down the road of fetishism. Michel Nedjar at one stage dipped his dolls into dirty water, a key part of a creative process viewed as

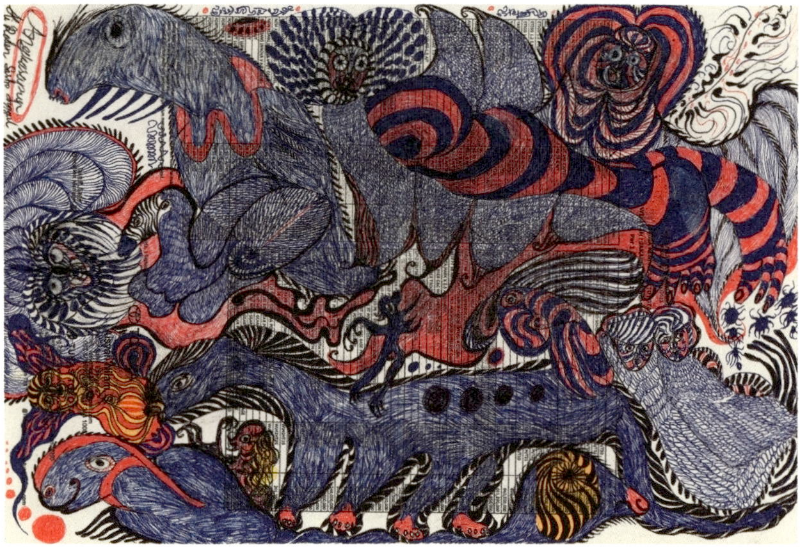

Novadi Angkasapura
untitled, 2014
ballpoint pen on paper
21.6 x 33 cm
ni-9845

a ritual of childbirth. Whatever it is that coagulates or is activated or 'loaded' in these operations not even the artist himself can say. Dalla Valle made his own abstract or unidentified fetishes with anything that came to hand, stretching the enigma to the utmost and leaving one clueless, with no hope of interpreting them. We are forced to assume some sort of 'magic' is involved in all this, but once again (as with the term 'belief'), this is just a way of underlining our inability to grasp what is going on in these objects that behave like electrical gadgets that are charged and then run down. Dalla Valle took his secret with him to the grave, leaving us to wonder about his universe that perhaps had nothing to do with our physics and the laws that govern the conduction of electricity. And he was not alone.

The exhibition offers an array of alternatives: kits for activating magic, cosmo-telluric traps that only their creator knows how to operate, unheard-of gods and fetishes or variants that don't quite match idols already encountered, alembic-like circuits of cause and effect, and indecipherable cryptographies and encoding systems that nonetheless seem to have an undeniable inner coherence. These bear weird witness to processes that are no less weird, by means of which new theories are generated about what vibrates, cries, or writhes in the blind spots of perception, in the deepest recesses of the earth, in the hollows of the air and at the outermost limits of the cosmos. And since some of these artists are dead, taking with them the keys to unlock the secrets of their cosmologies, we have to draw our own conclusions about these esoteric inventions, some of which will remain incomprehensible forever. It is up to us now to go out on a limb of belief and risk making hypotheses about them. Are there any trends to be found in this cosmo-telluric turmoil? Any reasonably distinguishable impulses or contradictory fancies?

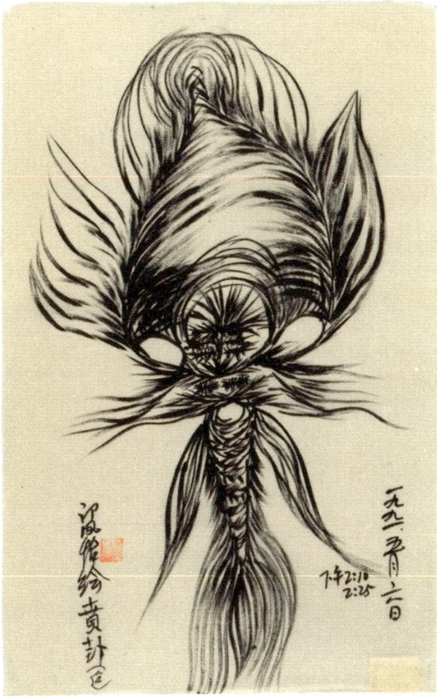

Guo Fengyi
La divination de Bo, 1991
India ink on Japanese paper
81 x 51.5 cm
cab-15040

The hubbub of celestial voices

It is hardly surprising that many of the artists appearing here should have flirted with spiritism and mediumism (Augustin Lesage, Fernand Desmoulin, Jane Ruffié, Raphaël Lonné, Madge Gill, etc.), sometimes claiming to be on intimate terms with highly personal powers, such as *Myrninerest*, the invisible force that guided Madge Gill in her drawings, or the guides with whom Lesage said he communicated. It is thanks to a guiding spirit acting as a messenger who transmits 'divine vibrations' that Noviadi Angkasapura conjures up what amounts to a whole biotope of entities and new creatures that can in no sense be compared to the existing pantheon of Javanese spirits. When one views oneself more as a go-between or a medium acting under dictation as it were — the toy of the spirits — than as the author of these works, it becomes in a certain sense the best way of connecting to the invisible systematically and, together, to set up a little engine of creation. What looks like 'belief' from the outside is in fact a relationship, a system of communication, even transcommunication. One listens to celestial voices and lets oneself be engulfed by messages and information of all kinds and translates them. There are almost as many states of receptiveness or hyperreceptiveness here as there are artists. For instance, Guo Fengyi uses *qi gong* to reach a state of mediumistic responsiveness. But the most surprising aspect of these states is that one can have fun swapping roles: slipping from simple go-between to patron or beneficiary of one's own drawing or painting, the issuer, receiver, and transmitter of information or 'fluids' (as in the case of Lesage). It is not a matter only of establishing an intimate relationship with a gaggle of entities that reply in varying degrees, and with whom one establishes an exclusive dialogue; the exchanges make it possible to change position regularly, revitalising the bond thus created until the 'occult powers desert you', as Desmoulin expressed it.

Making oneself the spokesman for a garden of spirits or for a biotope of entities has a price, for one is never just a representative; one becomes part of it, one lives it. One has to look after it, cultivate its presences, letting oneself be permeated and even possessed. The multitude of spirit contacts and the inventiveness of the procedures and techniques used to invoke and provoke them all bear witness to this invasion of spirits, which is sometimes chaotic, experienced as a revelation or possession, and sometimes more channelled or controlled by what amount to communication devices or protocols. There can be no creation here without opening channels of transmission, techniques of connection, contact procedures, invocations or incantations, without swaying from ventriloquy and mediumism, and, when other voices can be heard, without confusion, requiring an urgent 'who's speaking?' or 'who's there?' A real hubbub of celestial and terrestrial voices. The price to pay for this fantastical repopulating is an invasive overload of spirits speaking in waves and sometimes acting directly on someone who is quite willing to listen to them, through a profusion of sensations: shoves, waves, bumps, shakings, vibrations. And what is really striking, as the exhibition illustrates quite clearly, is the intensity of these events. All kinds of beings, entire pantheons crawling with new deities, suddenly emerge from everywhere. Adolf Wölfli repopulates Christ's crucifixion with a crowd of small animals (see p. 145). Hyperpresences, omnipresences. Observant, active, sometimes discreet, at other times monstrous, vampire-like, presences burst onto the scene, or, on another scale, lie simply curled up at the very ends of the universe, like Janko Domsic's creatures stretched out like spaghetti.

Delirious with power

Nobody can say in advance who it was that Domsic enjoyed depicting — God in person, himself, someone else. He himself was happy to say that his works were coded, studded with religious and masonic symbols. His creatures are strangely reminiscent of the *purusha*, the anthropomorphic depiction of the cosmos of the Hindus, as well as suggesting the spaghetti man envisioned by Stephen Hawking,[3] who believed that, attracted by the huge force of gravity, an intrepid astronaut would be stretched out like a piece of spaghetti as he approached the surface of a black hole! It's true that raving about or liberating God in all His mechanical, animal, and vegetable forms is a highly contrived approach when it comes to giving a work a cosmic dimension. The science-fiction writer Philip K. Dick opined that God is the only theological entity one can find everywhere, 'in the gutter' and 'in the stars'. He enjoyed speculating about new forms of divine intelligence in his journal *Exegesis*, which filled thousands of pages. The thing is that one cannot think of God without inventing a god of one's own, as the artists in this exhibition illustrate to perfection. Dick maintained that in March 1974 he gained access to a vast mental entity, an entity that he described variously as a 'weak, vegetable-level field', an AI system that responds only to what it is asked, so it is up to us to ask it questions, and a hereto undiscovered body in the field of reality. Elsewhere, he speaks of a force that encompasses each of us and acts through avenues that we cannot know, an engendered, profoundly evolving and non-static mind that has never been seen and that could be worshiped as something new that does not proceed through miracles but employs means we cannot understand. Dick started to stalk God everywhere, at the bottom of the gutter, in trash, believing Him to act everywhere; he sought the new ways He announced His presence, always uncertain as to His nature, form, and modes of communication and manifestation, basically everything that constituted His truly living parts. Dick felt one had to be prepared to see the living unknown proceed along the most crooked pathways, and this is exactly the kind of attitude one needs in order to appreciate the artists in this exhibition. Their work is their message, a message of conversion to states of belief and intense receptiveness that induce one to draw and paint, and in this way acknowledge unknown gods. If only Dick had been able to draw, he would certainly have depicted them, just like Domsic and others, who dreamt up cosmo-telluric traps and various procedures to get the invisible to speak in some other way. Indeed, Dick himself imagined a god whom one could carry around like a walkie-talkie. Some of

[3] Stephen Hawking, *A Brief History of Time* (New York: Bantam Press, 1989).

the artists included here went even further. They take God's place themselves. They don't invoke any god, they *are* God or a saint, as in the example of Adolf Wölfli, the author of an invented 25,000-page autobiography: *The Legend of St. Adolf.*

How can one fail to be moved by the complexity of what is played out in these creative processes doped with religious feeling and nourished by what are often highly bizarre beliefs? What we call Art Brut is without a doubt a great mystic laboratory, consisting of heretical acts and blasphemous gestures. It is filled with crackling voices that pass Jesus and the Bible off as feeble inventions of a God with no imagination and apparitions of the Virgin as scenes from an old B movie. They know how to bolster their faith. Their own blind beliefs wend their way down unexplored cosmo-telluric paths and reposition the creative act. They sometimes consider themselves possessed, behaving accordingly, propelled by 'occult' forces, acted upon rather than acting, but they may also believe they are entrusted with various missions, the bearers of arcane knowledge, a unique symbolism, or secret codes that will never be revealed (Domsic, Walla, etc.). What happens to us when, like the visitors to the exhibition, we find ourselves transported to totally encrypted universes, to a world that has been re-encoded or given fresh coordinates, new cosmo-telluric layers or networks? Some encourage us to look into the sky, some to delve into the earth, some to search the waters and others to make traps to attract powers to one, while still others to encrypt the universe with a riot of symbols.

Delirious with codes

'Cosmo-telluric' art is yet to be invented. The artists featured in this exhibition often create their own personal type of cartography and coding, trawling through the earth and the air, as well as the body. They turn themselves into visionaries of this form of art to be deciphered, guards on the paths of the unknowable. Some have internalised this stance by never purely and simply repeating the existing system of codes, preferring to create their own. While for example Guo Fengyi's delicate bodies are influenced by Chinese medicine, they are never reduced to it. Even when making use of a divining technique as a research instrument, as does Jules Godi, who paints with a pendulum, dotting his sheets with astral bearings, or Werner Hertig, who reveals invisible vortices and whirlwinds, the code is impenetrable to us, and must remain so. We thus find that the world has an underside, a rear-world, an 'undercoat'. The creator becomes detector, amplifier, 'antenna-man', a thoroughgoing crypto-cartographer or geographer of parallel spaces that at first glance are not necessarily inhabited, but become so by means of the technique employed.
What is striking is the breadth of the encrypting performed, the tendency to concoct entire systems of coding, alchemies with their own set of symbols, sacred architecture and mandalas, the desire to devote oneself to meticulous,

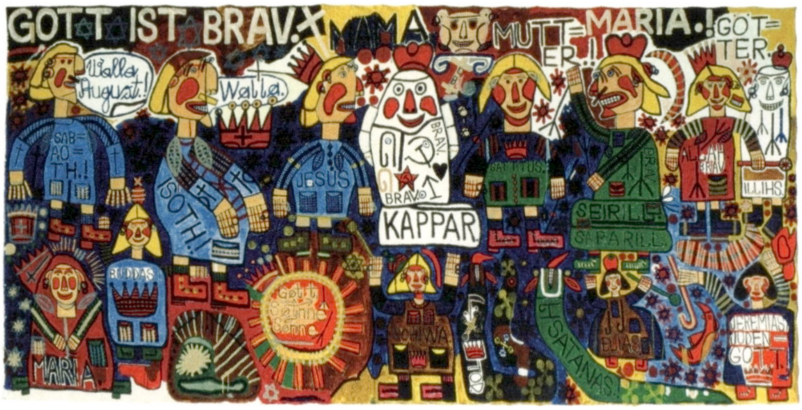

August Walla
Götter, 1986
acrylic on canvas
260 x 532 cm
cab-7650

painstaking calculations. The religious realm acts here as a source of inspiration for a multitude of different forms of research, re-coding, over-coding, and the miscegenation of codes and symbols that seem able to expand forever. This sometimes gives rise to astonishing cosmologies, whose codes and coherence might well always remain impenetrable to us. In order to make sense of Adolf Wölfli's vast oeuvre, for example, commentators do not hesitate to speak of 'cosmology', of the creator of a 'universe', and have long striven to decipher the motifs and symbolism of Wölfli's figurative music in the hope of finding the key that would explain everything.[4] 'What if the guiding principle of the cosmos were music?' asked Allen Weiss in this regard. After reading Prinzhorn's famous 1923 book discussing the works of patients in a psychiatric hospital, Rilke wrote to Lou Andreas-Salomé: 'The Wölfli case will enable us to obtain new explanations for the origins of creativity.' Almost one hundred years later, we continue to wonder about the 'music of the spheres' that secretly inspired the inmate who described himself as a 'composer', played a paper trumpet in the hospital, made 1300 drawings, and filled 44 exercise books setting out his scientific and religious theories, while distorting the words and mangling the vowels and consonants. Of course, there is something fundamentally religious about Wölfli's undertaking. It takes the form of a great act of piracy: he borrows religion's codes and even its urge to overcode, just as others distort the Bible (Elijah), remodel reliquaries (Marc Moret), or try to reawaken other telluric powers, entities emerging from the earth (Guyodo).

When one tampers with icons, borrows religion's motifs, invents rituals and cryptographies, and attributes intentions to objects without explicitly using the terms 'spirit' when referring to some of them, or 'mysticism', what is one doing? One is anything but a victim of one's own belief. One is enjoying the freedom to play with it, to give it something to work on, to let oneself be metamorphosed by it, and this is how many of the works on display acquire their visionary breadth or their cosmological dimension. For us visitors or art lovers, unprecedented gaps appear in the universe, hitherto unseen links are created, connections are forged; where the sky, the earth, and the cosmos meet, one gets lost in the folds and recesses, right where no one has ever

[4] See the works by K. Keller and P. Streiff (1970), as well as those by B. Odo Polzer and E. Förster.

Werner Hertig
Geht mit Monde, 1980
graphite and felt-tip pen on tracing paper
50.5 x 80.5 cm
ni-7445

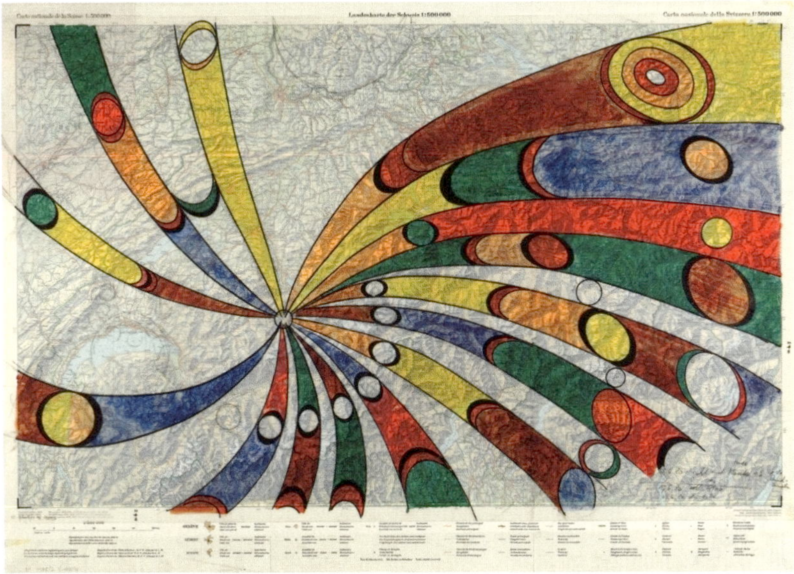

thought of looking for powers with which to consort. It will be clear by now that the very concept of belief is too weak to encompass all these experiences, these interactions with the invisible, these esoteric adventures. How can it do justice to these celestial languages, which seek each other out as they make contact with matter, and these gestures that imply different kinds of architecture (Crépin) and conjure up codes on a cosmic scale, or new kinds of cartography or geography that have no earthly equivalent (Hertig), to explore other forms of resonance? It is up to us to learn how to decipher them and to develop a suitable state of receptiveness, for the unknowns they address are ours too.

Emmanuel Grimaud
ANTHROPOLOGIST, RESEARCHER AT CNRS,
CENTRE NATIONAL DE LA RECHERCHE SCIENTIFIQUE

Catalogue

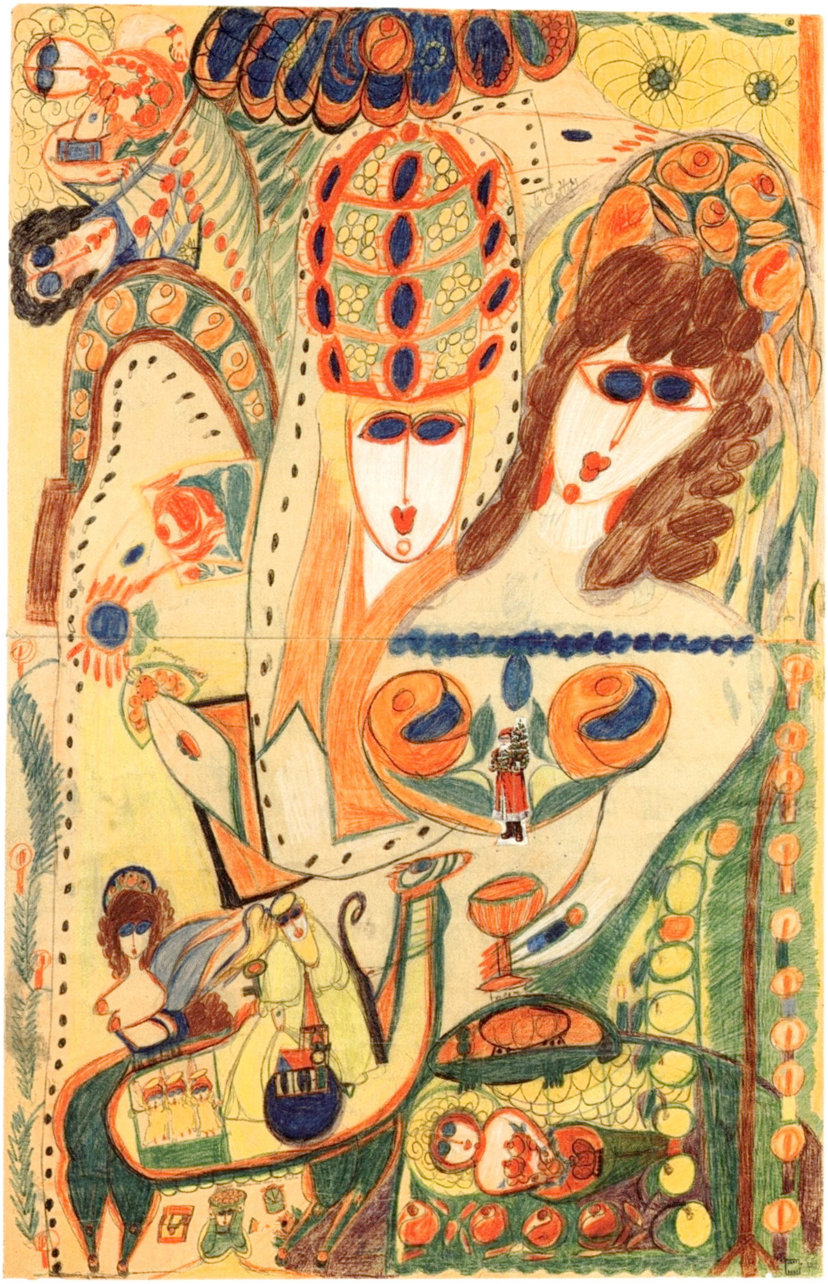

Aloïse [Corbaz]
Mme Cotty - bracelet retrouvé, ca. 1954
Crayon de couleur et papier cousu
sur une feuille de papier d'emballage
coloured pencil and paper sewn
on sheet of wrapping paper
150 x 99,5 cm
cab-2159

Aloïse [Corbaz]
Duchesse d'Albe, 1950
mine de plomb, crayon de couleur
partiellement aquarellé, papiers cousus
et papiers collés sur deux feuilles de papier
d'emballage cousues ensemble graphite,
coloured pencil with partial wash, sewn
paper and paper glued onto two sheets
of wrapping paper sewn together
161 x 81 cm
cab-2161

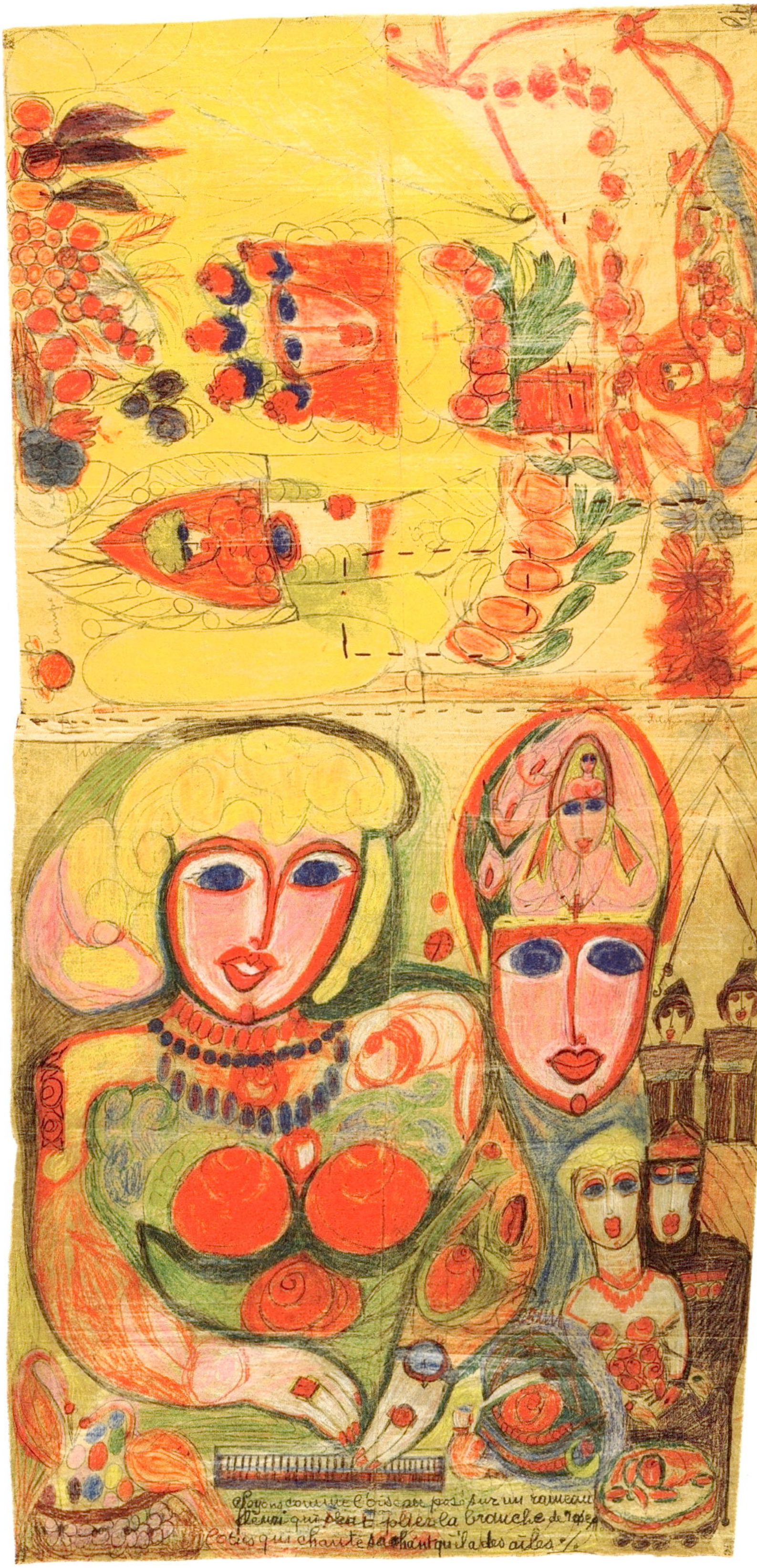
Soyons comme l'oiseau posé sur un rameau
qu'il a des ailes

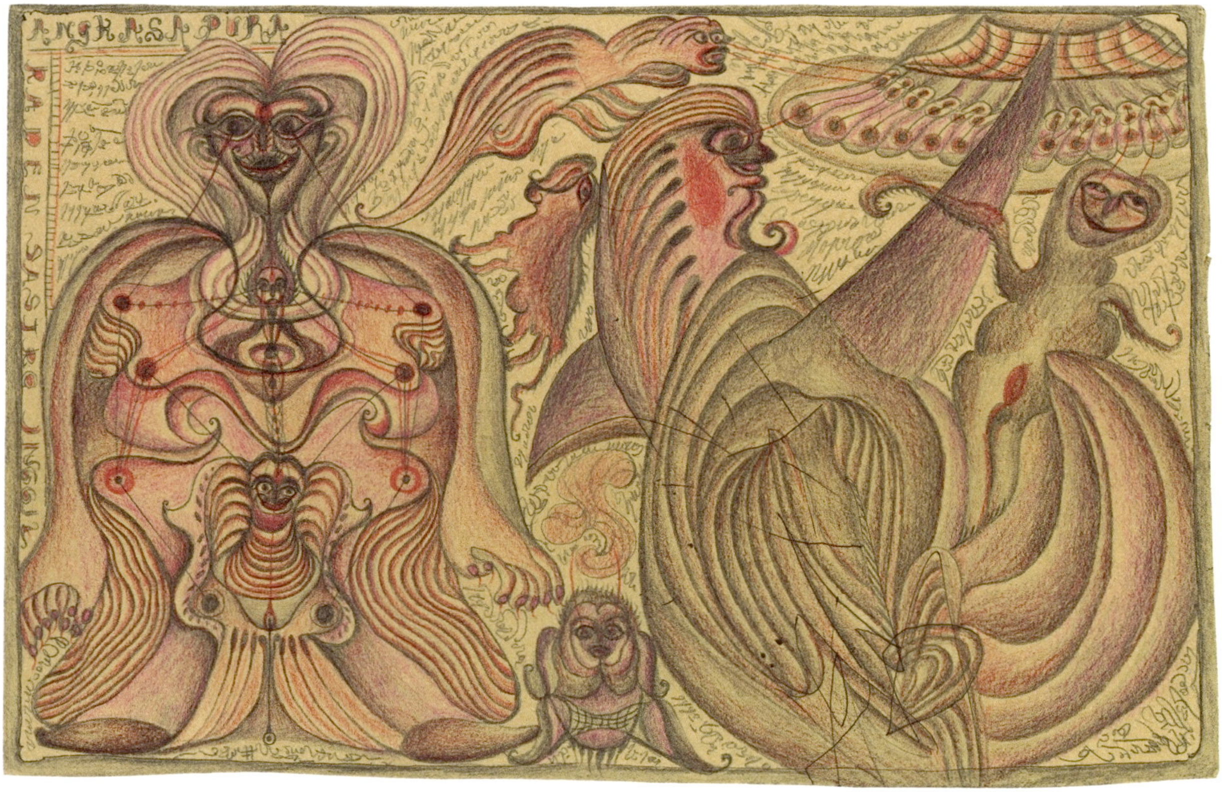

Noviadi Angkasapura
sans titre untitled, 2015
mine de plomb, stylo-bille et crayon de couleur sur papier graphite, ballpoint pen, and coloured pencil on paper
22,5 x 31,5 cm
ni-9846

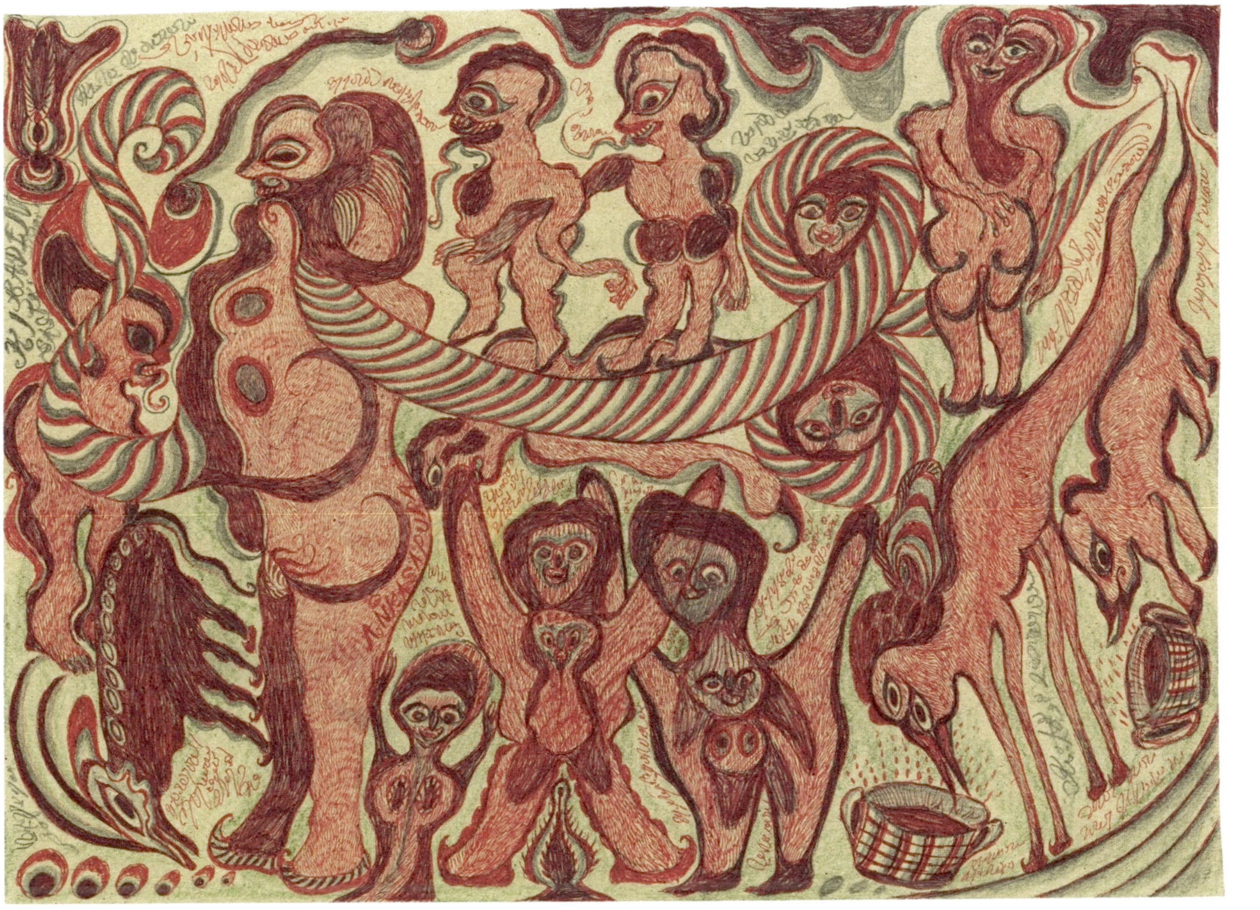

Noviadi Angkasapura
sans titre untitled, 2015
mine de plomb, stylo-bille et crayon
de couleur sur papier graphite, ballpoint
pen, and coloured pencil on paper
22,8 x 36,4 cm
ni-9847

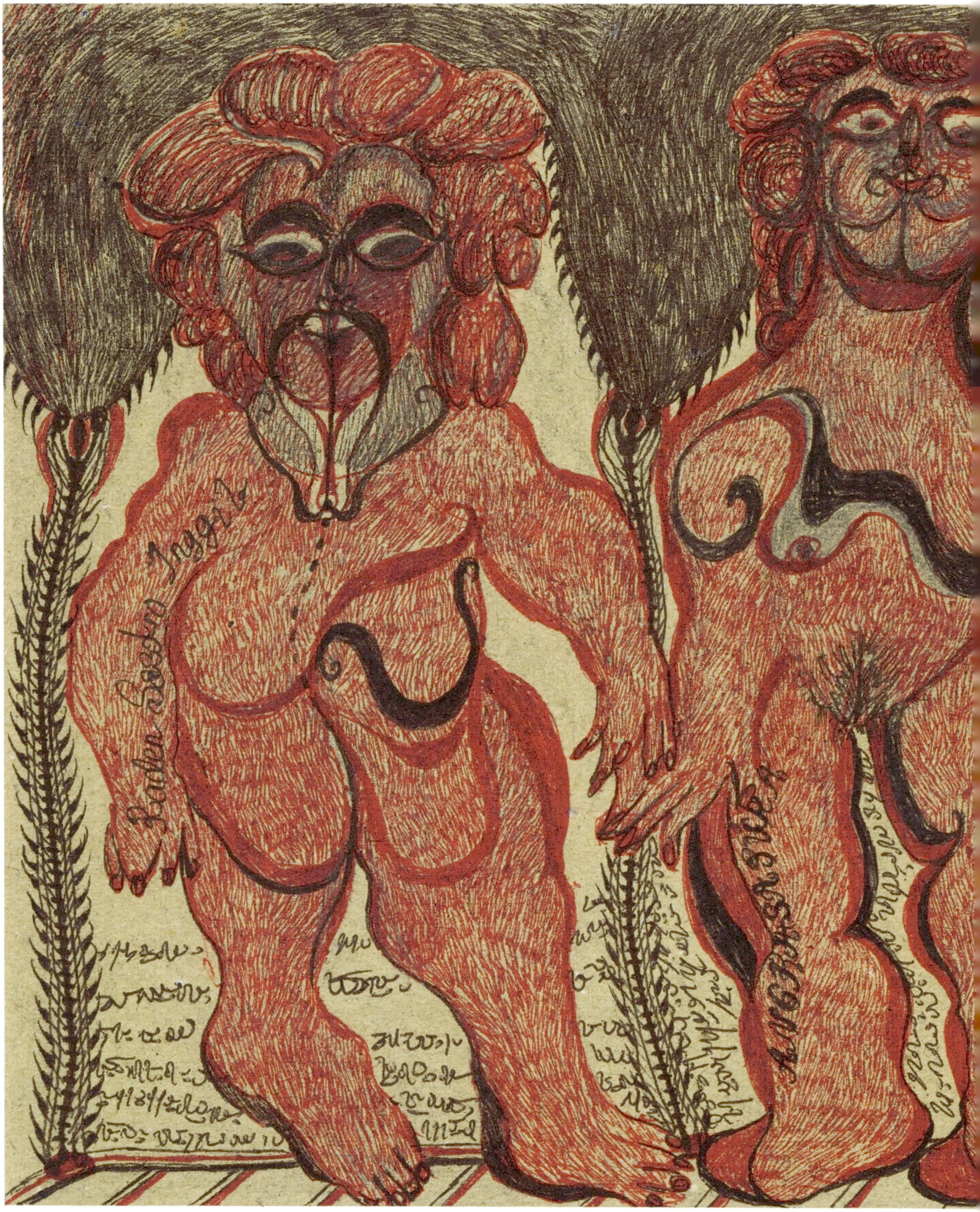

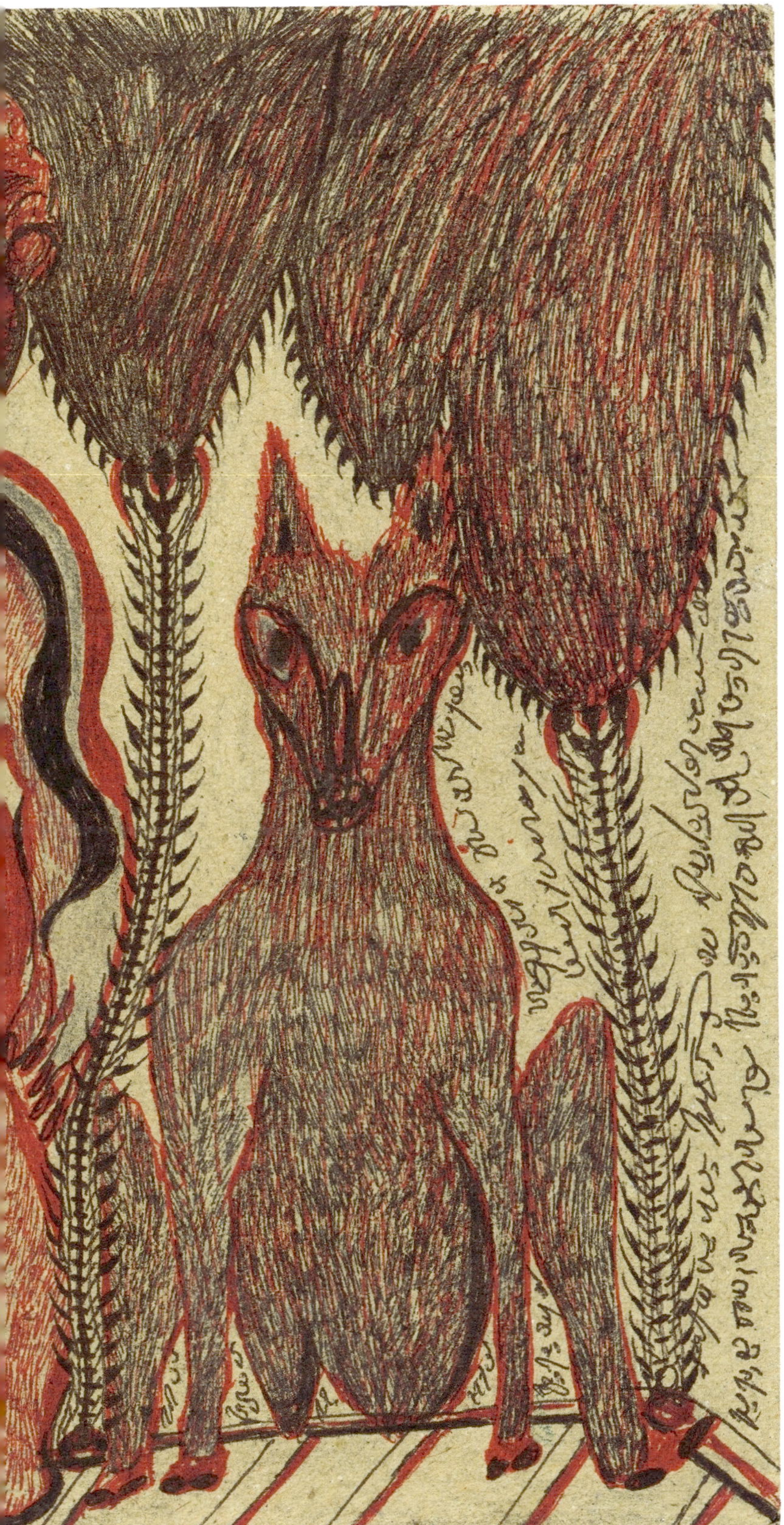

Noviadi Angkasapura
sans titre untitled, 2015
mine de plomb et stylo-bille sur papier
graphite, ballpoint pen on paper
14,8 x 20,9 cm
ni-9849

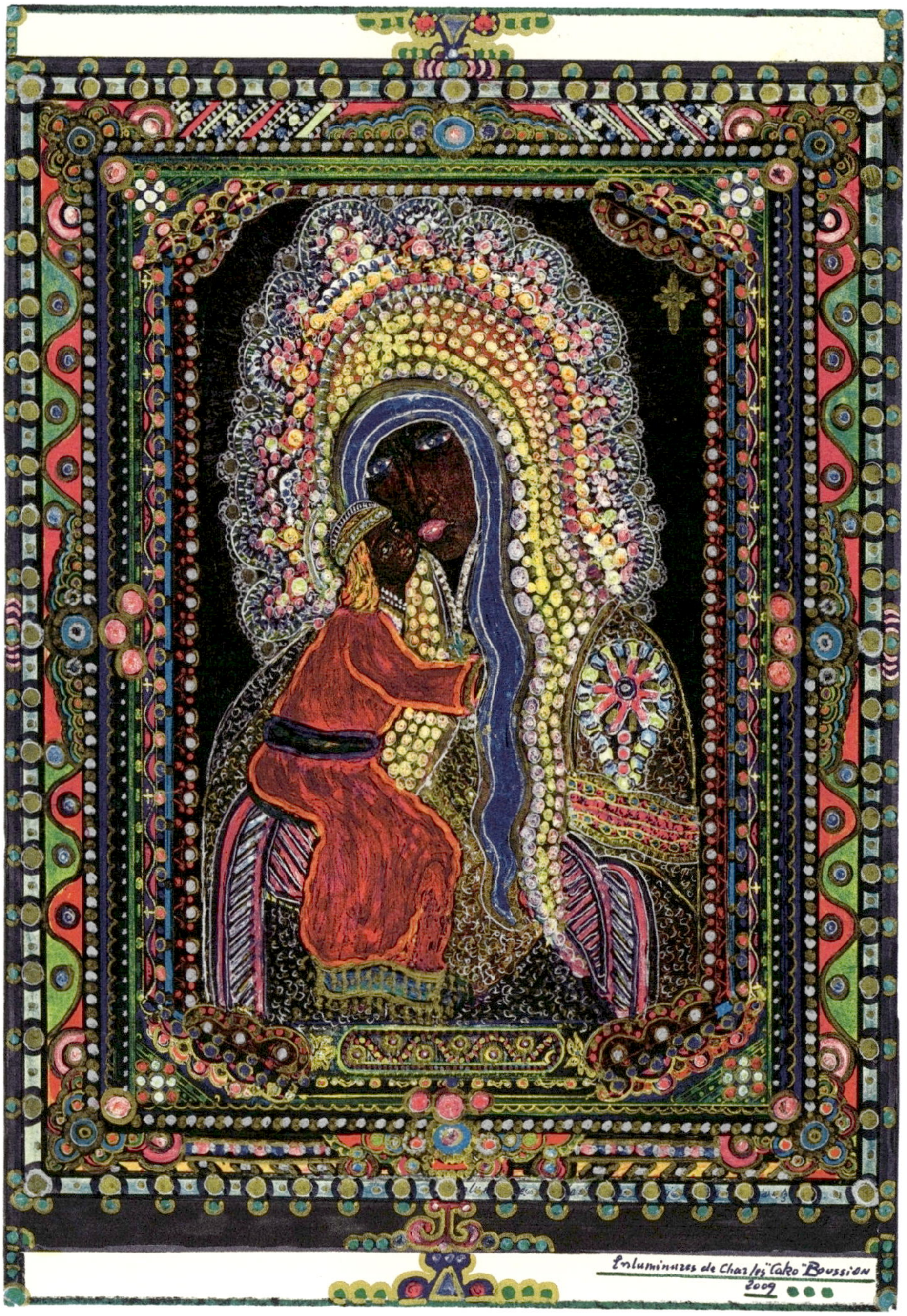

Charles Boussion
Virgen negra, Santa Madre del cielo y su niño divino, 2009
feutre, correcteur blanc et surligneur sur papier glacé felt-tip pen, white correction fluid, and highlighter on coated paper
42,1 x 29,6 cm
cab-16702

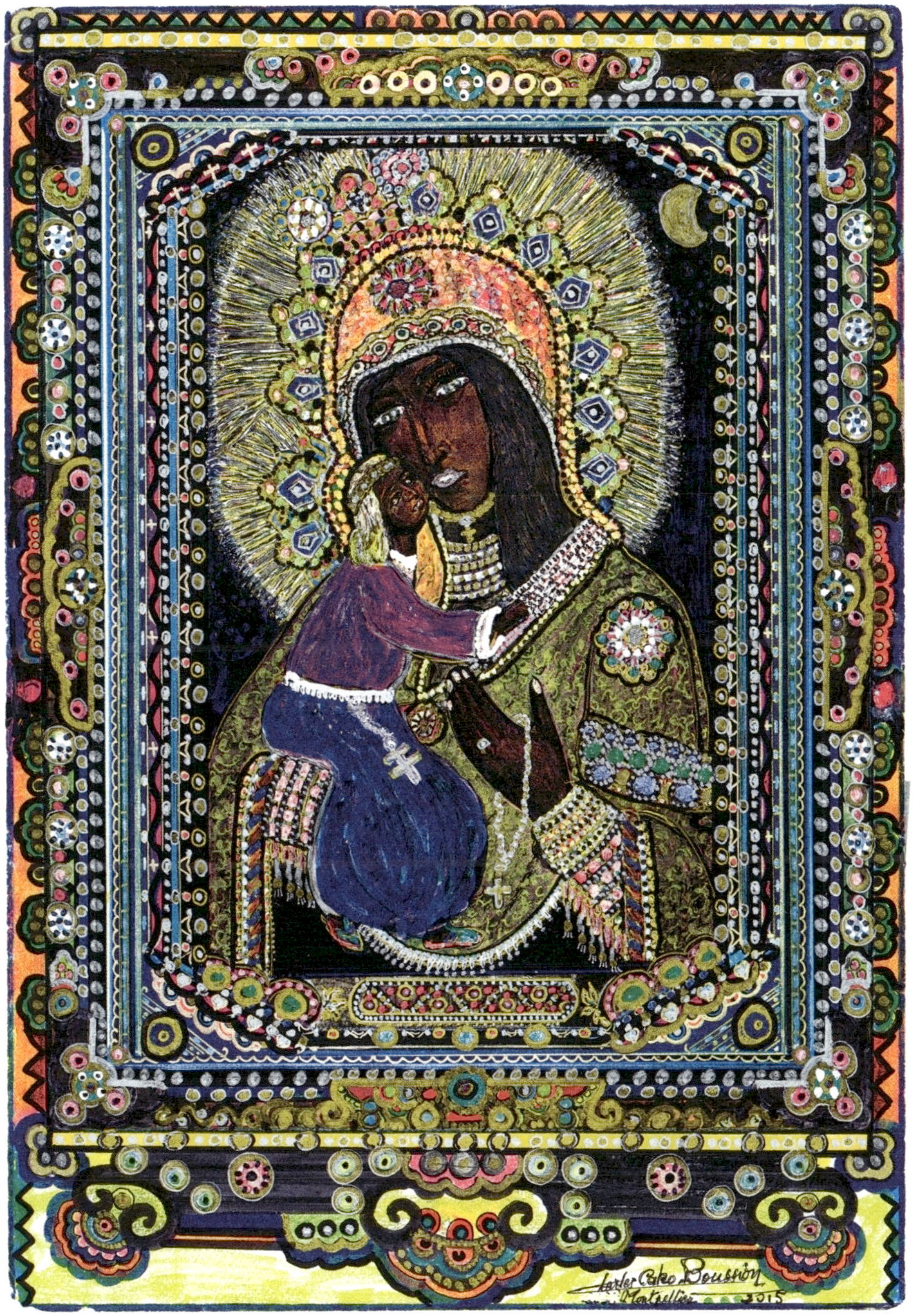

Charles Boussion
Icône revisitée Vierge noire à l'enfant Jésus, 2015
feutre, correcteur blanc, paillettes et surligneur sur papier glacé felt-tip pen, white correction fluid, sequins, and highlighter on coated paper
42 x 29,5 cm
cab-16704

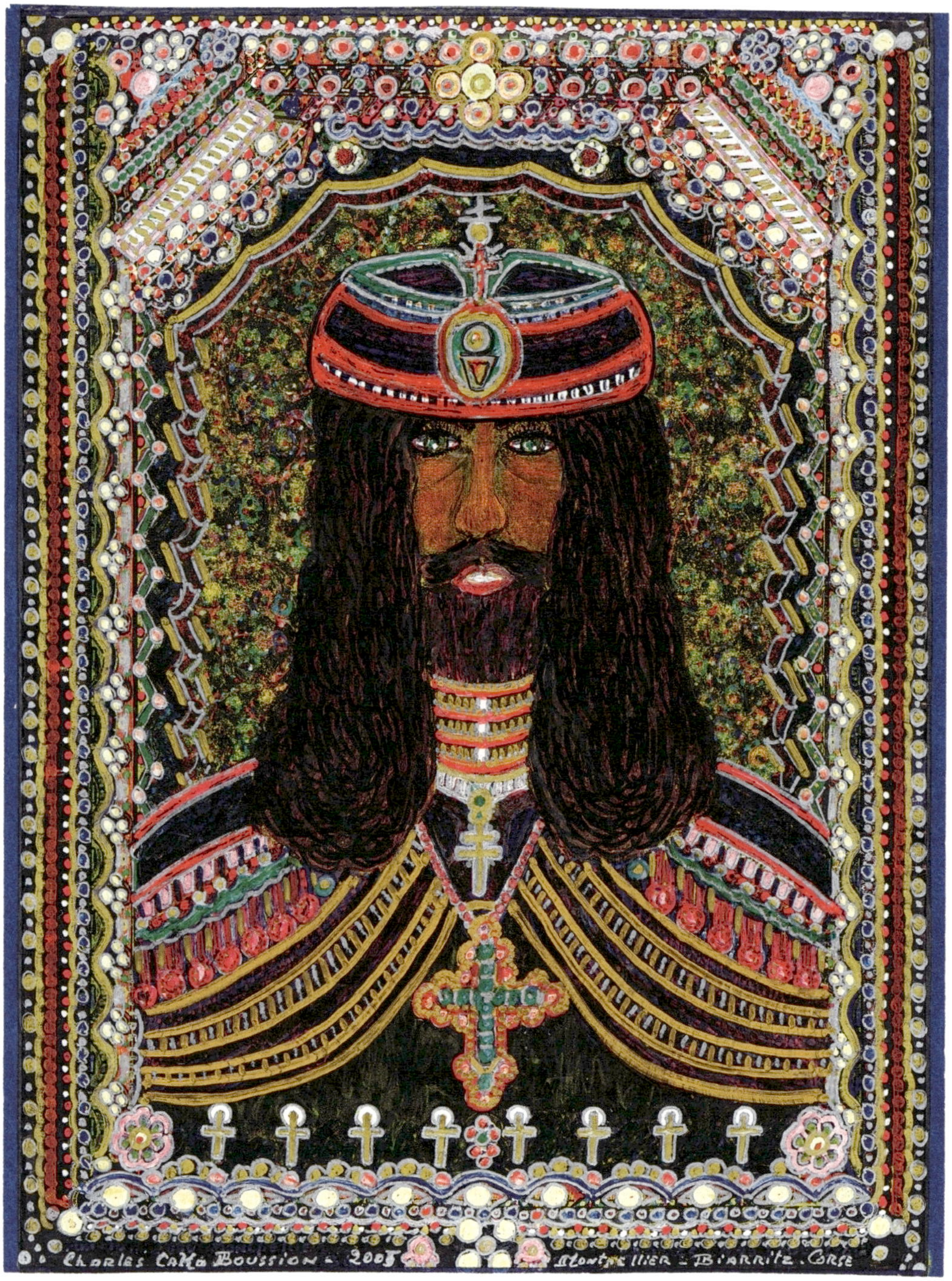

Charles Boussion
sans titre untitled, 2015
feutre et correcteur blanc sur papier glacé felt-tip pen and white correction fluid on coated paper
38,8 x 29,6 cm
cab-16706

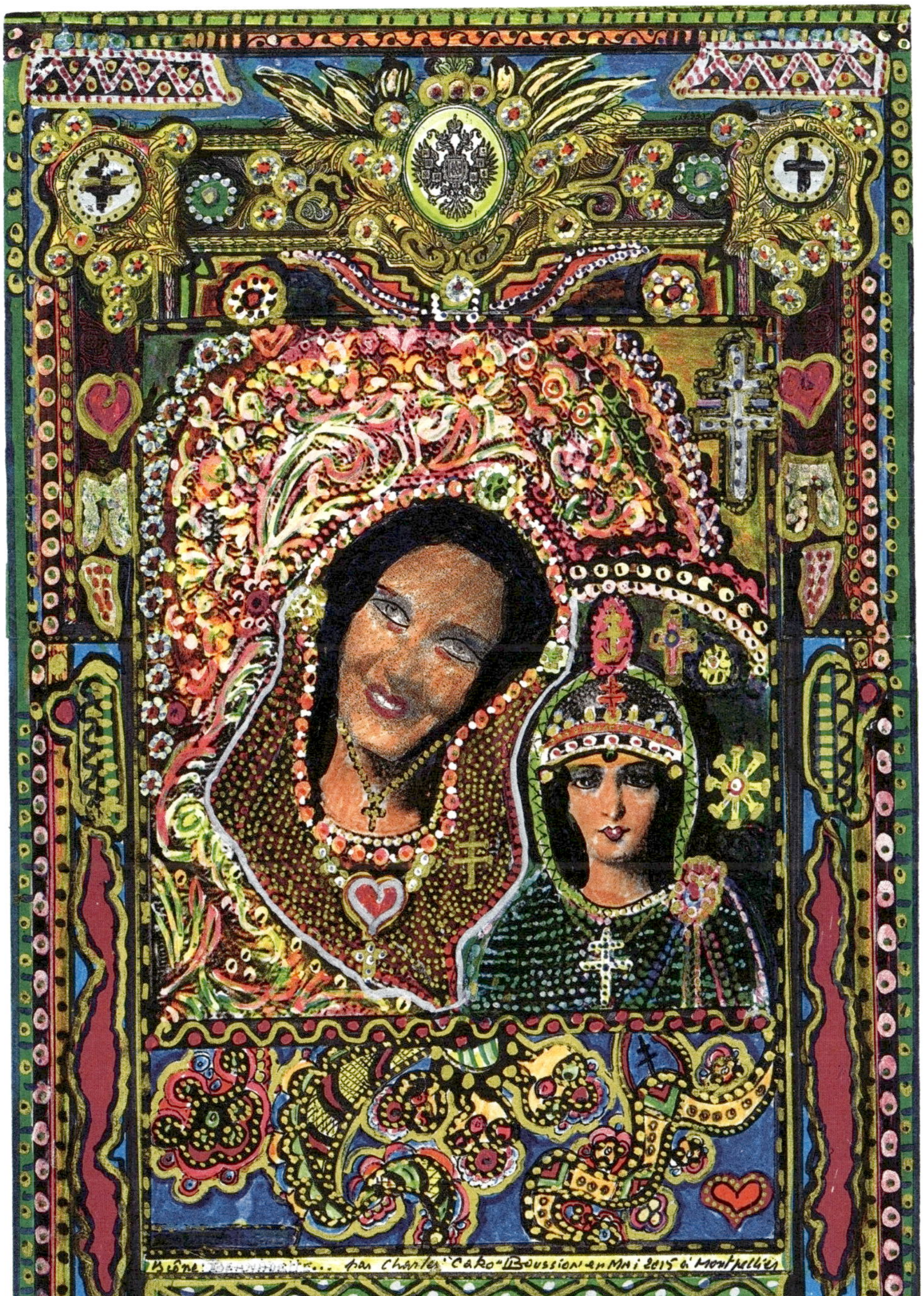

Charles Boussion
Icône Bernadette, 2015
feutre, correcteur blanc et collage sur papier glacé felt-tip pen, white correction fluid, and collage on coated paper
42 x 29,9 cm
cab-16698

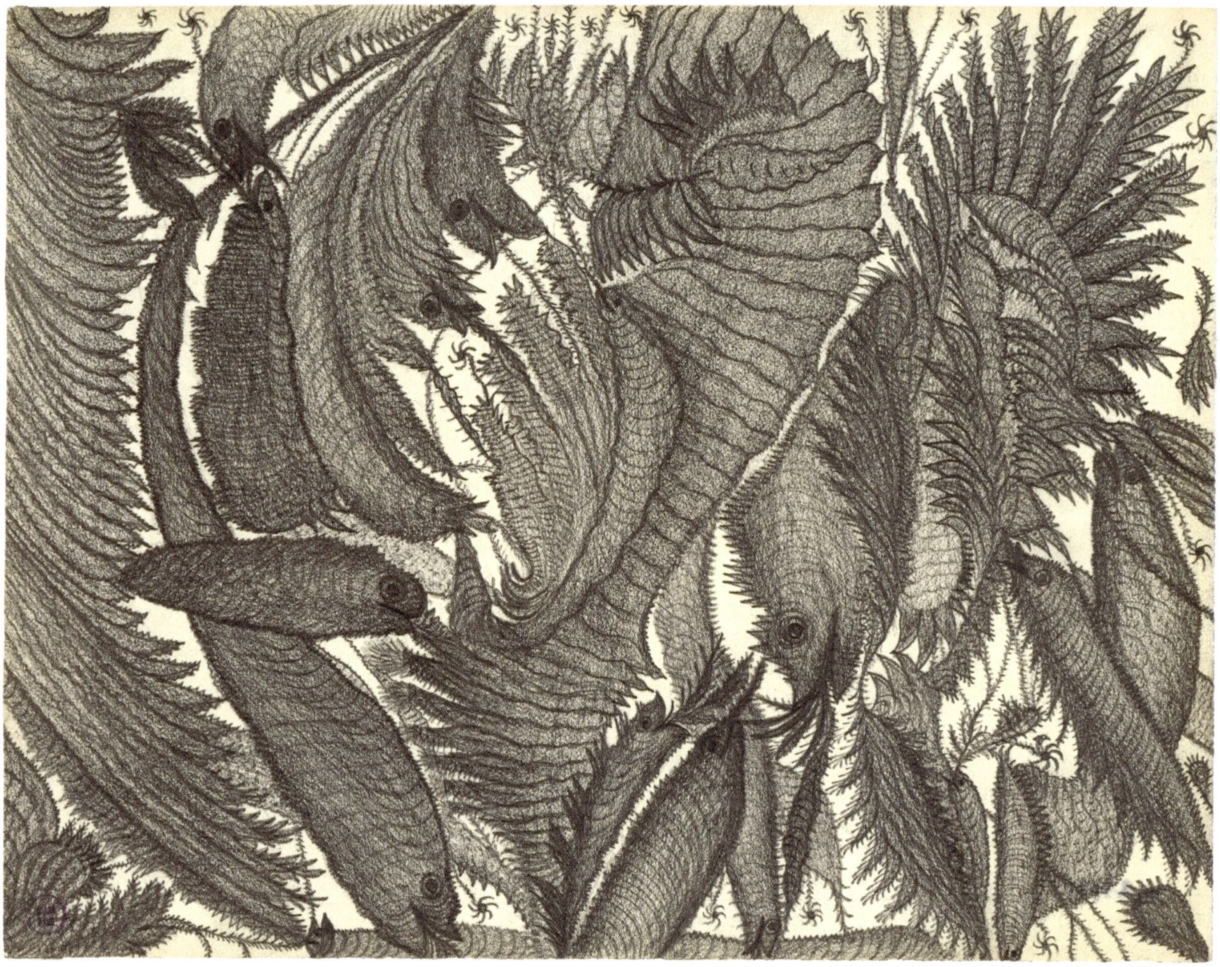

Marie Bouttier
sans titre untitled, 1899
mine de plomb sur papier
graphite on paper
25 x 32 cm
cab-3473-22

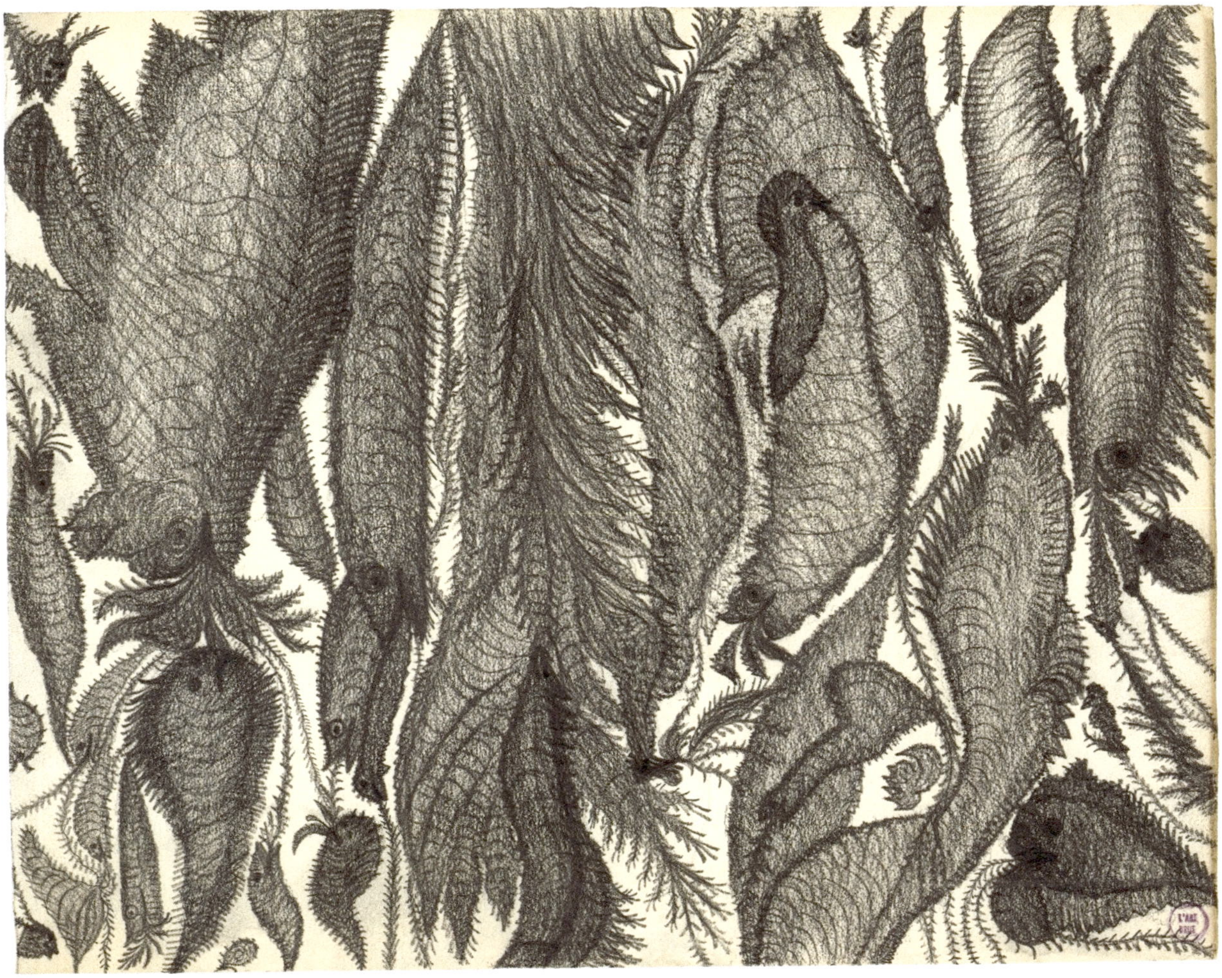

Marie Bouttier
sans titre untitled, 1899
mine de plomb sur papier
graphite on paper
25 x 32 cm
cab-3473-13

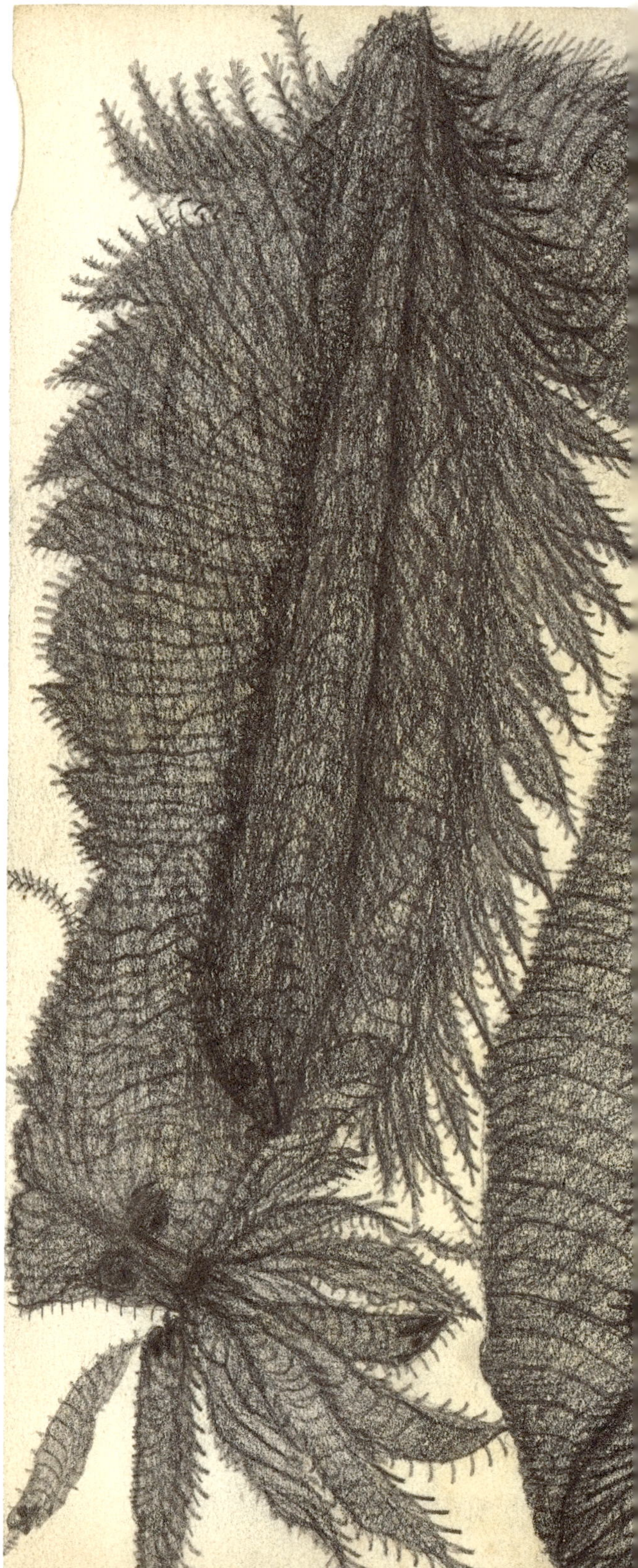

Marie Bouttier
sans titre untitled, 1899
mine de plomb sur papier
graphite on paper
25 x 32 cm
cab-3473-29

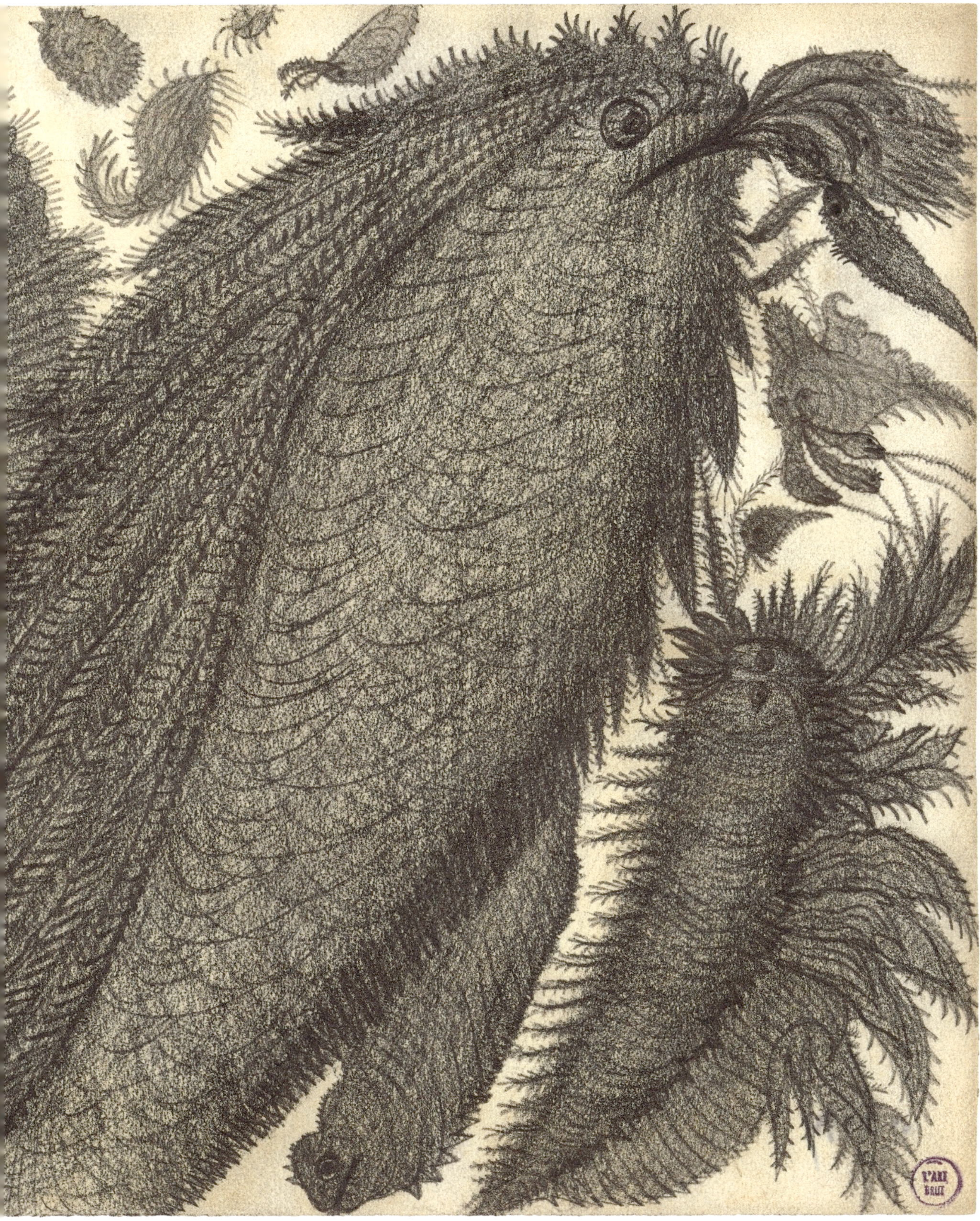

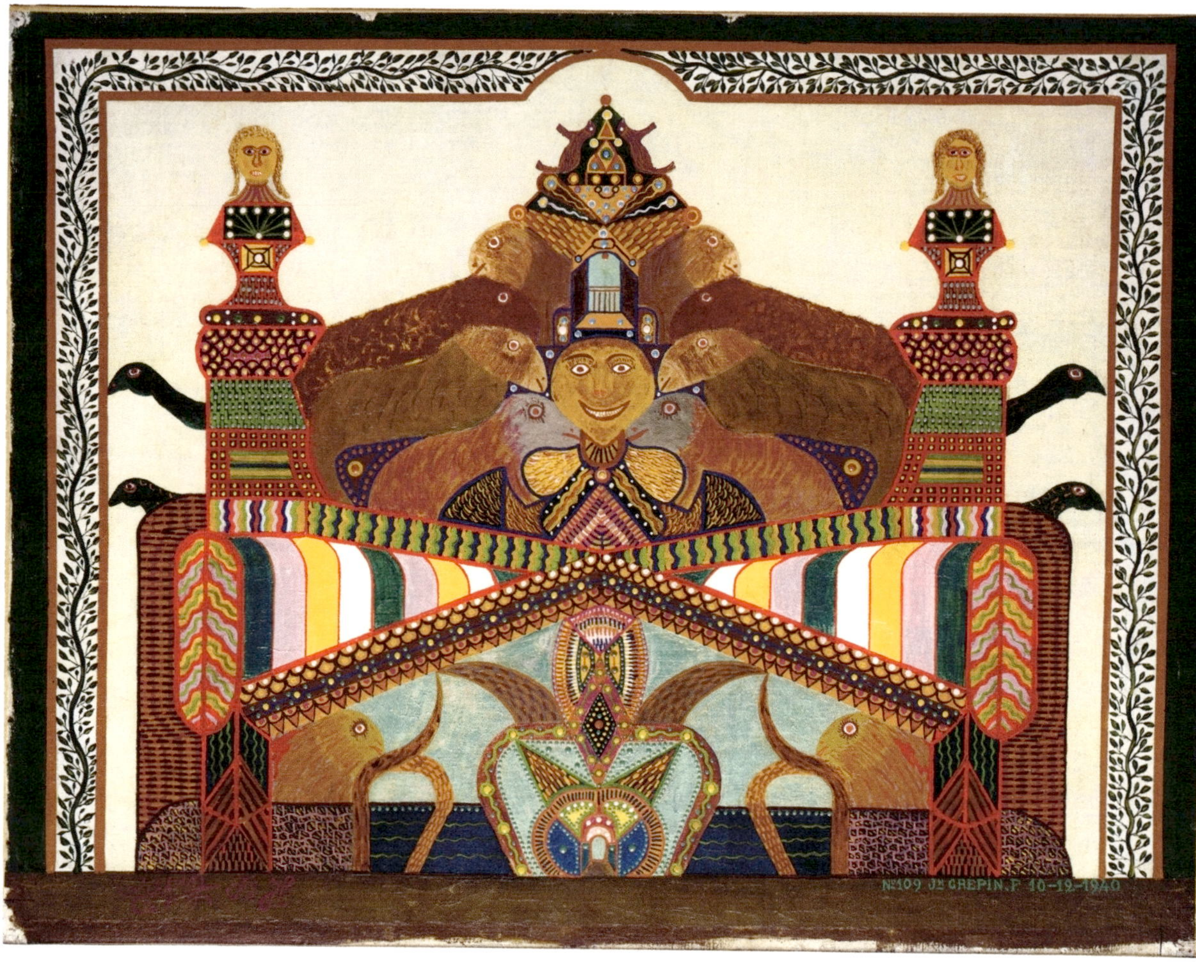

Fleury-Joseph Crépin
N° 109, 1939
huile sur toile
oil on canvas
58 x 75,5 x 3,5 cm
cab-A59

Fleury-Joseph Crépin
N° 43, 1939
huile sur toile
oil on canvas
51,5 x 35 x 1,5 cm
cab-A144

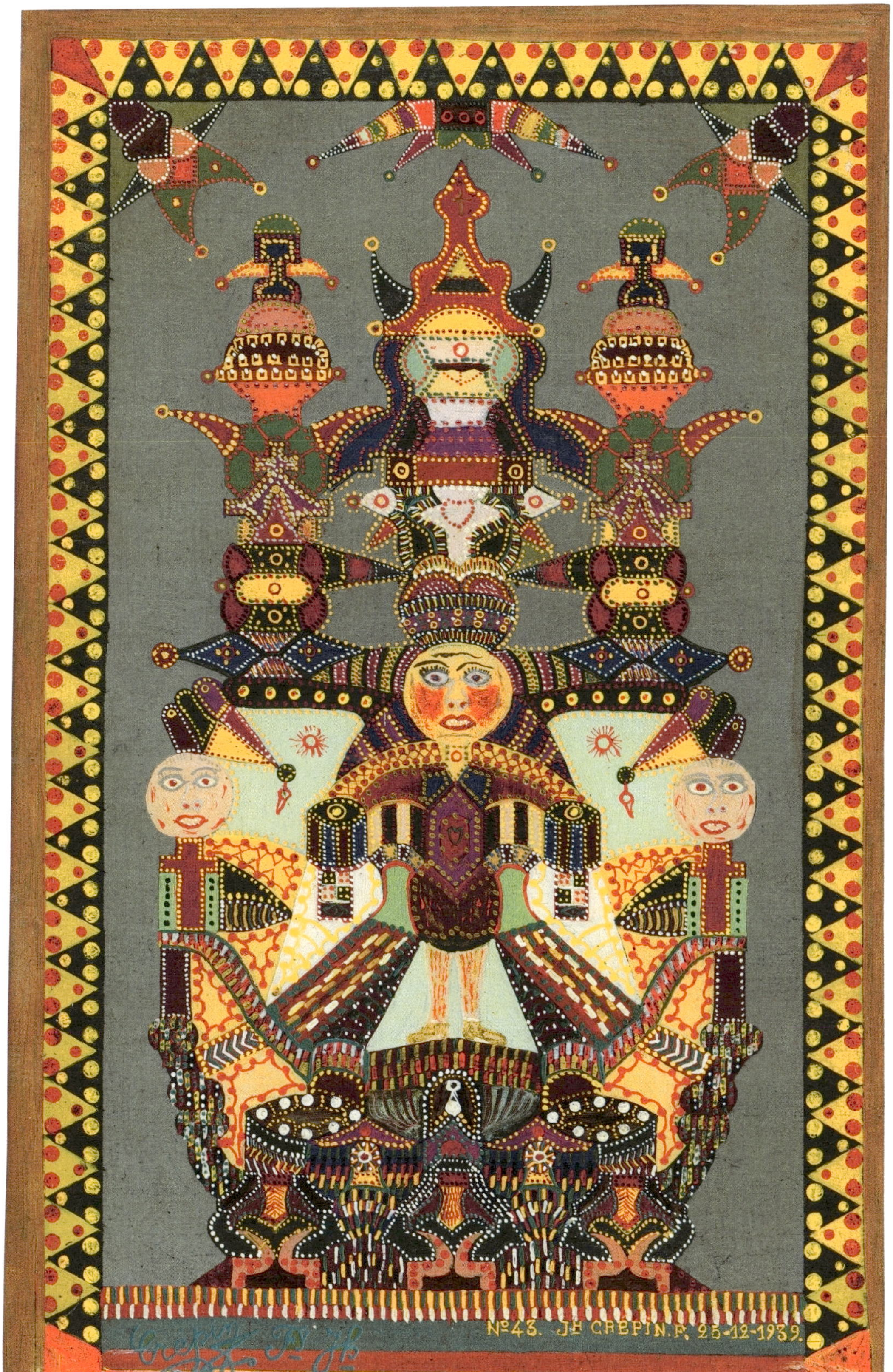
N°43. J. CREPIN. F. 25-12-1939.

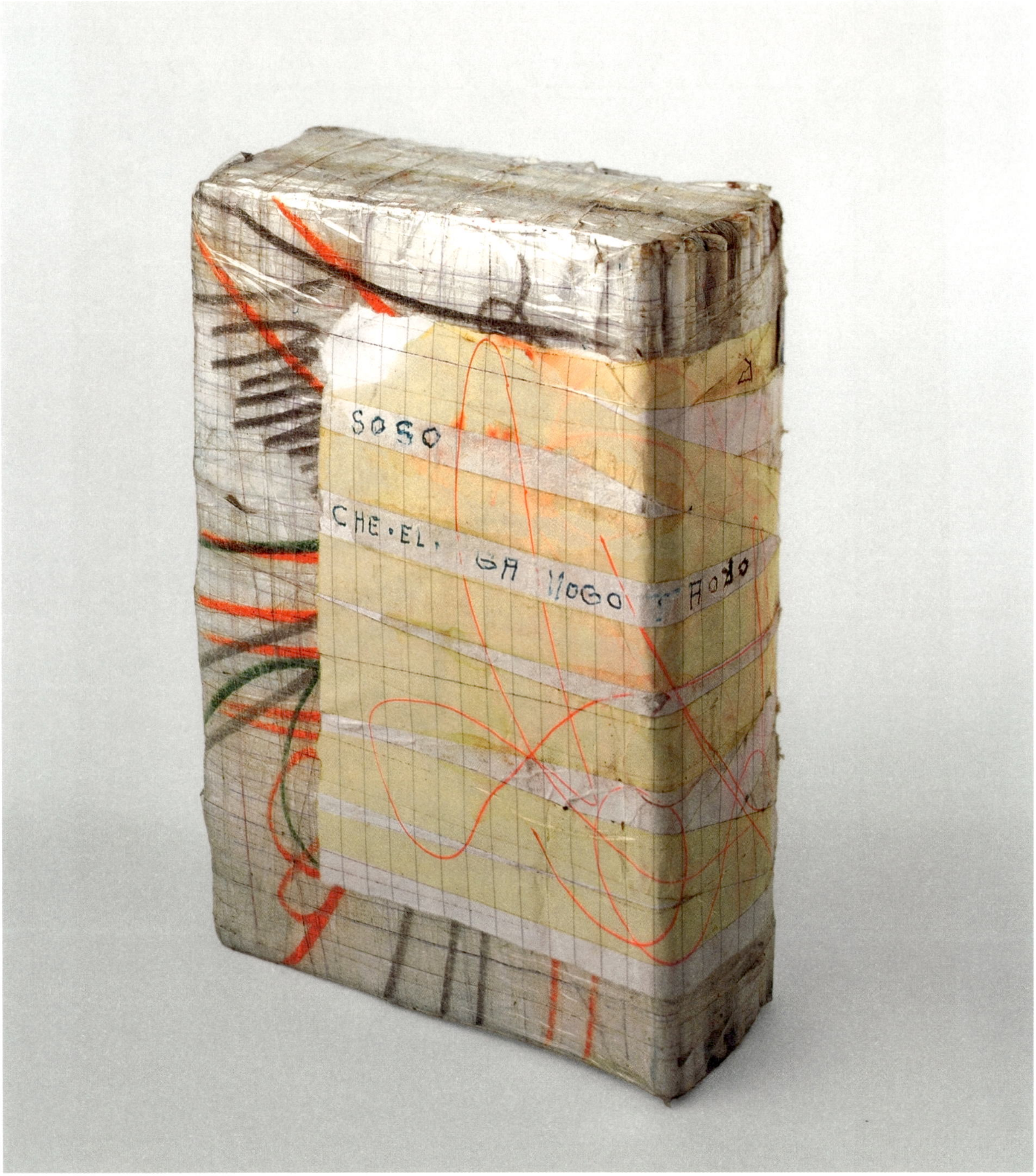

Antonio Dalla Valle
sans titre untitled, entre between
1997 et and 2003
assemblage de matériaux divers :
carton, papier, plastique, ruban adhésif,
tissu, … assemblage of miscellaneous
materials: cardboard, paper, plastic,
adhesive tape, cloth …
dimensions diverses various sizes
cab-13473-1-8, cab-13474
cab-13973, cab-13974
cab-13985, cab-13986

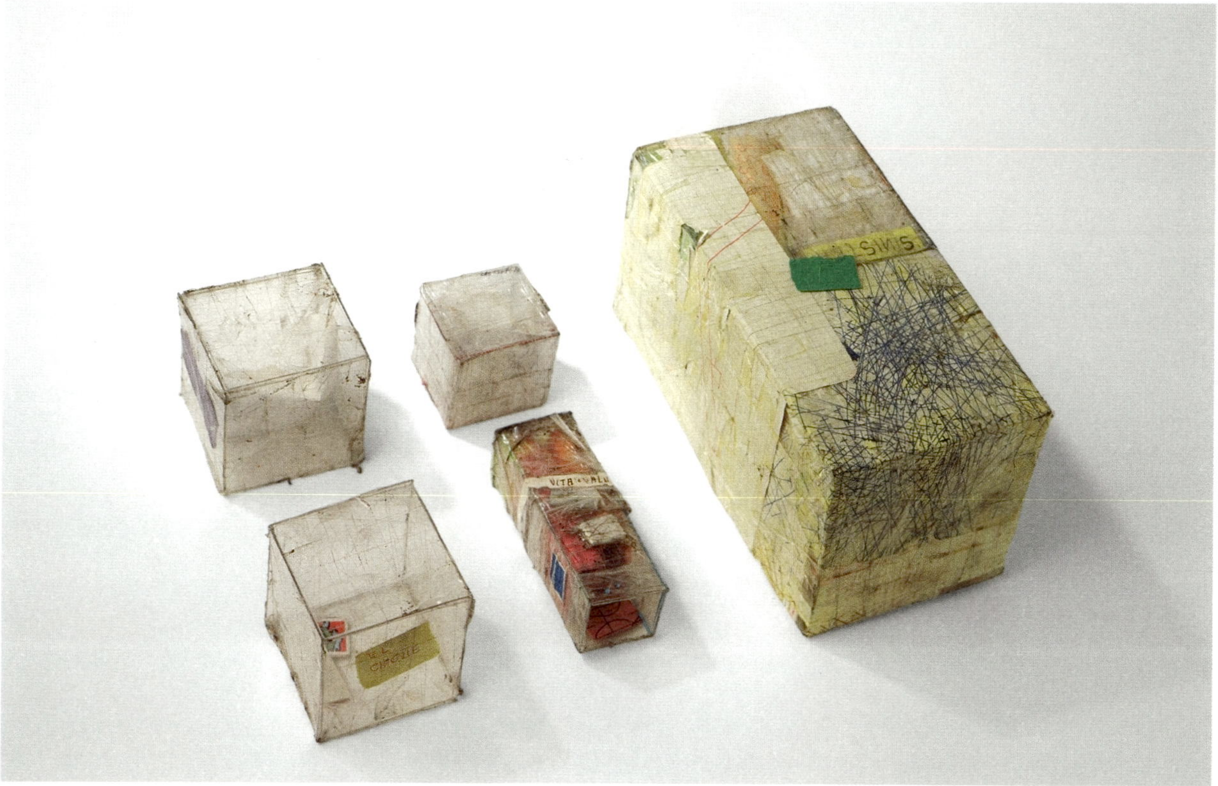

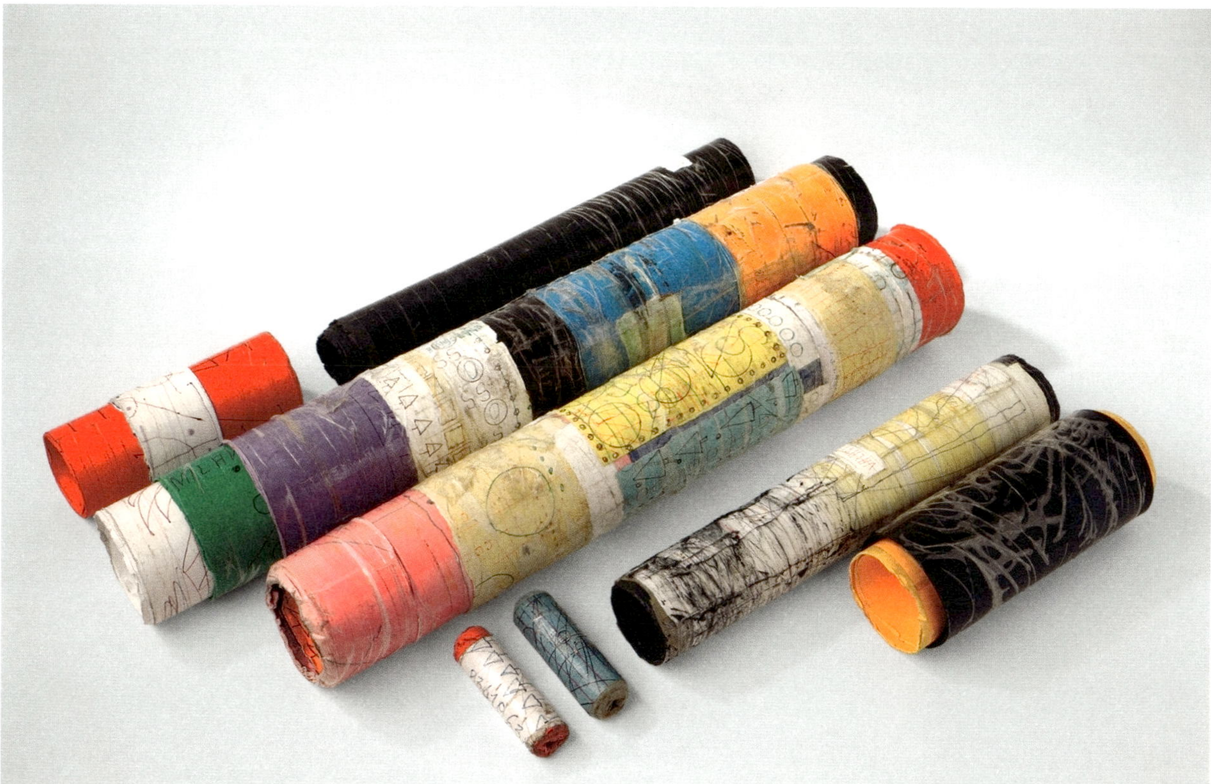

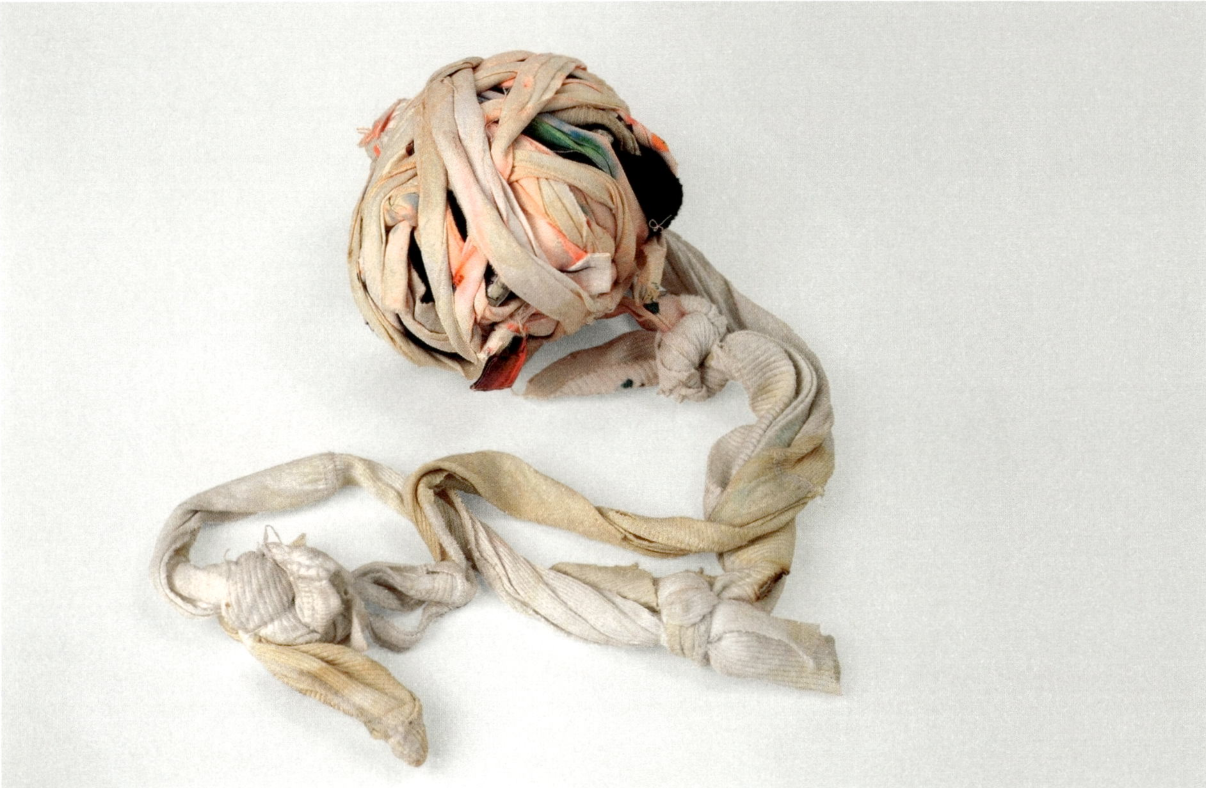

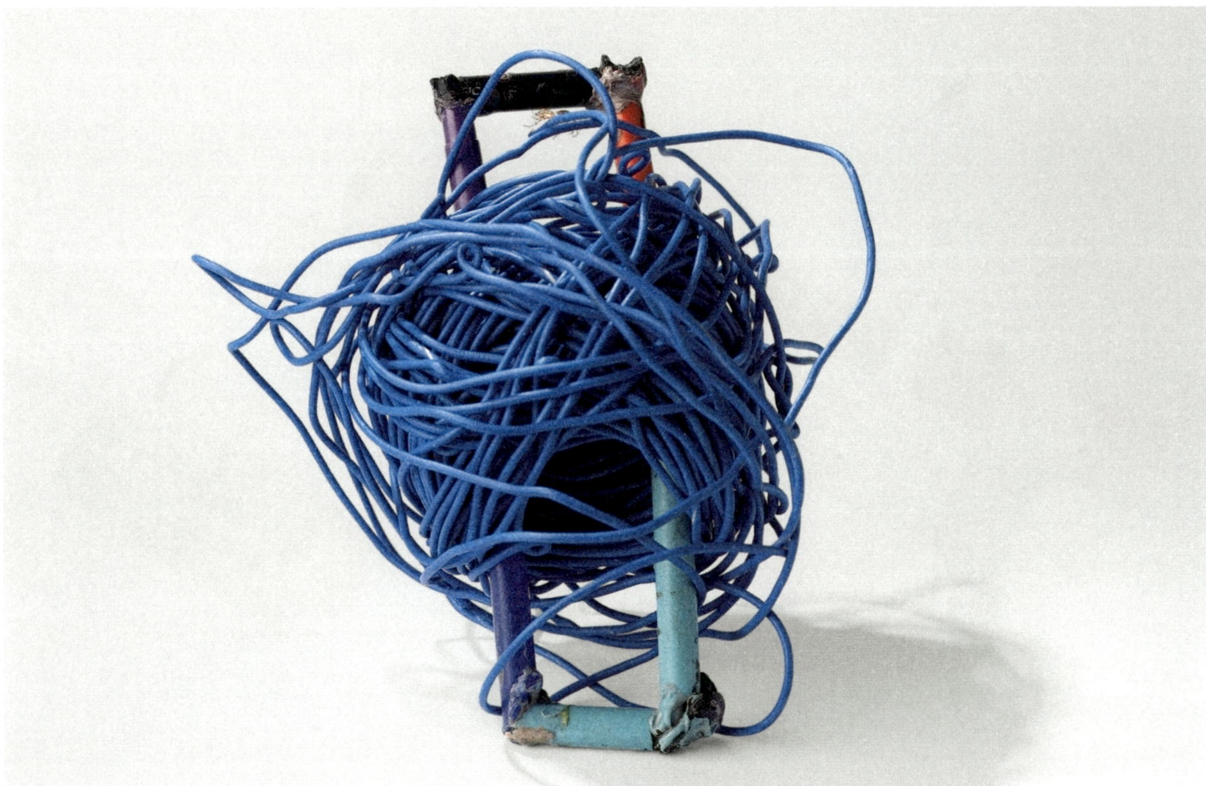

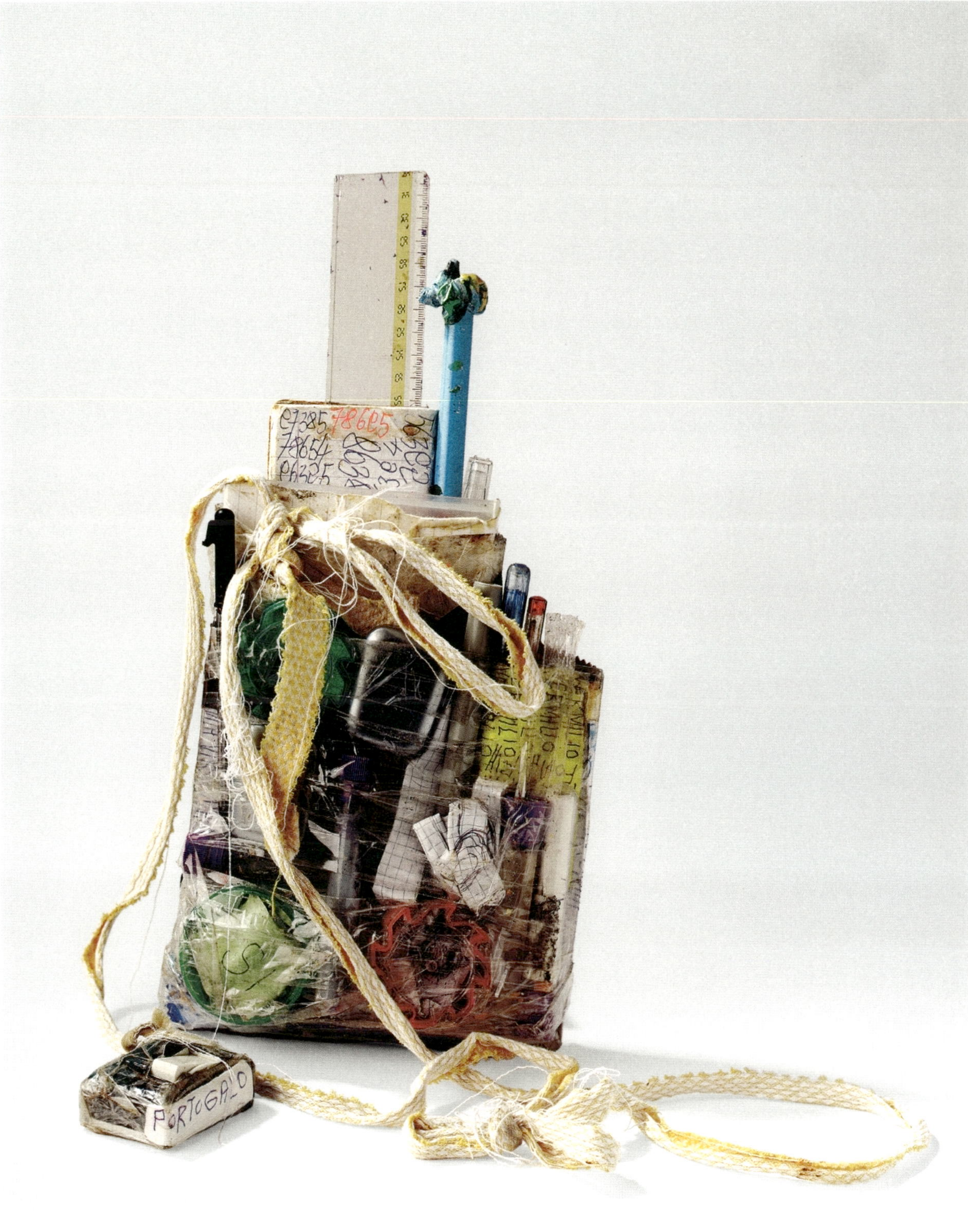

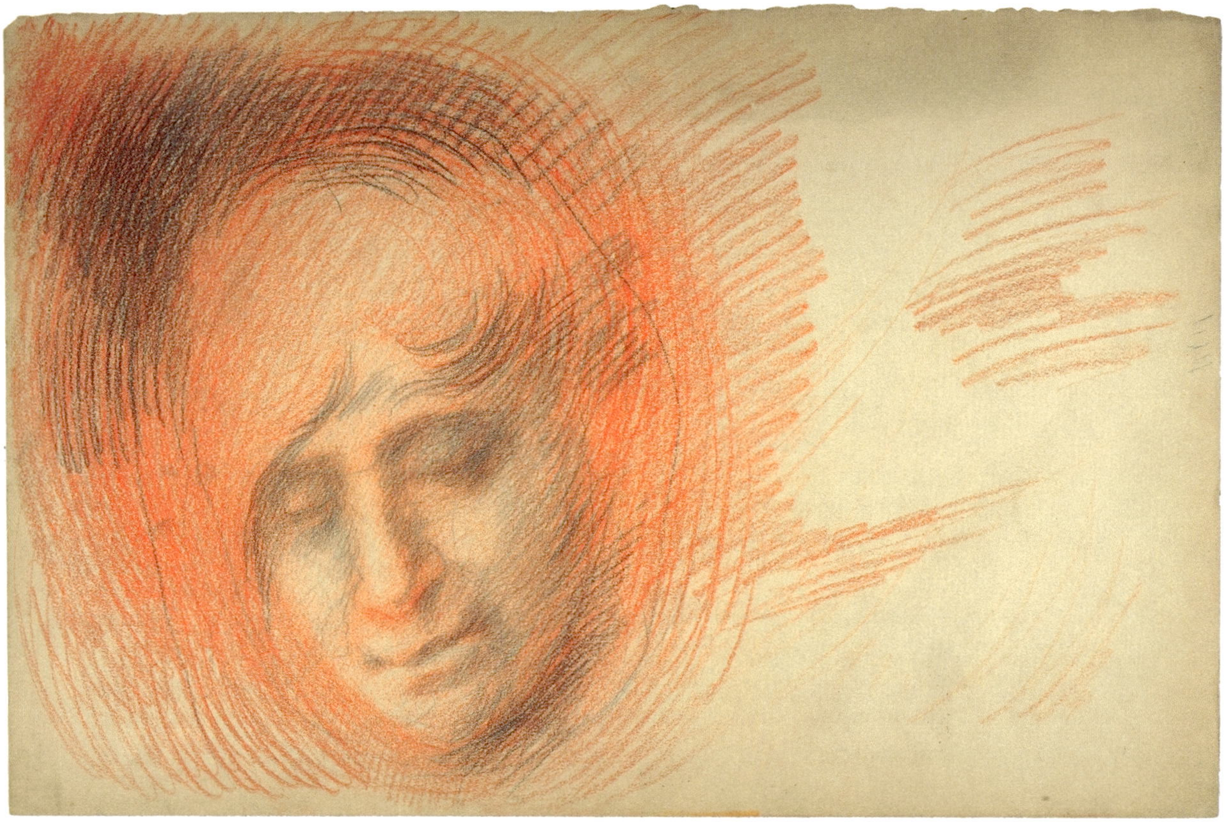

Fernand Desmoulin
Jeune homme au tourbillon,
entre between 1900 et and 1902
mine de plomb et sanguine sur papier
graphite and sanguine on paper
32,7 x 50,2 cm
ni-7747

Fernand Desmoulin
Visages endormis,
entre between 1900 et and 1902
mine de plomb sur papier
graphite on paper
50 x 32,5 cm
ni-7751

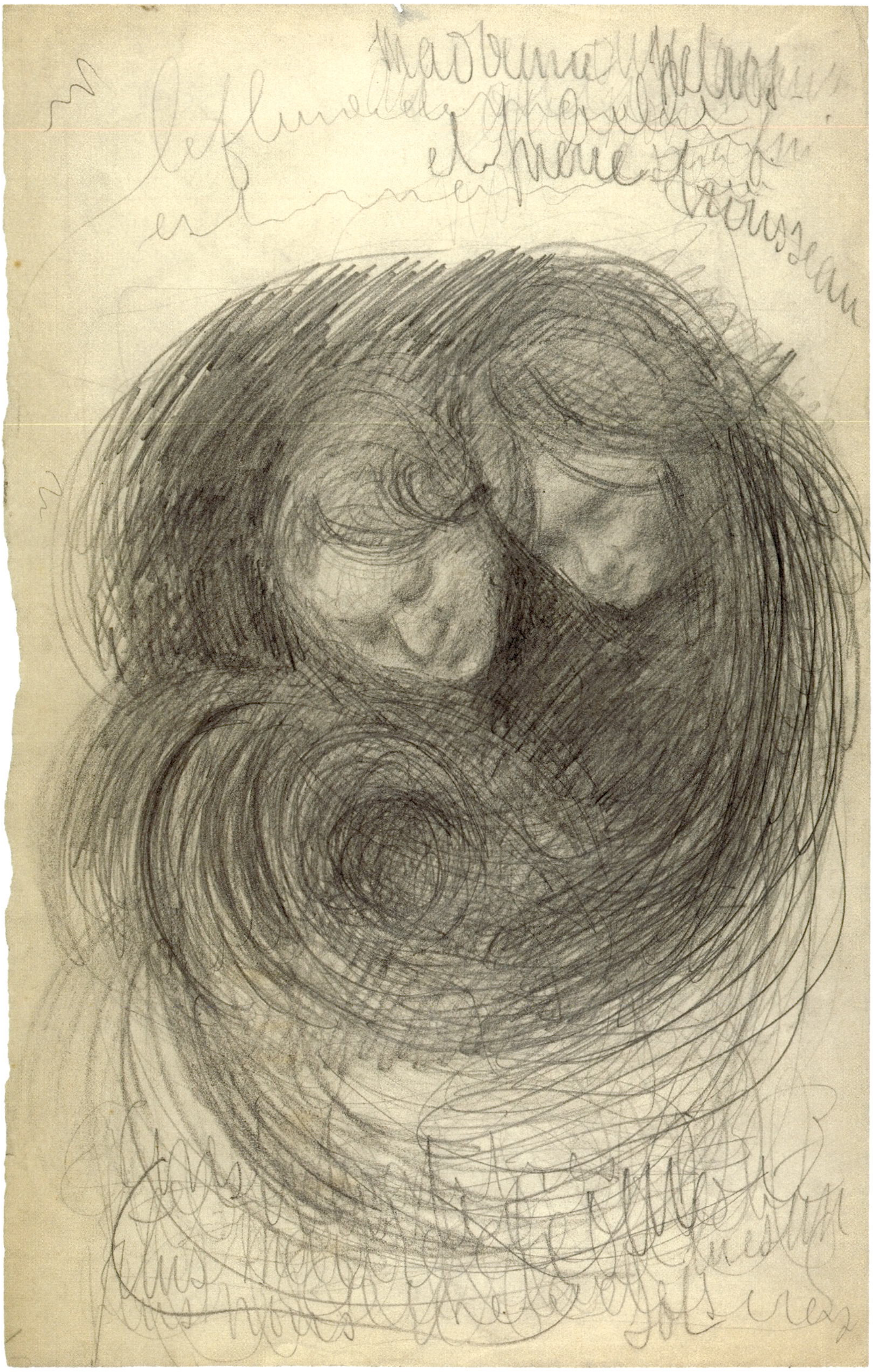

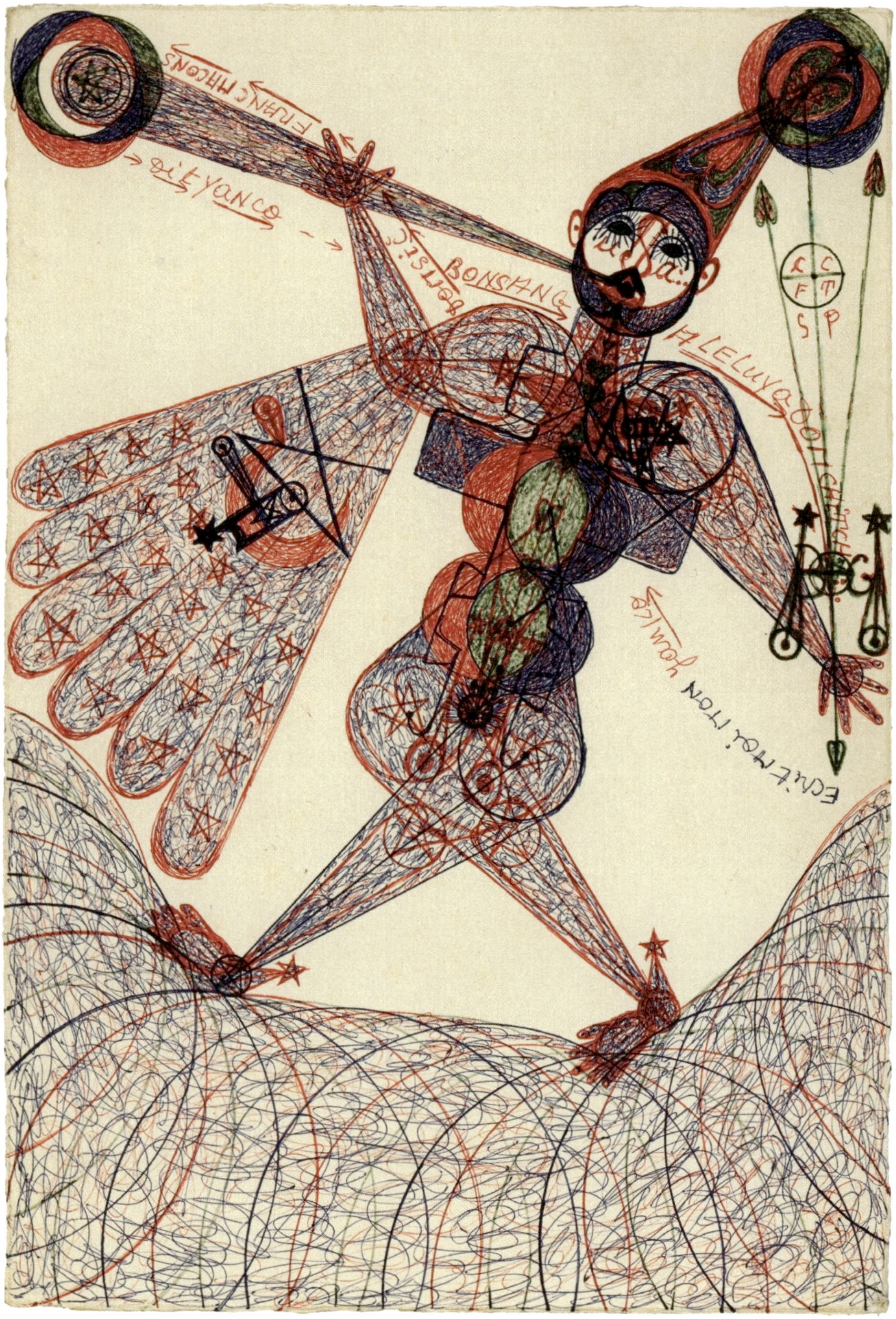

Janko Domsic
Écrit moi, ca. 1970
stylo-bille sur carton
ballpoint pen on cardboard
50 x 34,5 cm
cab-7597

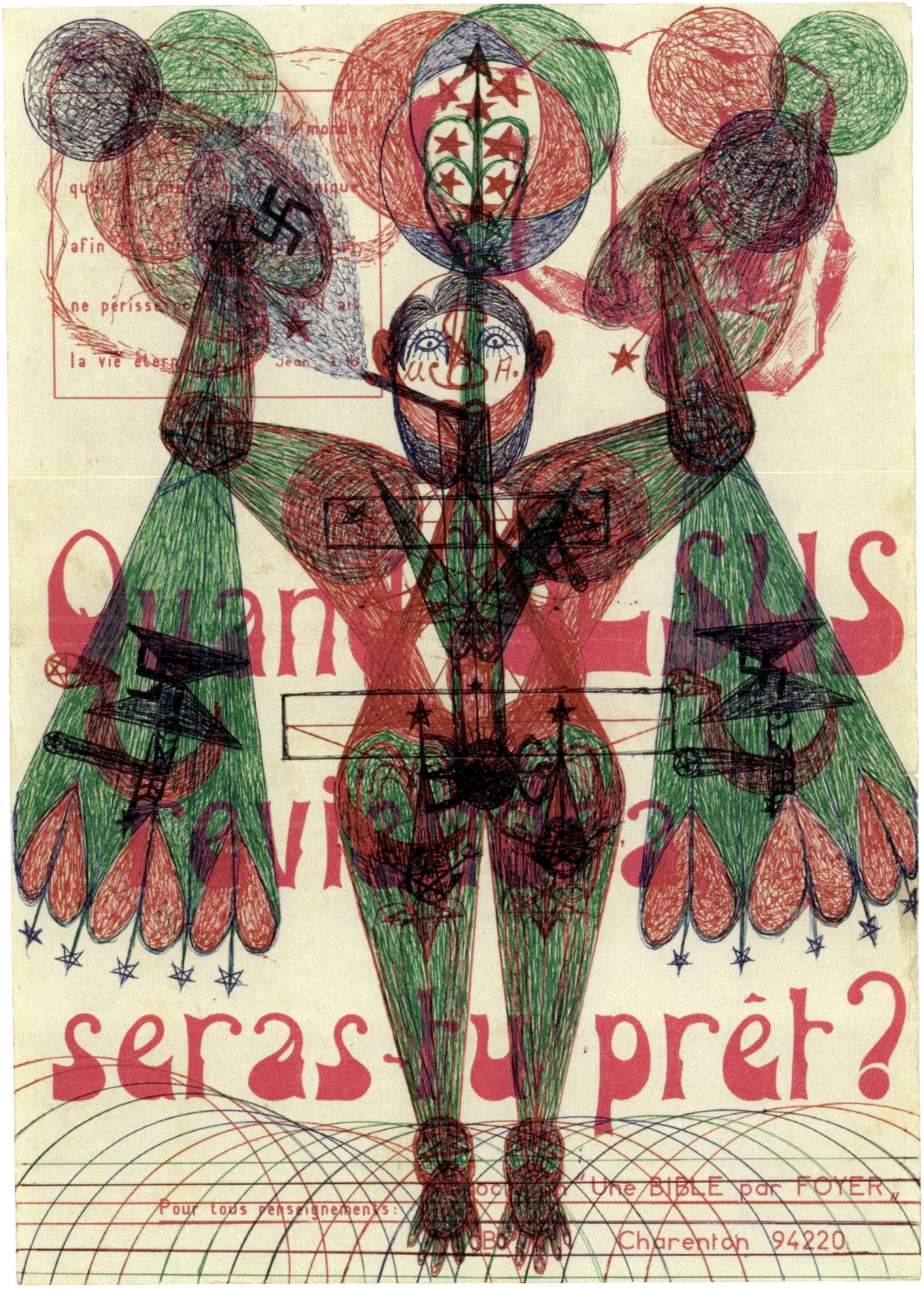

Janko Domsic
U$A, ca. 1970
stylo-bille sur papier
ballpoint pen on cardboard
44 x 32 cm
cab-7590

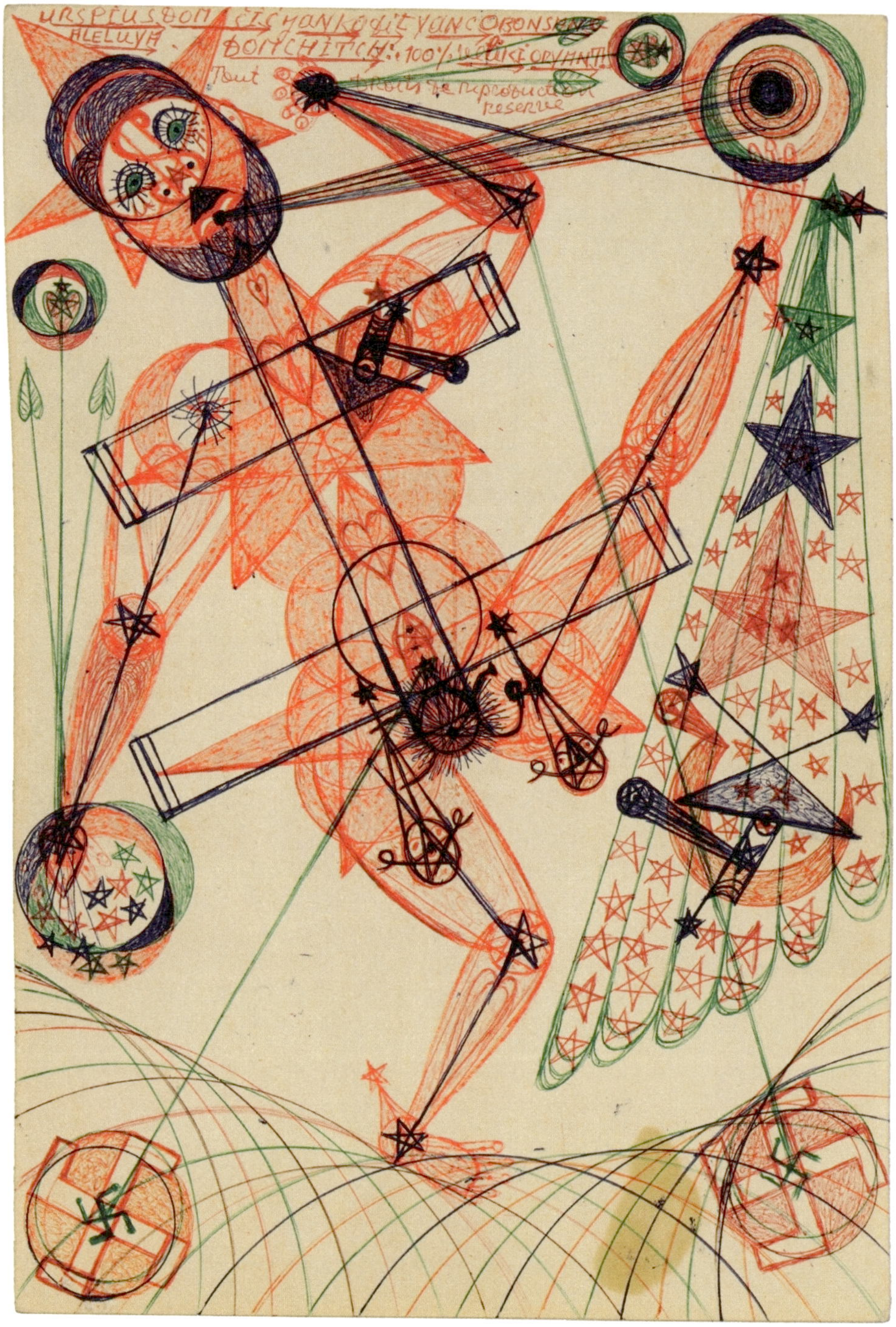

Janko Domsic
Tous droits de reproduction réservés, ca. 1970
stylo-bille et feutre sur carton ballpoint pen and felt-tip pen on cardboard
42,5 x 29 cm
cab-7589

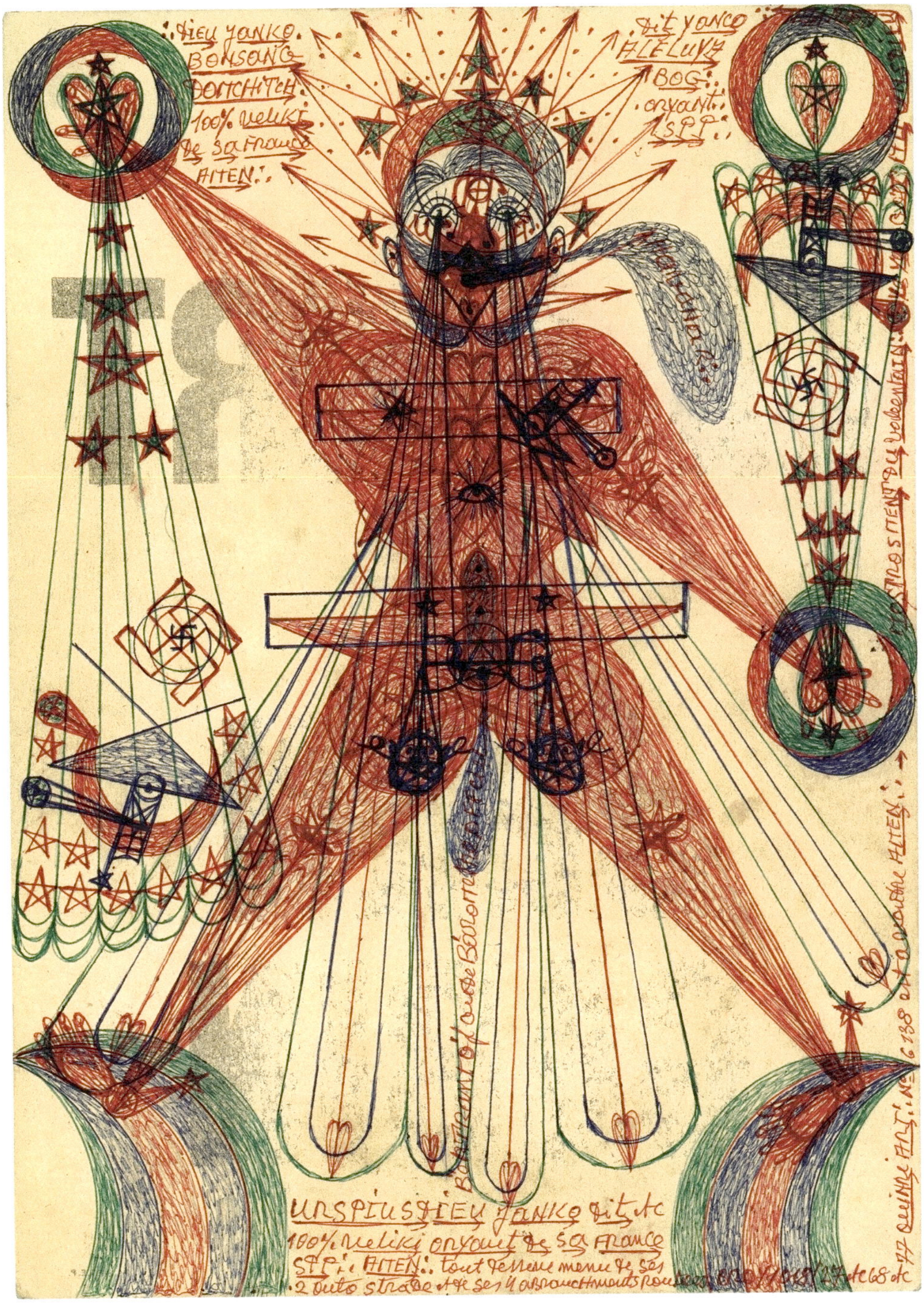

Janko Domsic
sans titre untitled, ca. 1970
stylo-bille sur papier
ballpoint pen on paper
41,5 x 30 cm
cab-7707

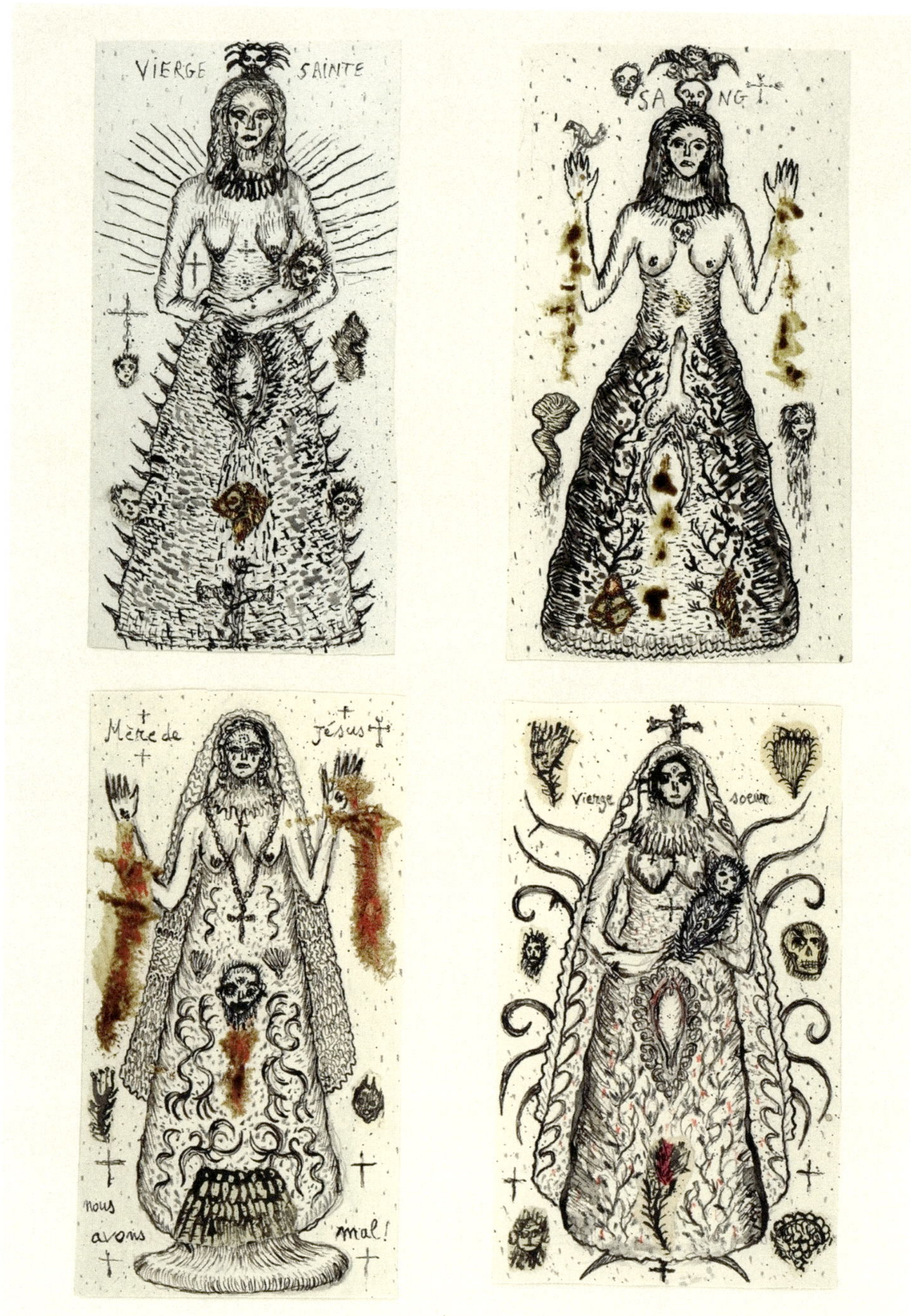

Philippe Ducollet-Michaëlef
Déesse - Mère, vierges saintes, vierges «hindoues», entre between 2006 et and 2020
mine de plomb, encre de Chine, crayon de couleur, sang et feutre sur papier
graphite, India ink, coloured pencil, blood, and felt-tip pen on paper
42 x 29,7 cm
ni-10322

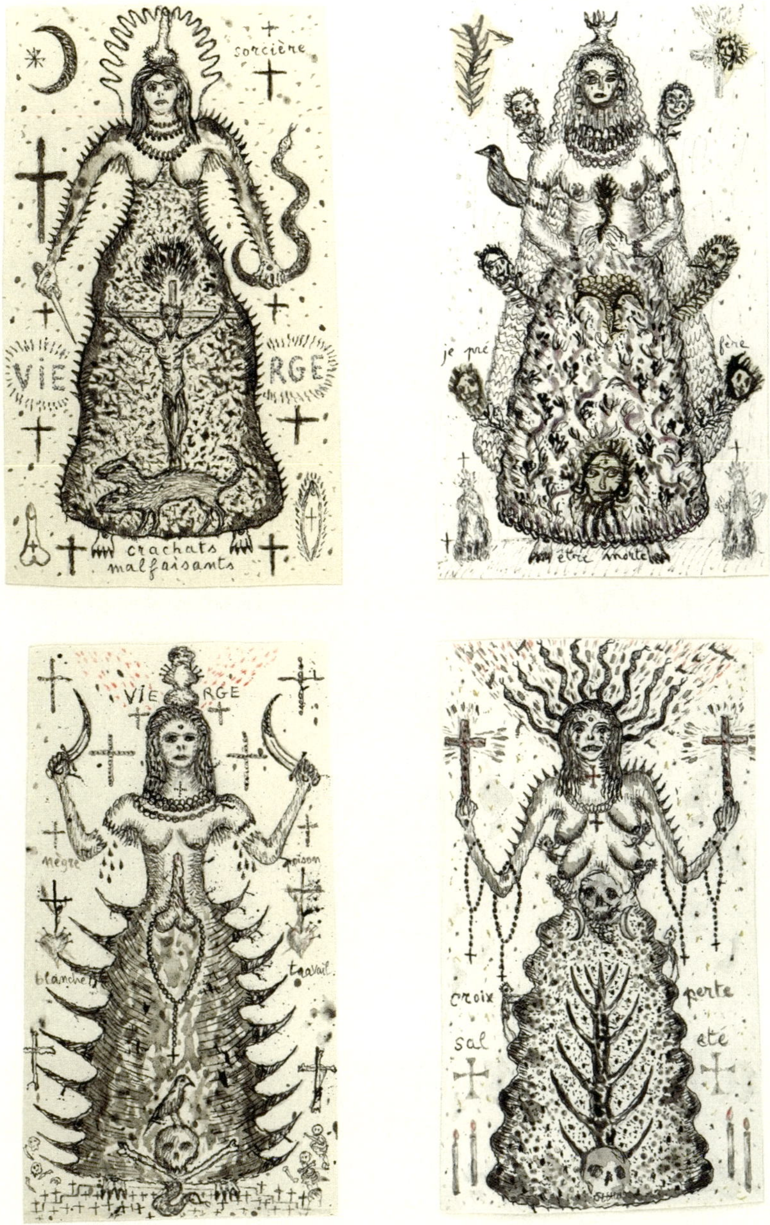

Philippe Ducollet-Michaëlef
Déesse - Mère, vierges saintes, vierges «hindoues», entre between 2006 et and 2020
mine de plomb, encre de Chine, crayon de couleur et feutre sur papier
graphite, India ink, coloured pencil, and felt-tip pen on paper
42 x 29,7 cm
ni-10316

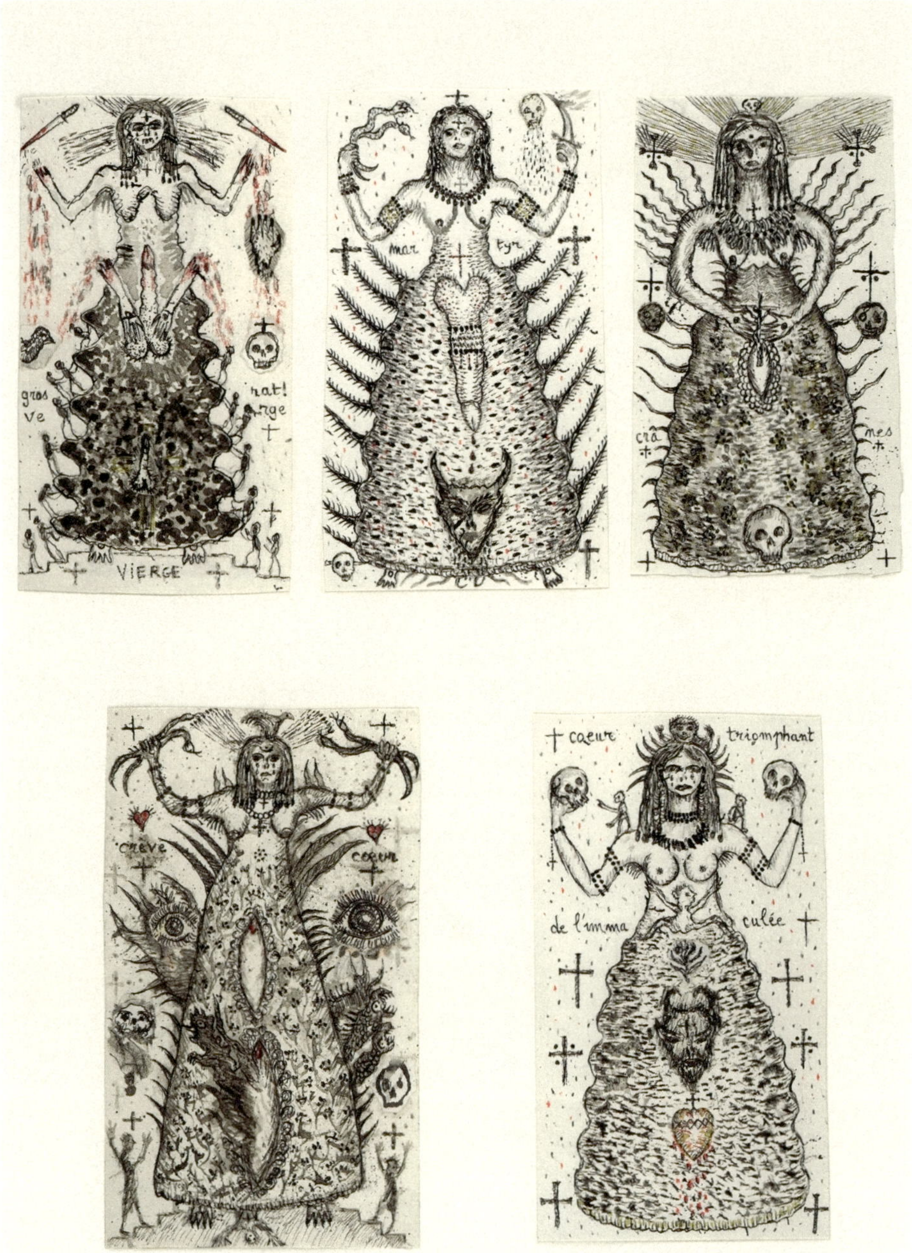

Philippe Ducollet-Michaëlef
Déesse - Mère, vierges saintes, vierges «hindoues», entre between 2006 et and 2020
mine de plomb, encre de Chine, crayon de couleur et feutre sur papier
graphite, India ink, coloured pencil, and felt-tip pen on paper
42 x 29,7 cm
ni-10301

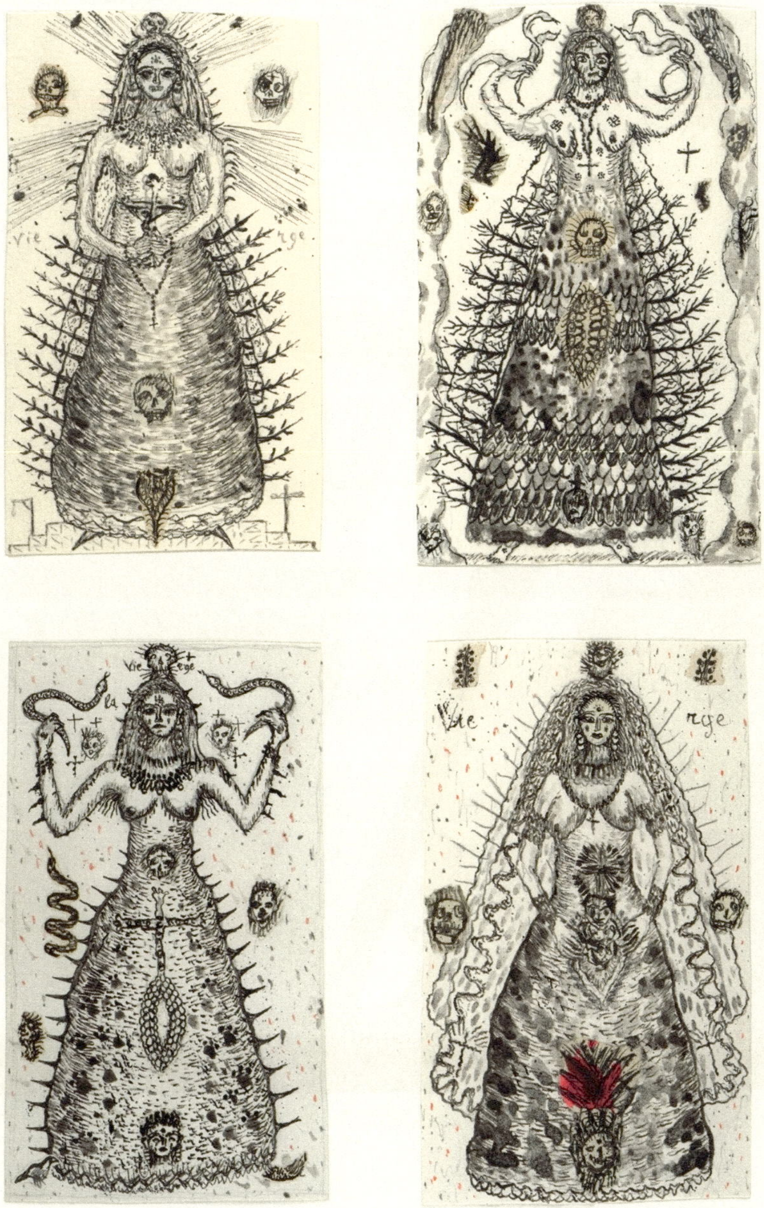

Philippe Ducollet-Michaëlef
Déesse - Mère, vierges saintes, vierges «hindoues», entre between 2006 et and 2020
mine de plomb, encre de Chine, crayon de couleur et feutre sur papier
graphite, India ink, coloured pencil, and felt-tip pen on paper
42 x 29,7 cm
ni-10313

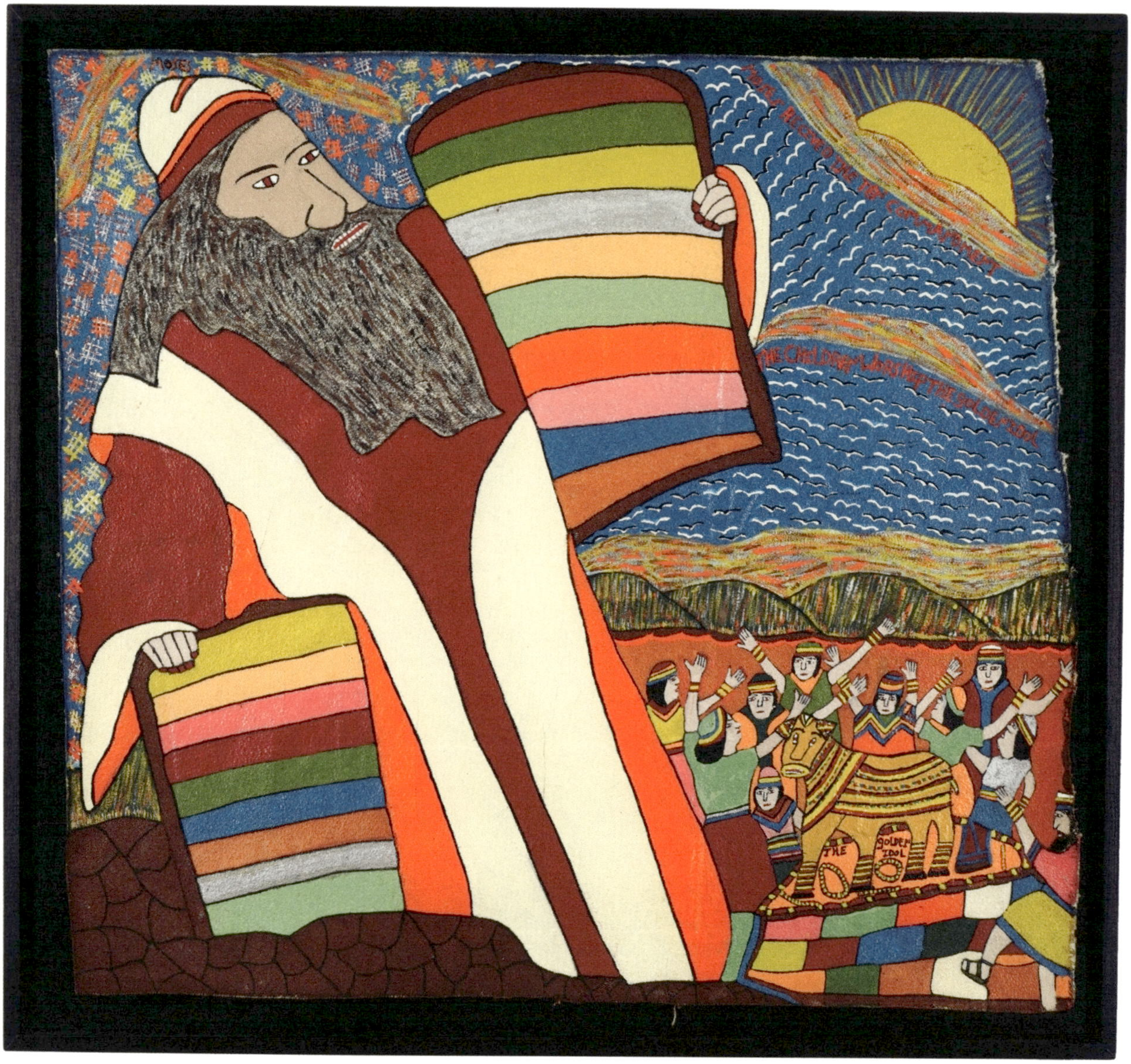

Elijah
Moses recived the Ten Commandment
entre between 1990 et and 2000
huile sur toile oil on canvas
66 x 72 cm
cab-12014

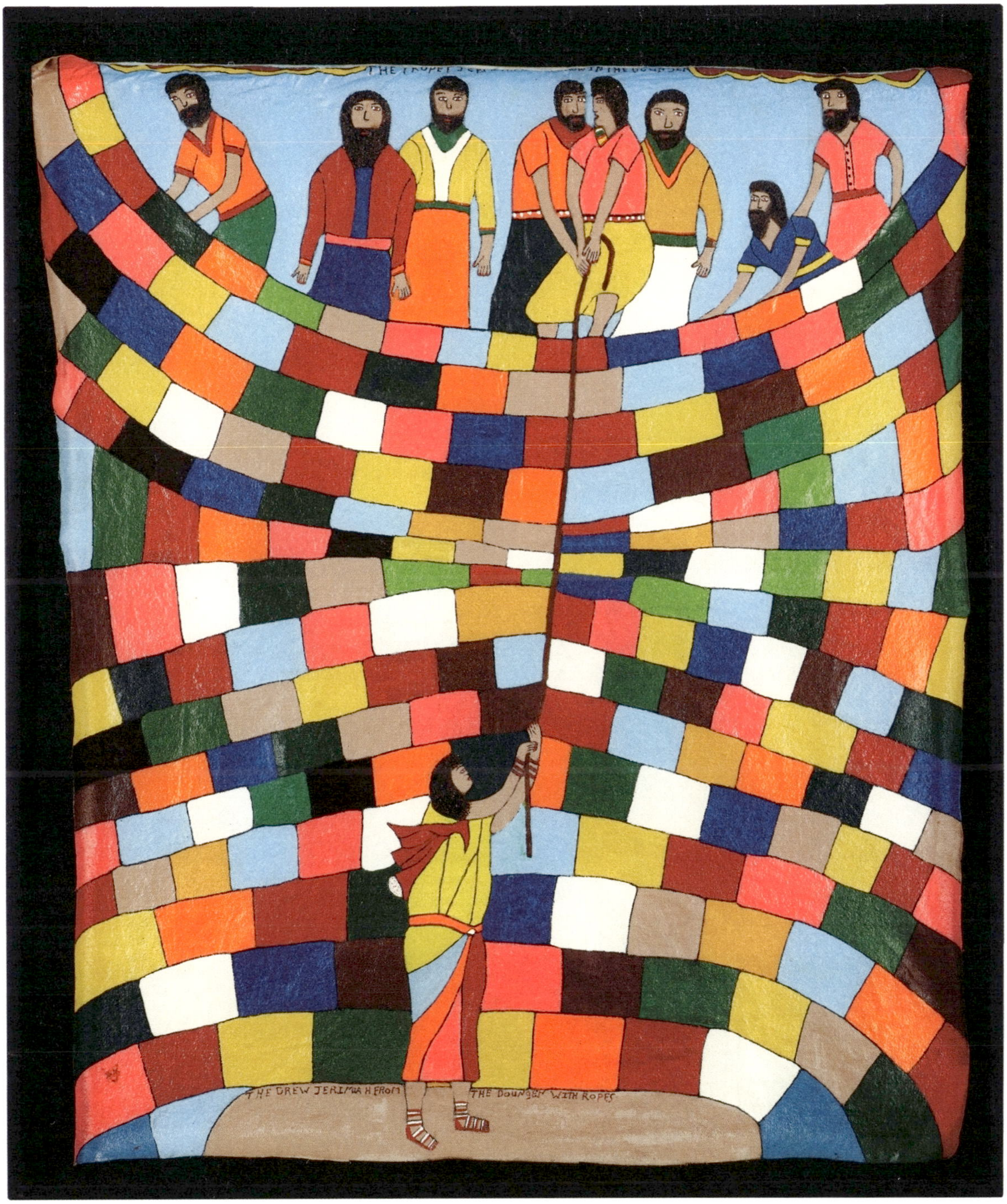

Elijah
The Propet Jermiah was throw in Dounjen, entre between 1985 et and 1993
huile sur toile oil on canvas
78 x 66 cm
cab-9902

> Elijah
The Crusifyxsion of Jesus Christ, entre between 1990 et and 2000
huile sur toile oil on canvas
68,5 x 108 cm
cab-12042

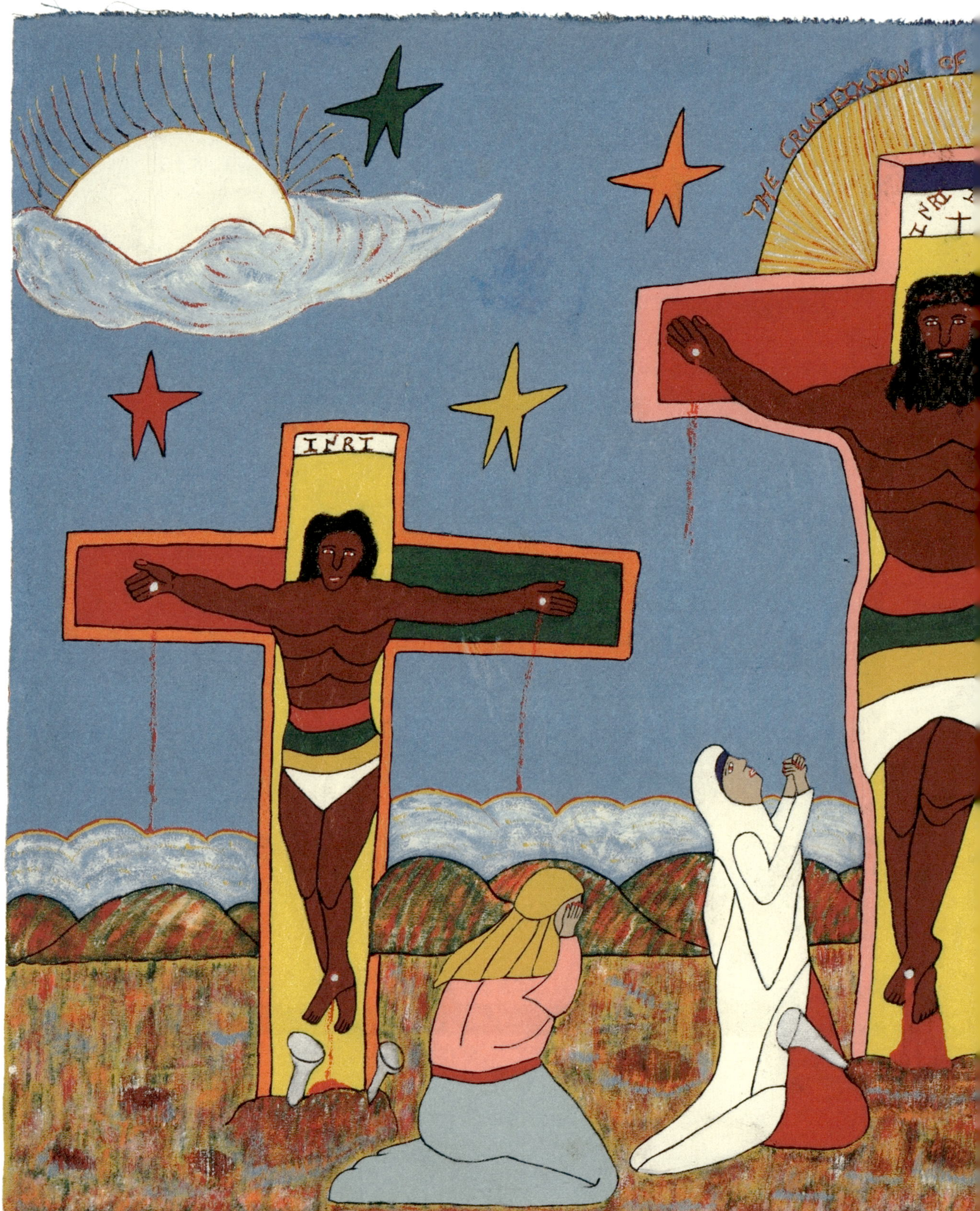
INRI

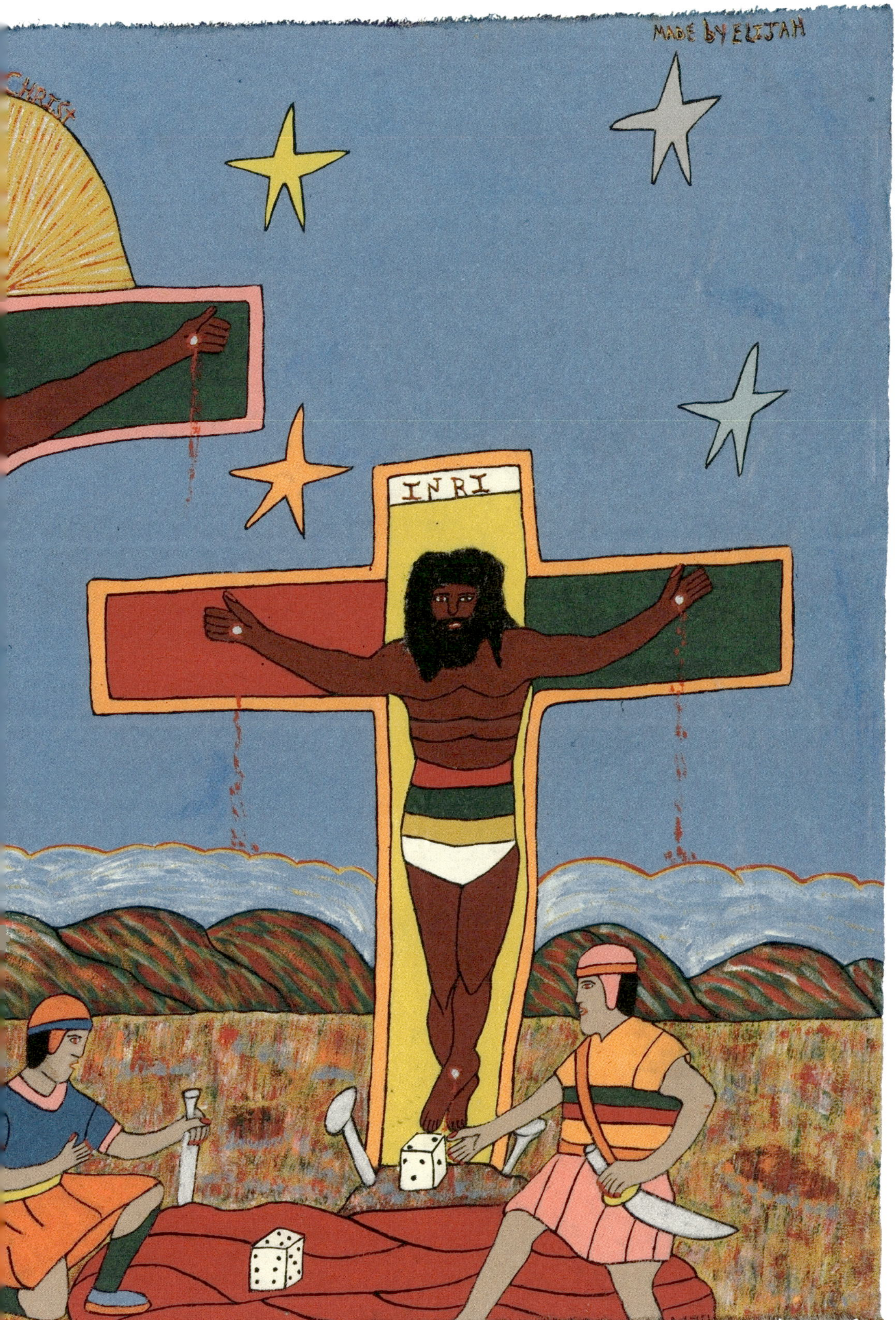
MADE BY ELIJAH
CHRIST
INRI

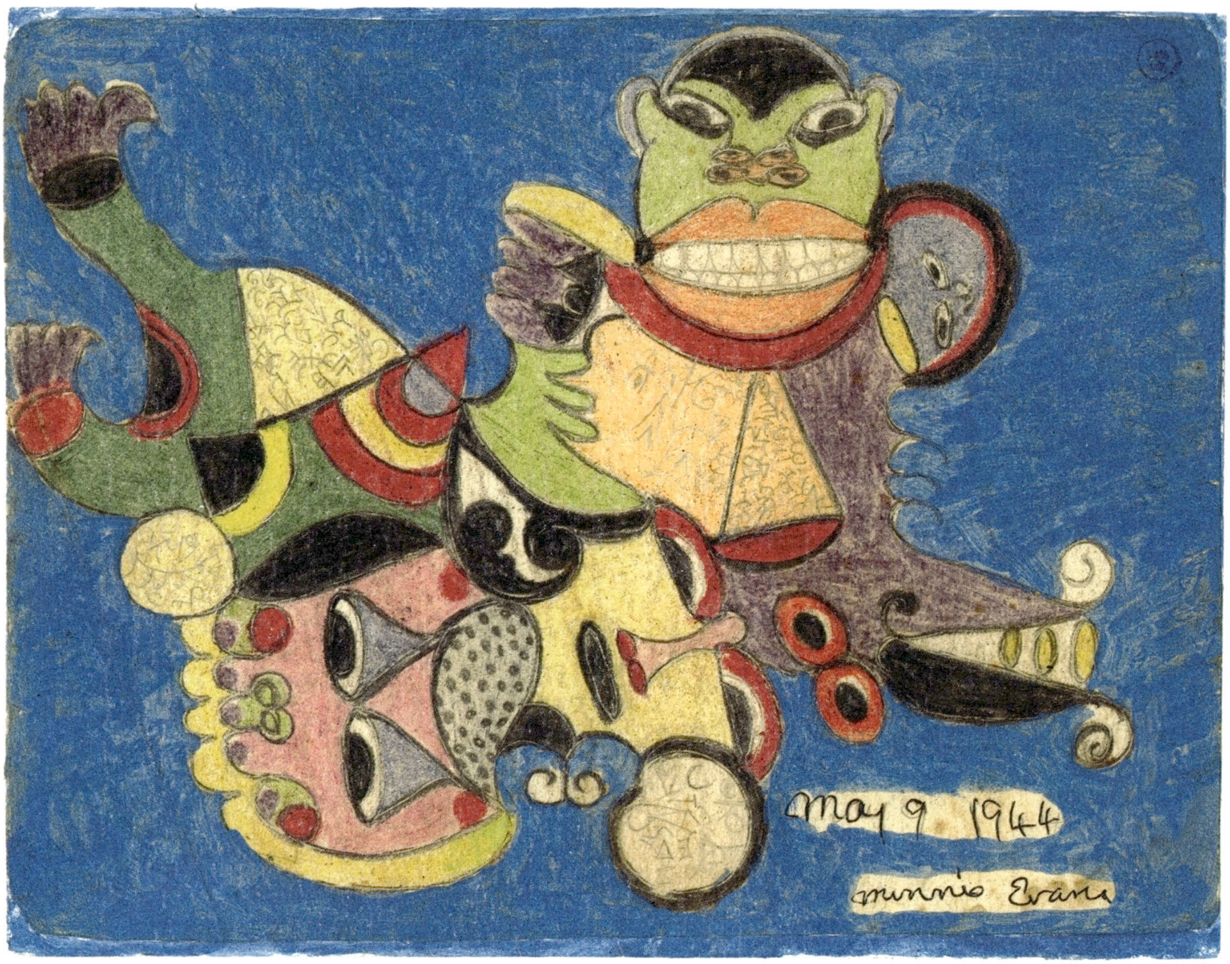

Minnie Evans
sans titre untitled, 1944
mine de plomb et crayon de couleur sur papier graphite, India ink, and coloured pencil on paper
23 x 30 cm
cab-3494

Minnie Evans
sans titre untitled, entre between 1935 et and 1973
mine de plomb, feutre et crayon de couleur sur papier graphite, felt-tip pen, and coloured pencil on paper
30,5 x 22,5 cm
cab-3493

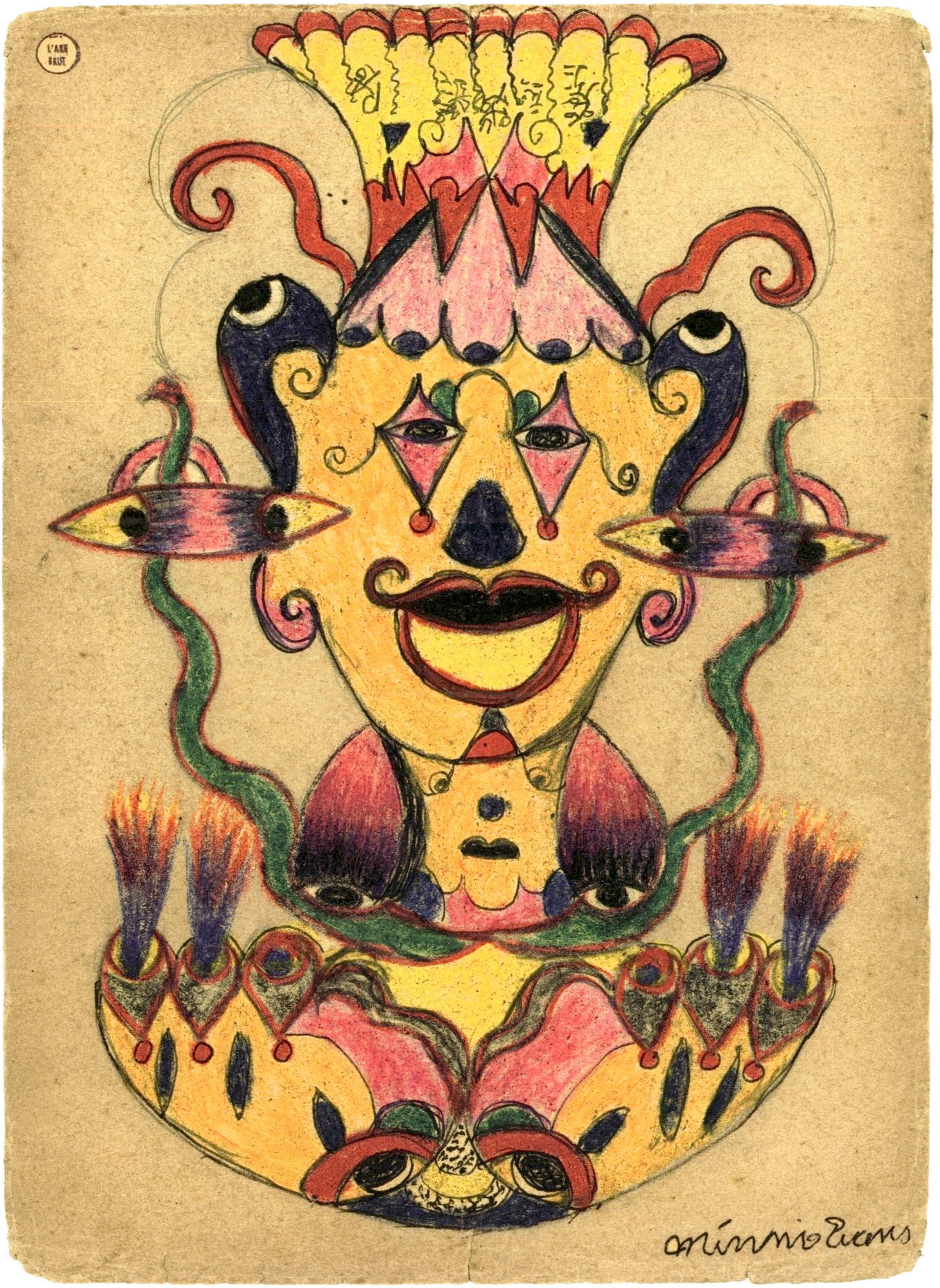

Jill Galliéni
sans titre untitled, ca. 1990
encre sur papier ink on paper
23,9 x 15,6 cm
ni-9984

Jill Galliéni
sans titre untitled, ca. 1990
encre sur papier ink on paper
23,9 x 15,6 cm
ni-9985

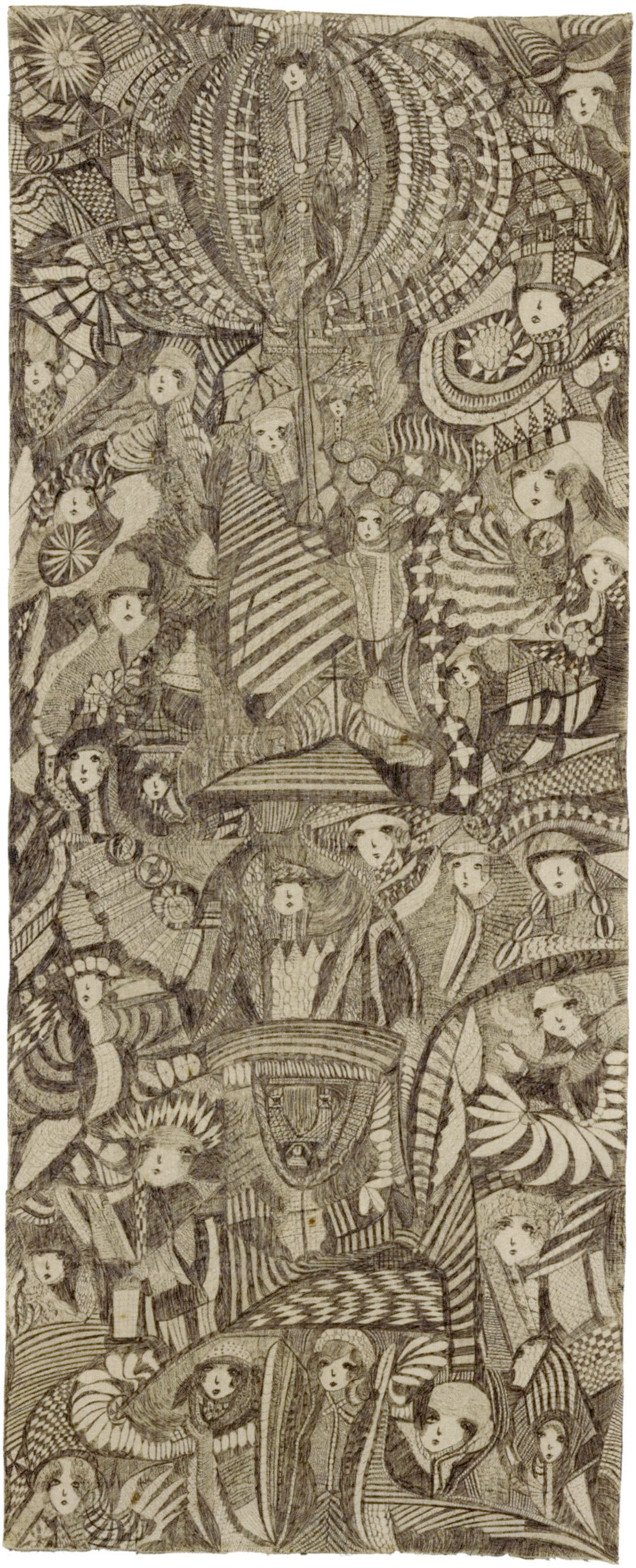

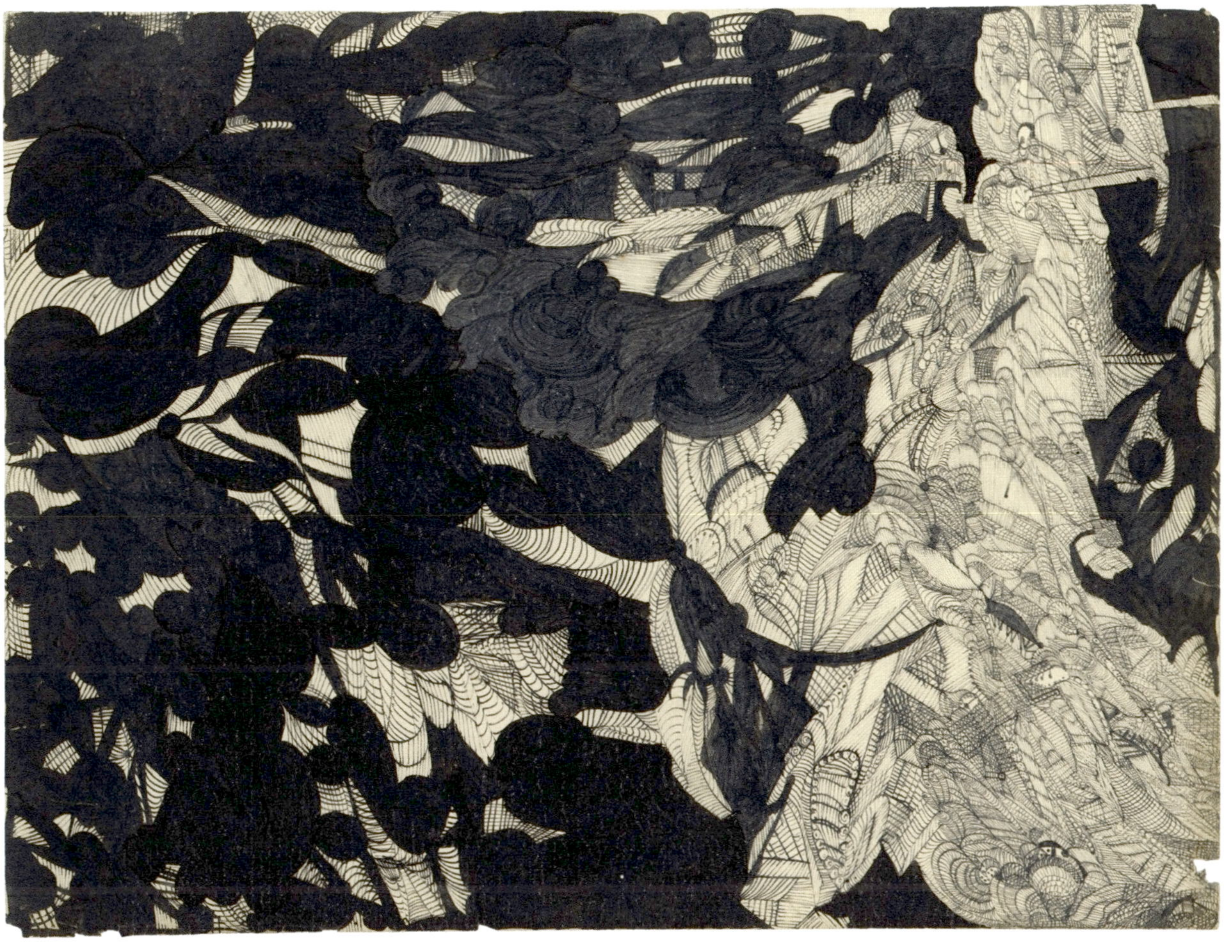

Madge Gill
sans titre untitled, s.d. n.d.
encre de Chine sur calicot
India ink on calico
213 x 86,5 cm
cab-6892

Madge Gill
sans titre untitled, s.d. n.d.
encre sur papier
ink on paper
55,5 x 76 cm
cab-9130

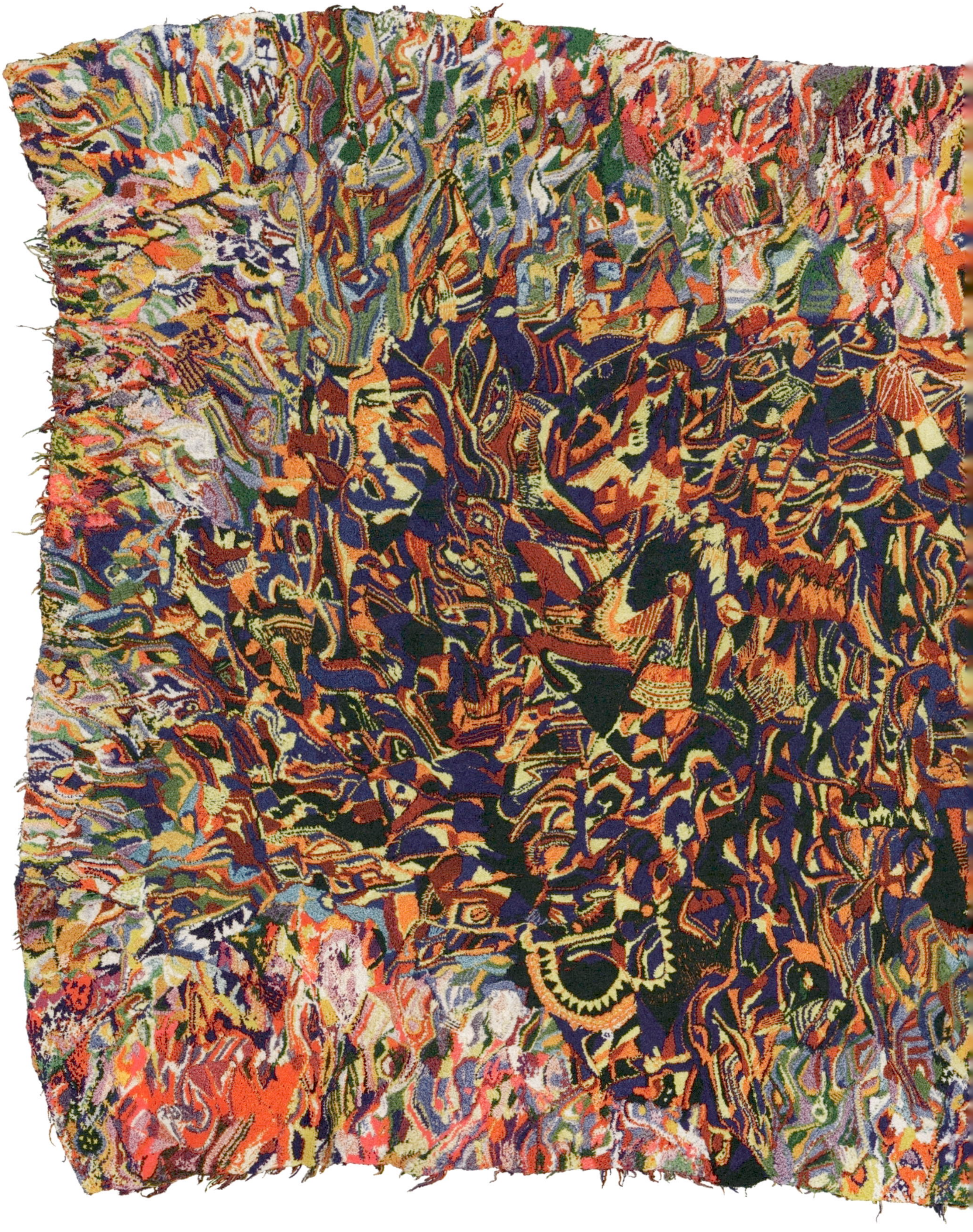

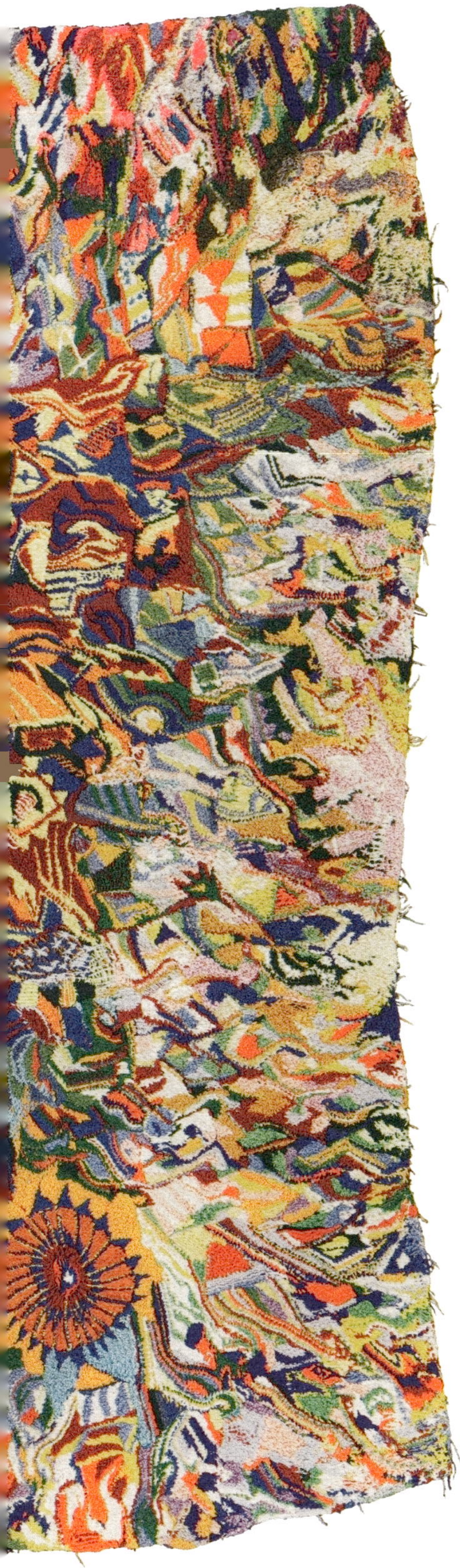

Madge Gill
sans titre untitled, s.d. n.d.
broderie de laine wool embroidery
125 x 150 cm
cab-3153

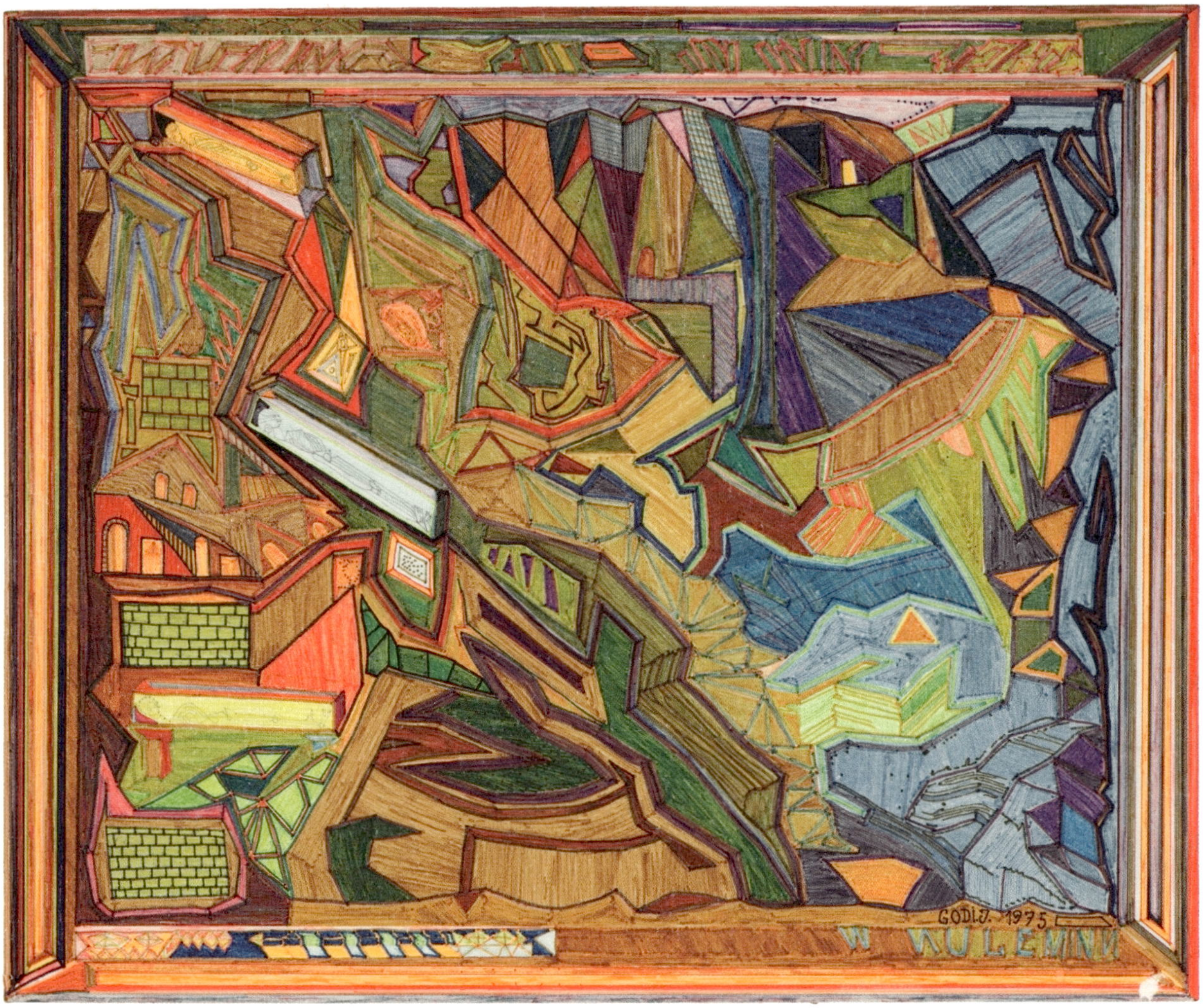

Jules Godi
W Wuleminn, 1975
feutre sur papier
felt-tip pen on paper
39 x 48 cm
cab-4154

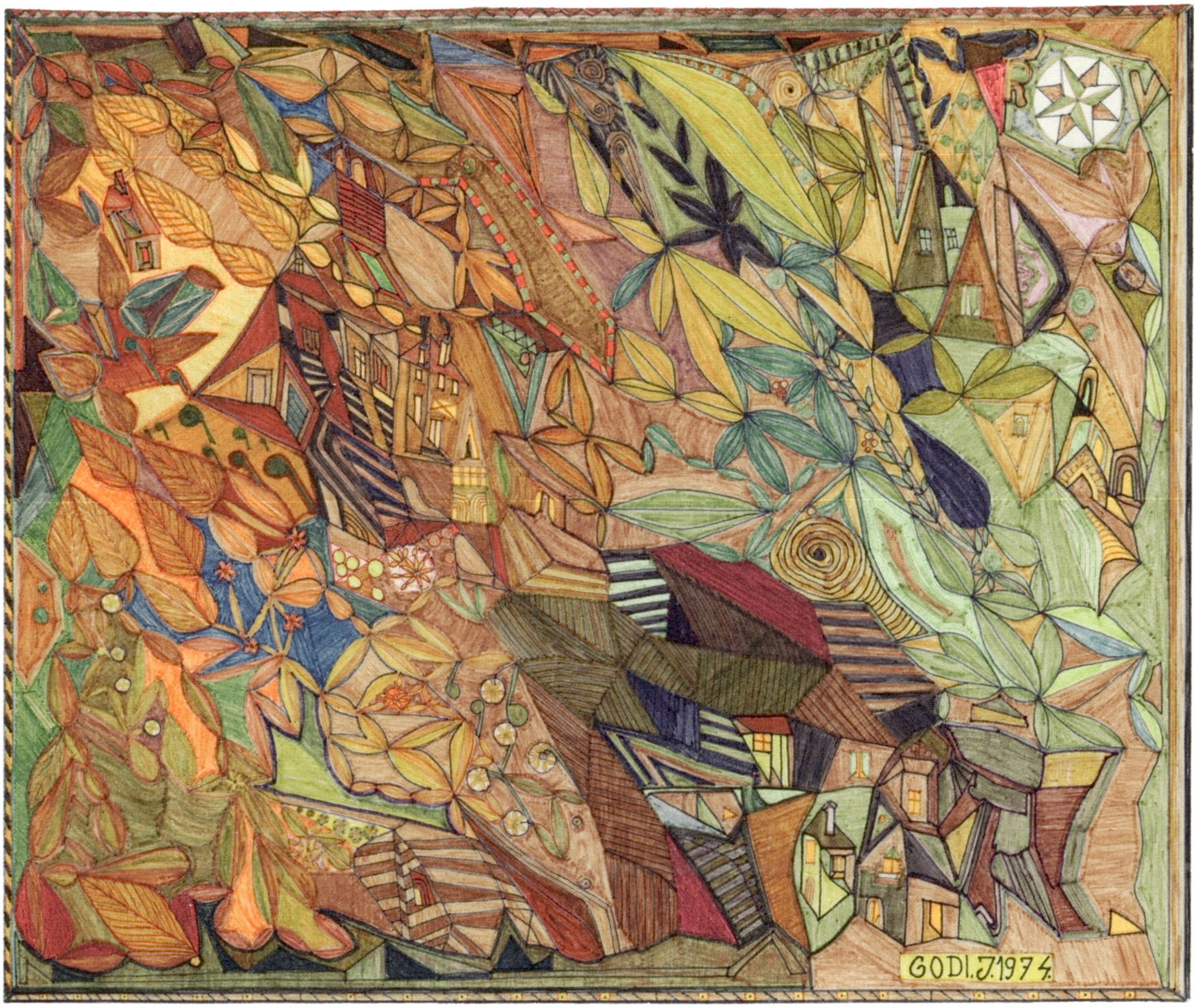

Jules Godi
sans titre untitled, 1974
feutre sur papier
felt-tip pen on paper
39 x 48 cm
cab-4157

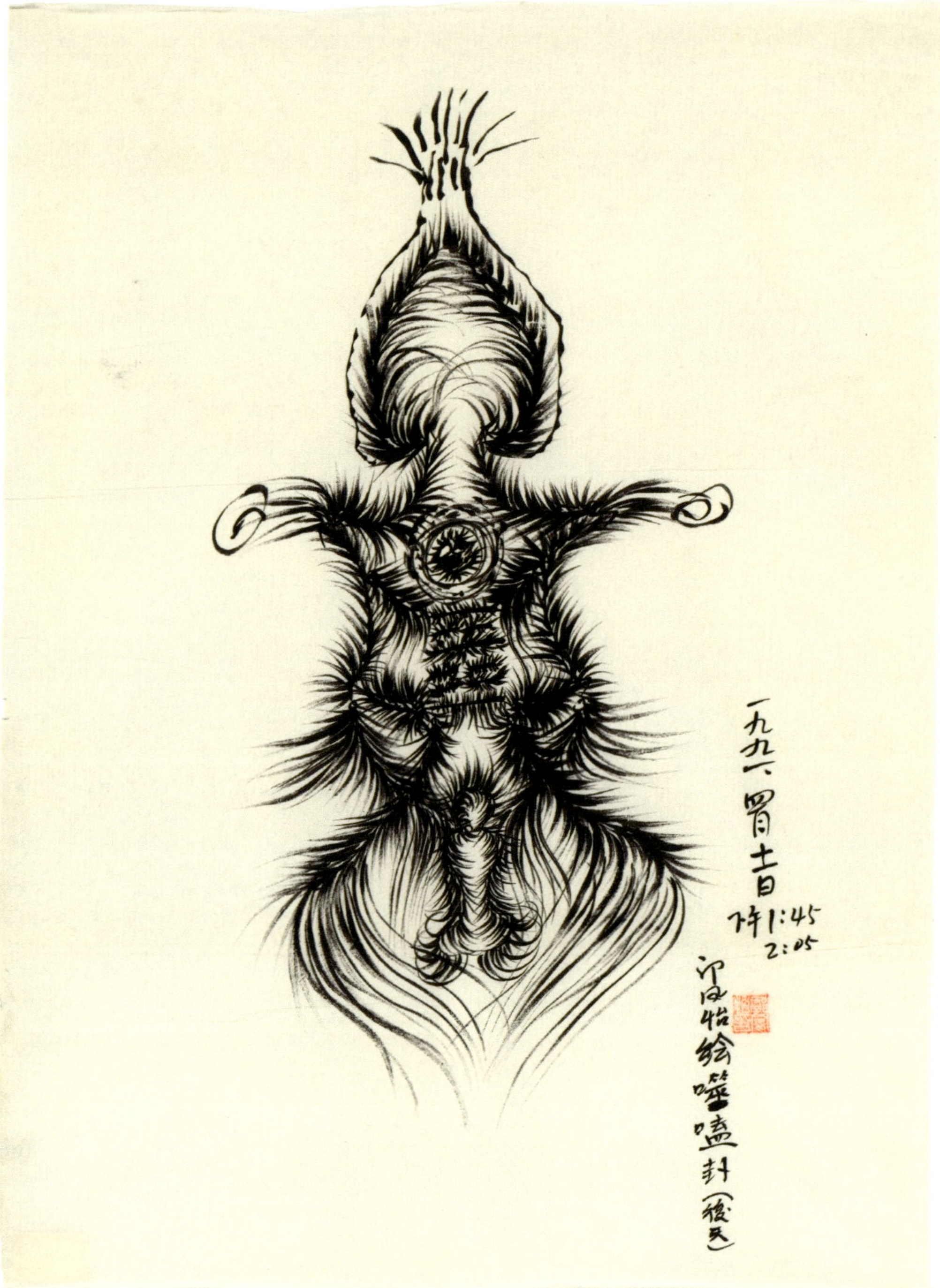

Guo Fengyi
La divination de Shihe peint par Guo Fengyi, 1991
encre de Chine sur papier Japon
India ink on Japanese paper
91 x 67,5 cm
cab-14941

Guo Fengyi
La divination de Zhen, 1991
encre de Chine sur papier Japon
India ink on Japanese paper
99,5 x 53,5 cm
cab-15022

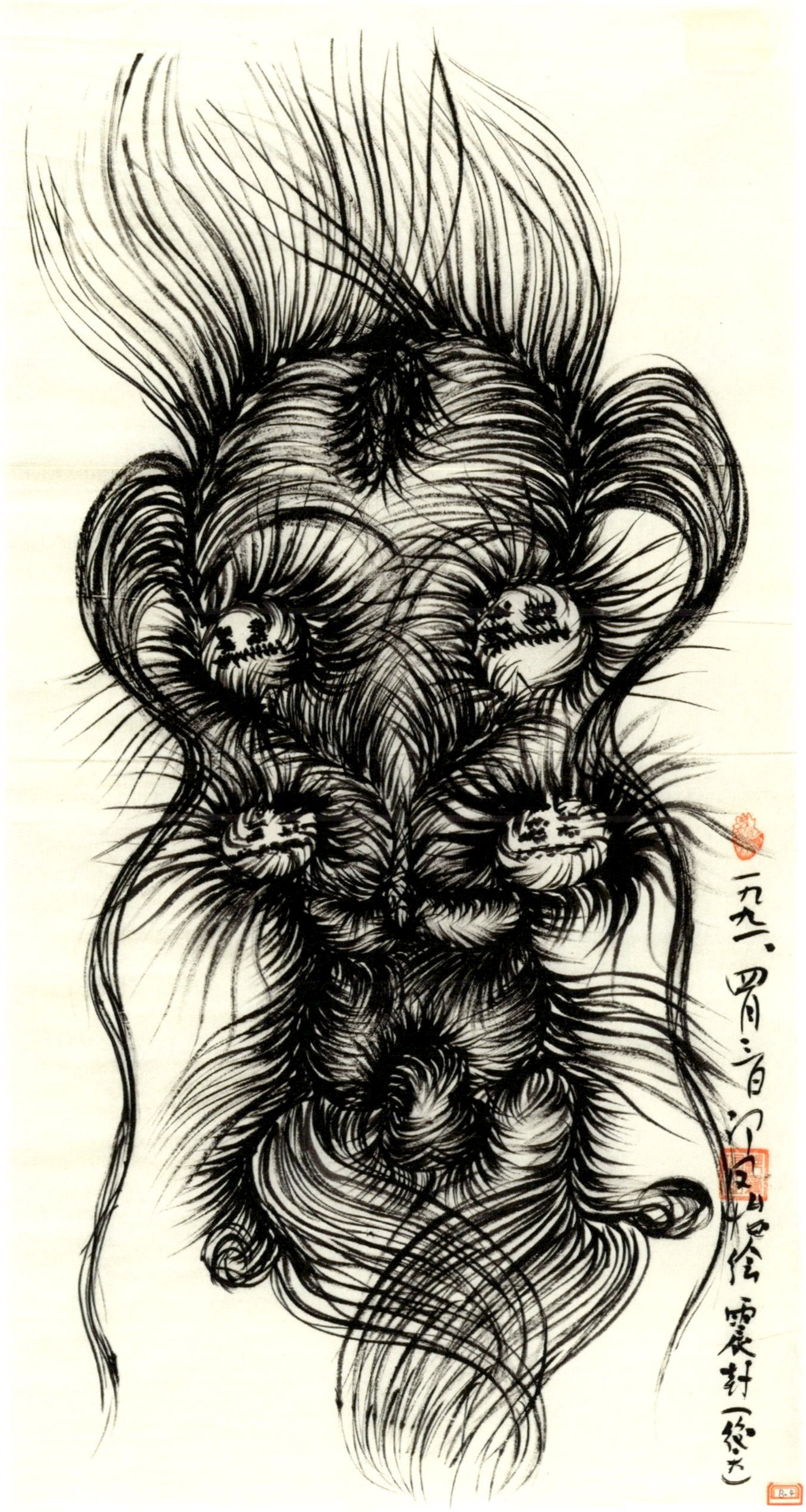

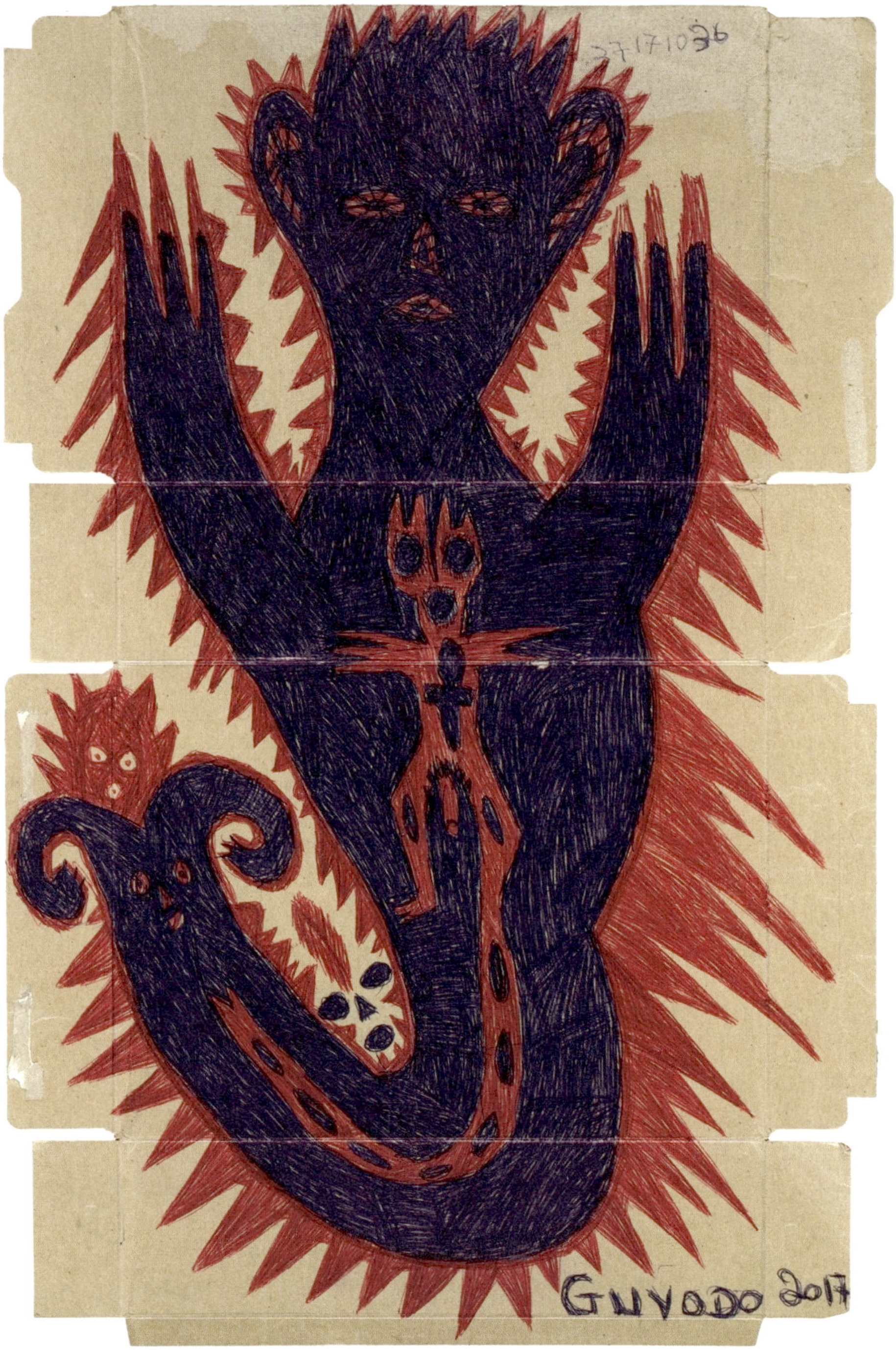

Guyodo
sans titre untitled, 2017
stylo-bille sur carton d'emballage
ballpoint pen on wrapping paper
59 x 40,3 cm
ni-9973

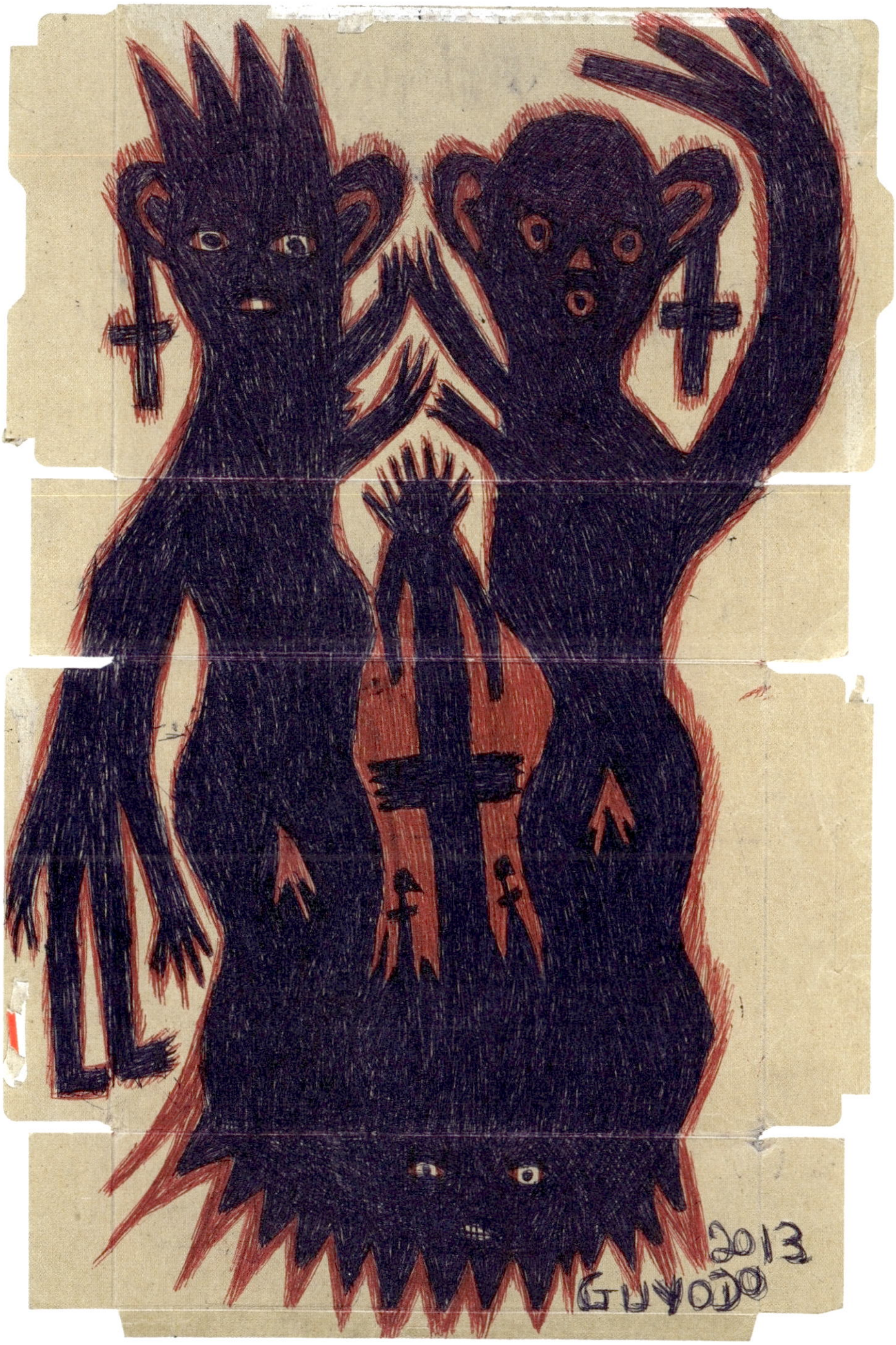

Guyodo
sans titre untitled, 2013
stylo-bille sur carton d'emballage
ballpoint pen on wrapping paper
59 x 40,3 cm
ni-9974

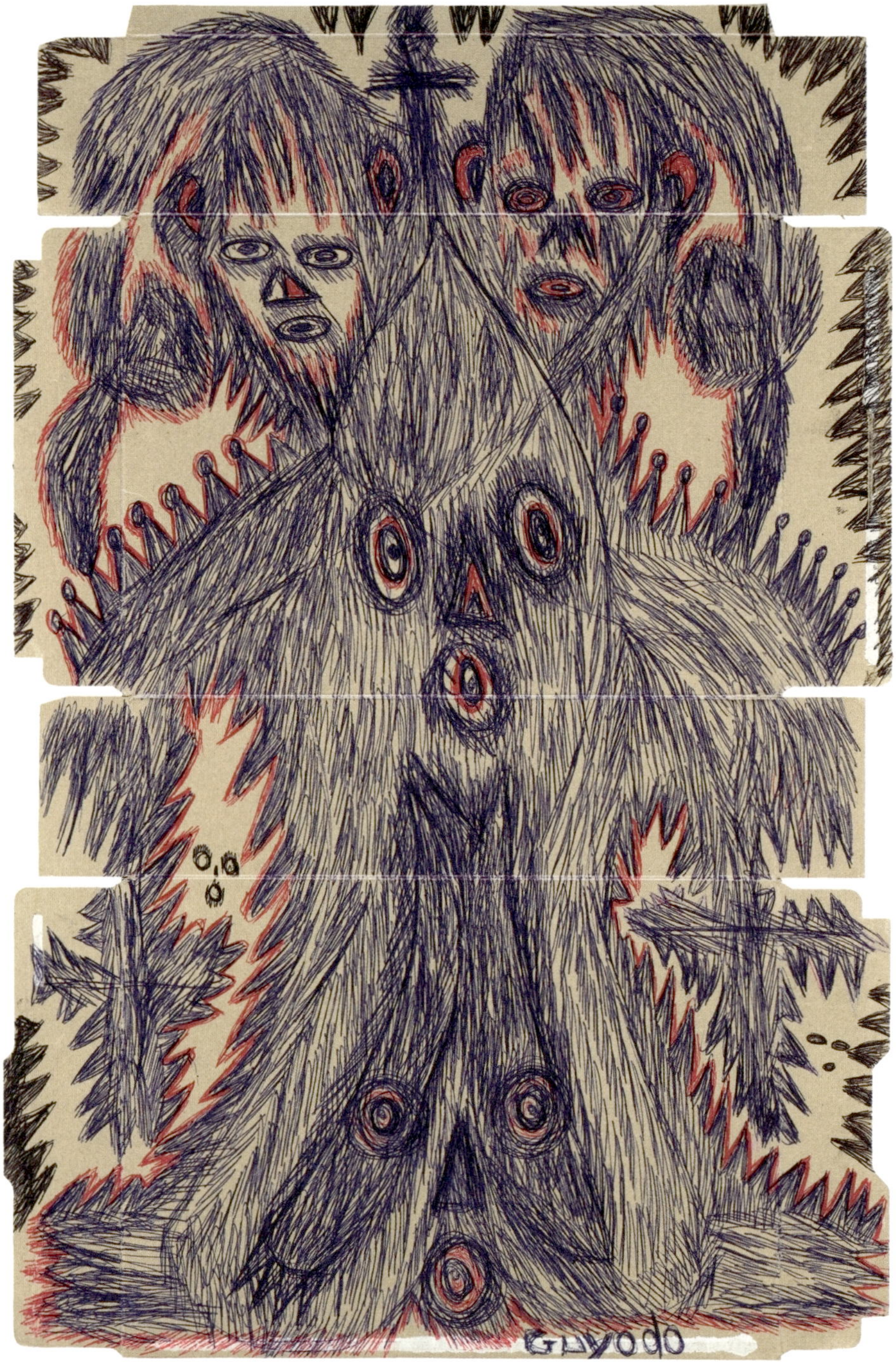

Guyodo
sans titre untitled, s.d. n.d.
stylo-bille sur carton d'emballage
ballpoint pen on wrapping paper
59 x 40 cm
ni-9980

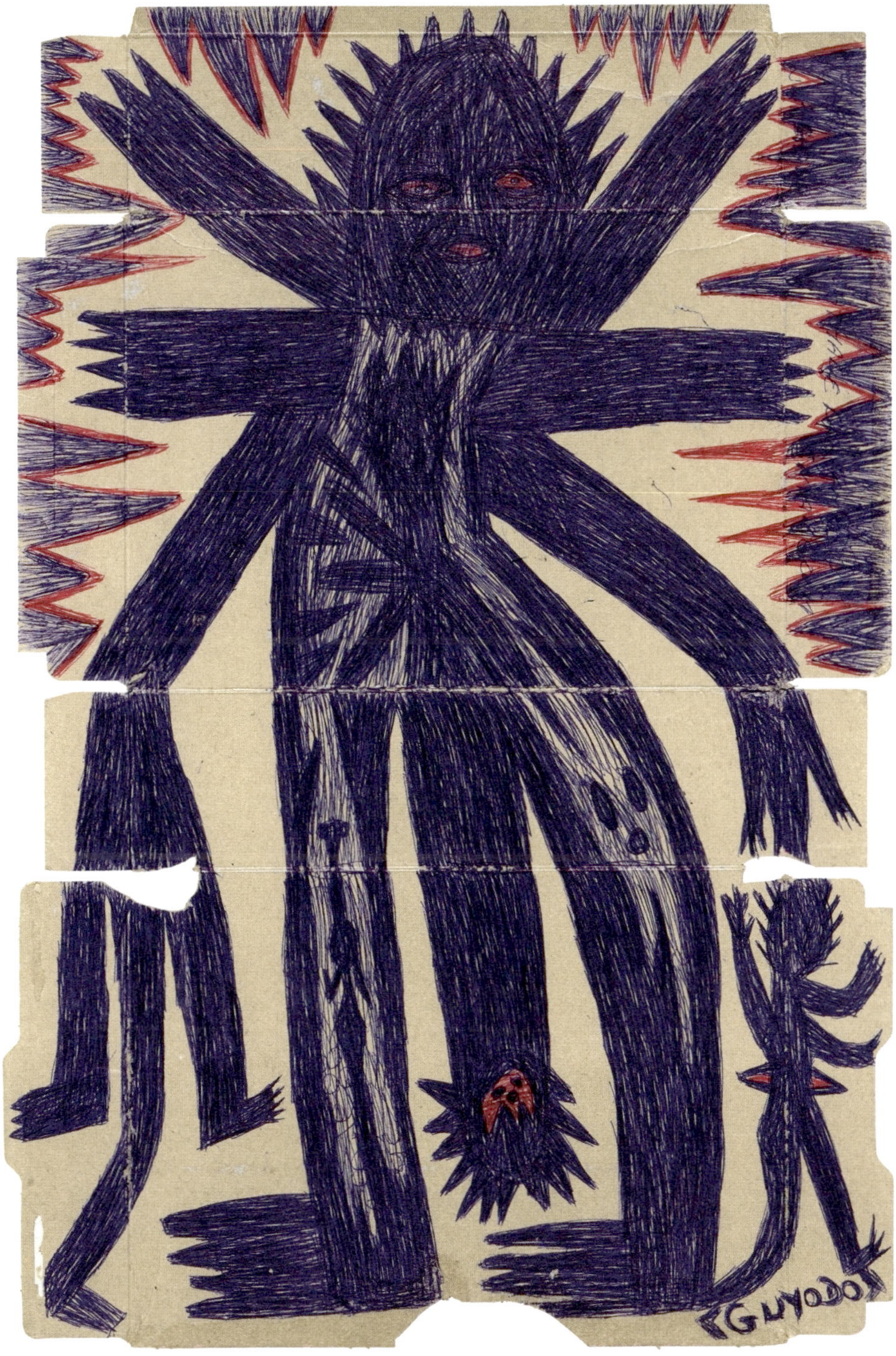

Guyodo
sans titre untitled, s.d. n.d.
stylo-bille sur carton d'emballage
ballpoint pen on wrapping paper
59 x 40,5 cm
ni-9982

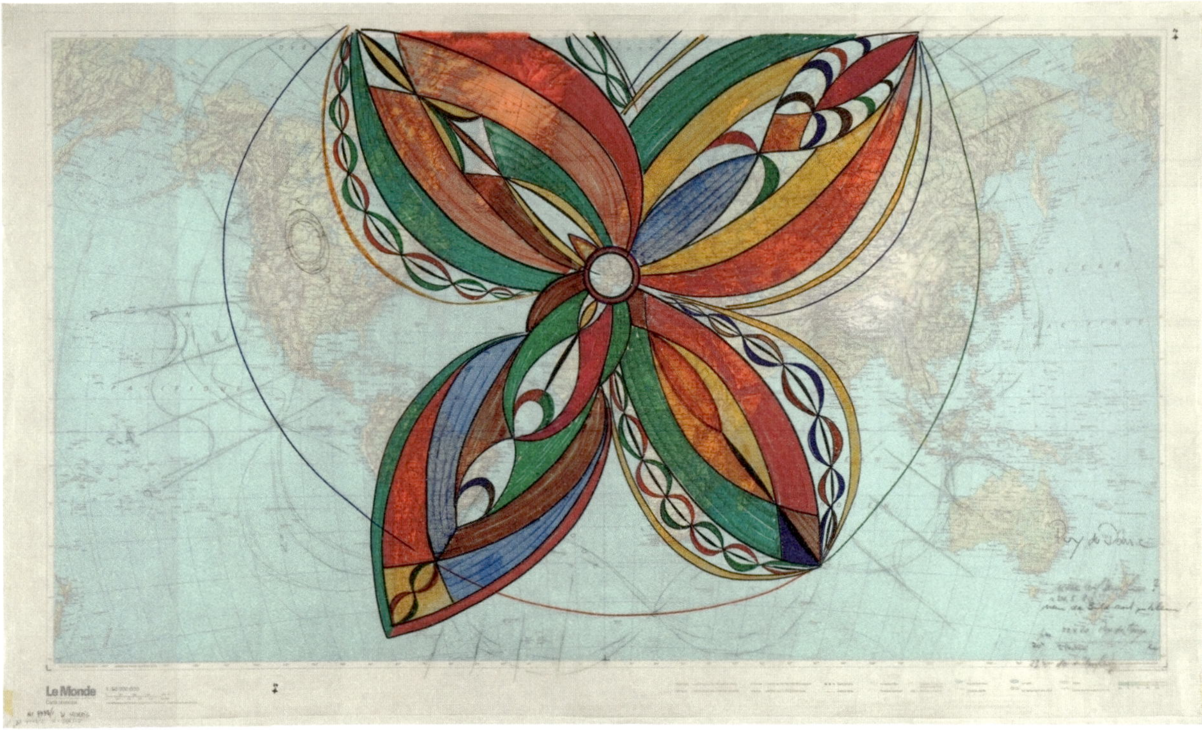

Werner Hertig
Puy de Dôme, 1980
mine de plomb et feutre sur papier calque, carte topographique
graphite and felt-tip pen on tracing paper, topographic map
51 x 87,2 cm
cab-7443/1-2

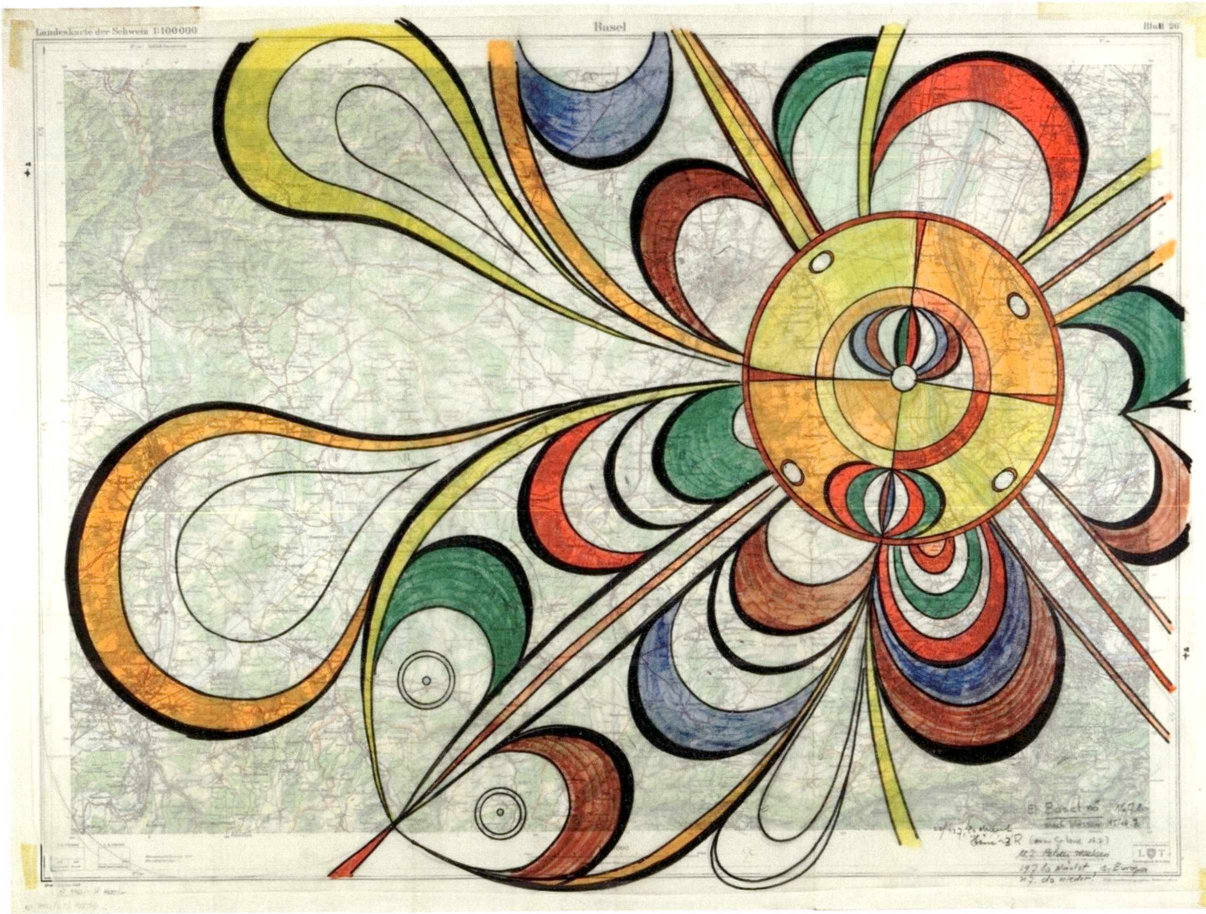

Werner Hertig
Basel, 1980
mine de plomb et feutre sur papier
calque, carte topographique
graphite and felt-tip pen on tracing
paper, topographic map
57 x 78 cm
cab-7462/1-2

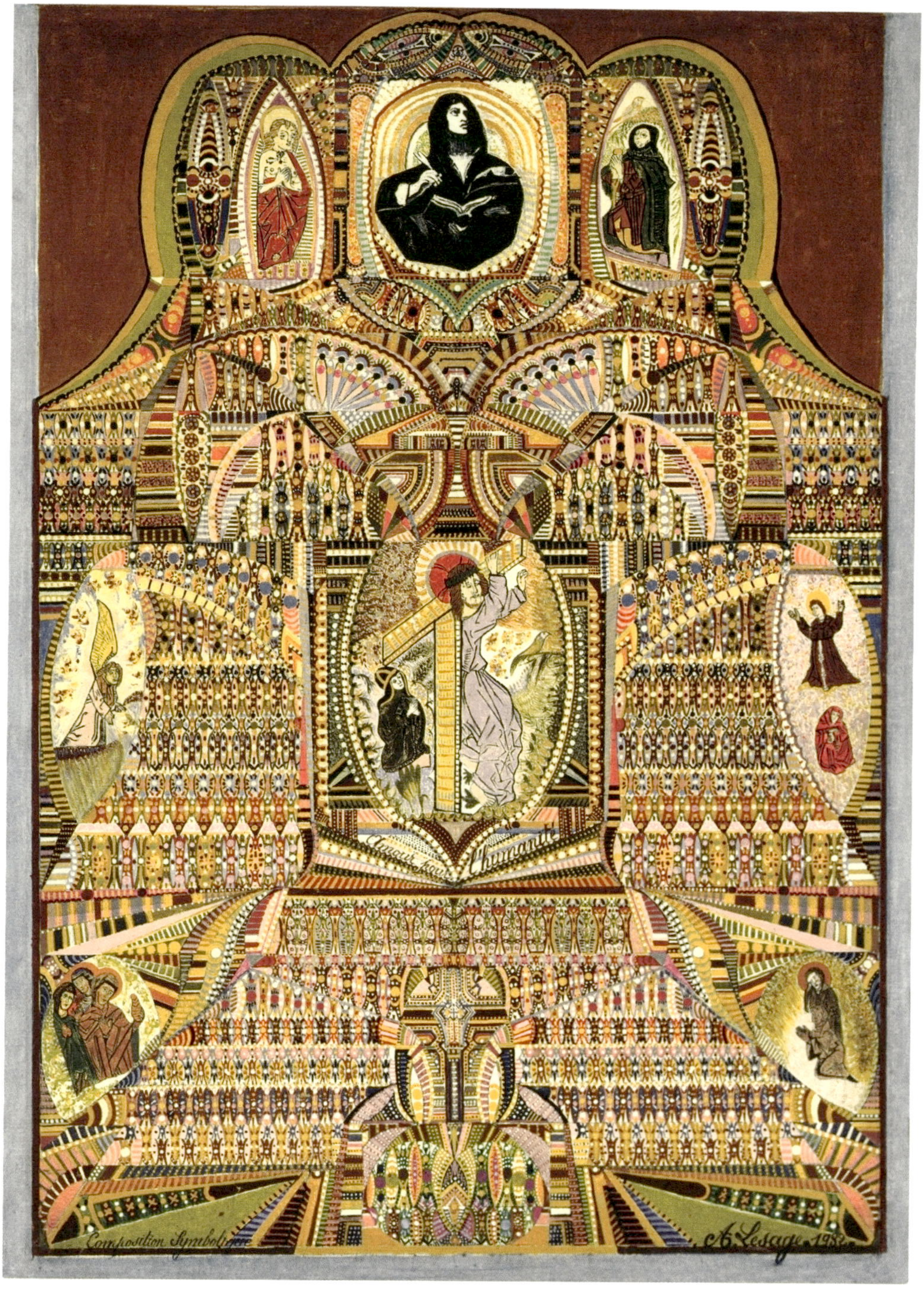

Augustin Lesage
Composition symbolique, amour pour l'humanité, 1932
huile sur toile oil on canvas
97 x 70 cm
cab-1111

Augustin Lesage
sans titre untitled, 1941
huile sur toile oil on canvas
190 x 140 cm
cab-9957

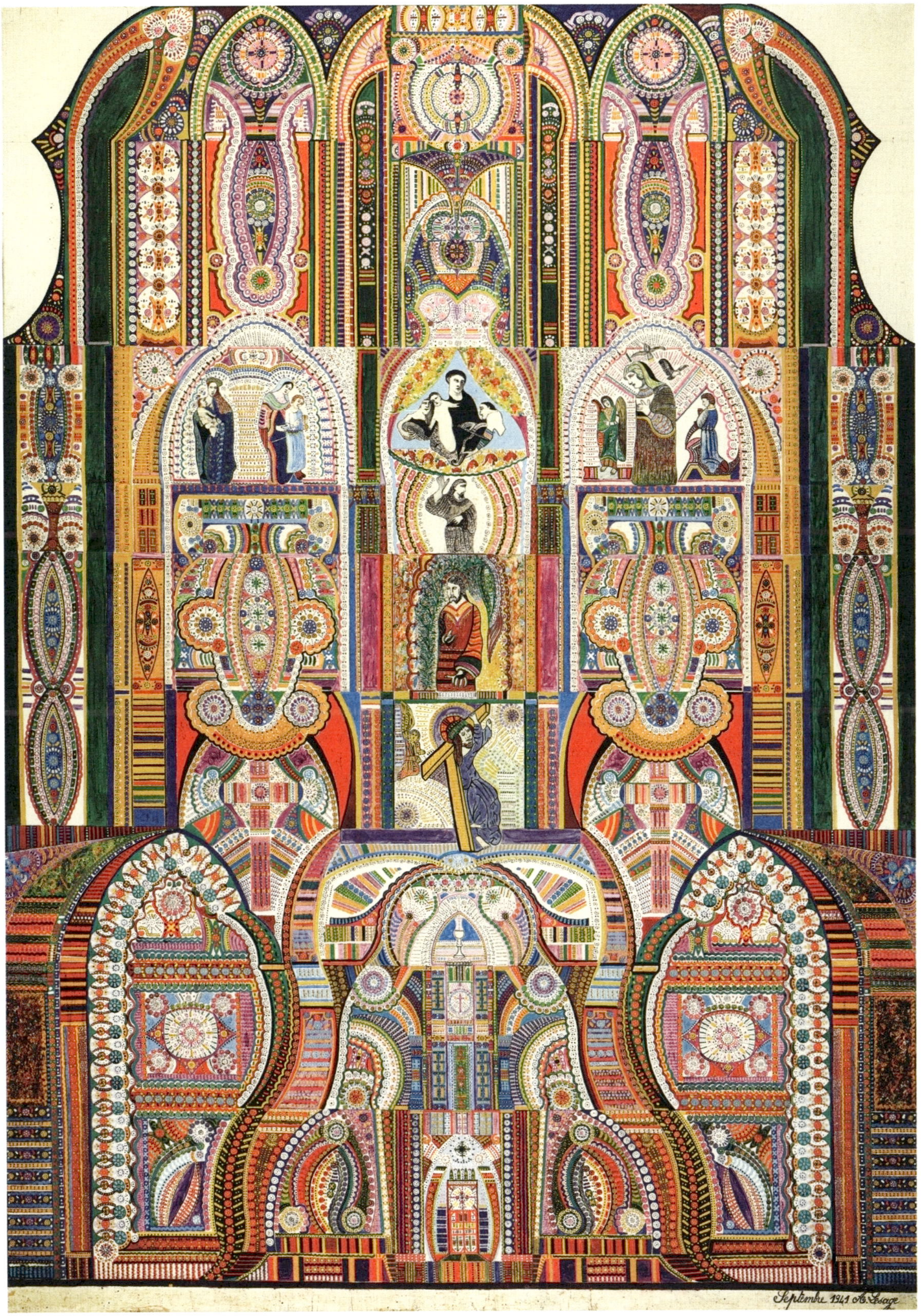
Septembre 1941 A. Lesage

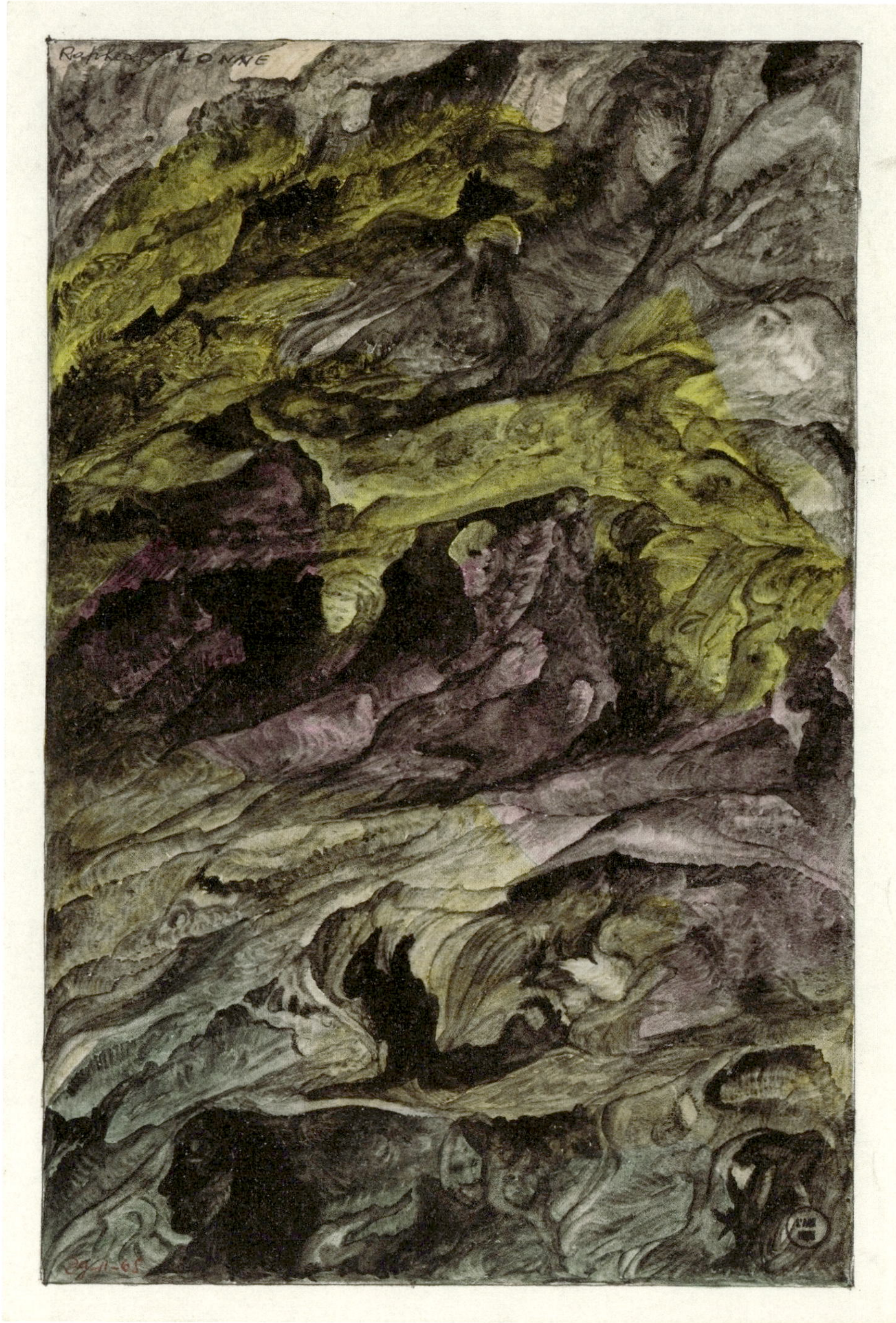

Raphaël Lonné
sans titre untitled, 29.11.1965
peinture à l'eau sur papier
watercolor on paper
32 x 22 cm
cab-2452

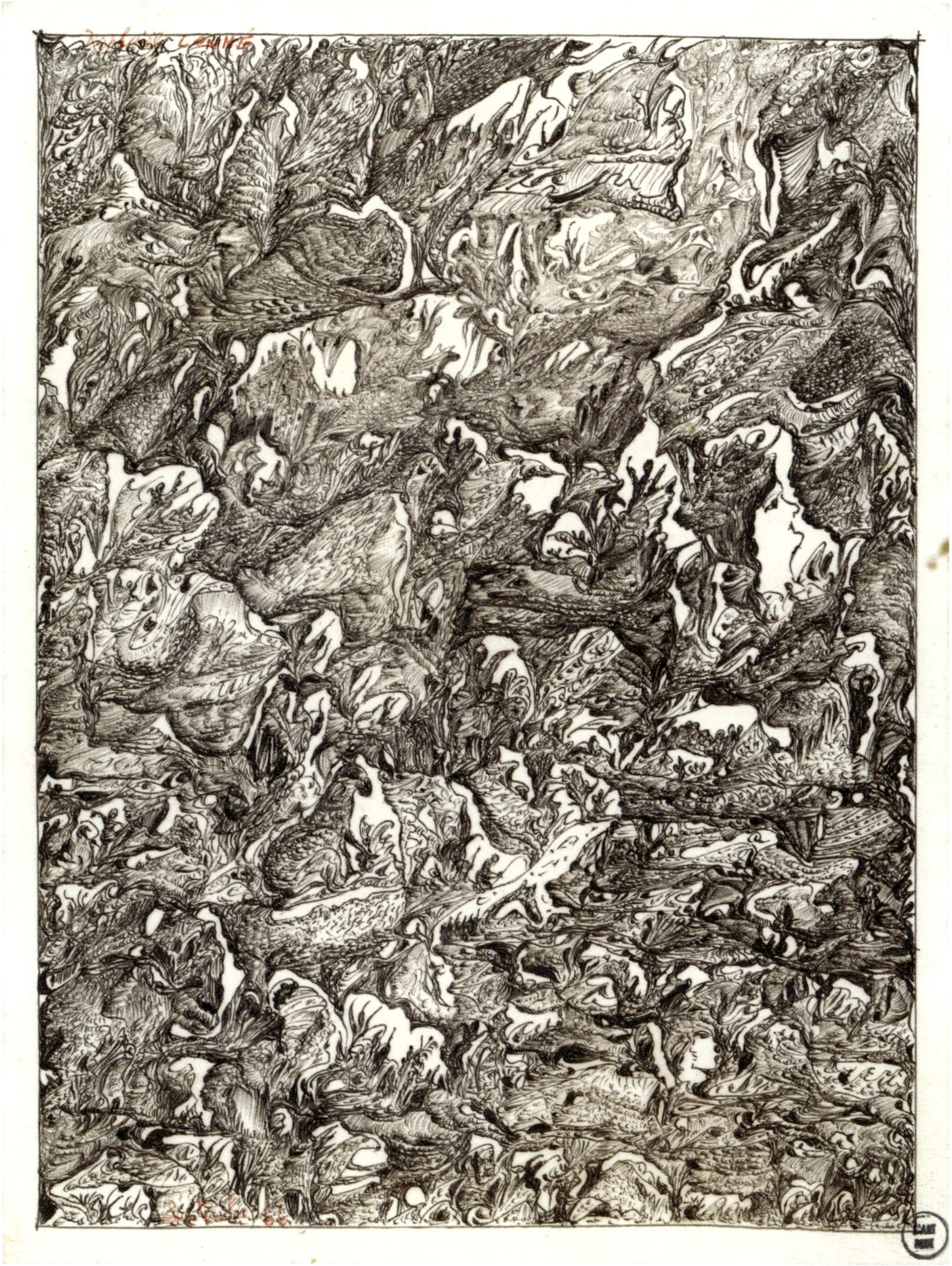

Raphaël Lonné
sans titre untitled, 1966
stylo-bille sur papier
ballpoint pen on paper
27 x 21 cm
cab-2625

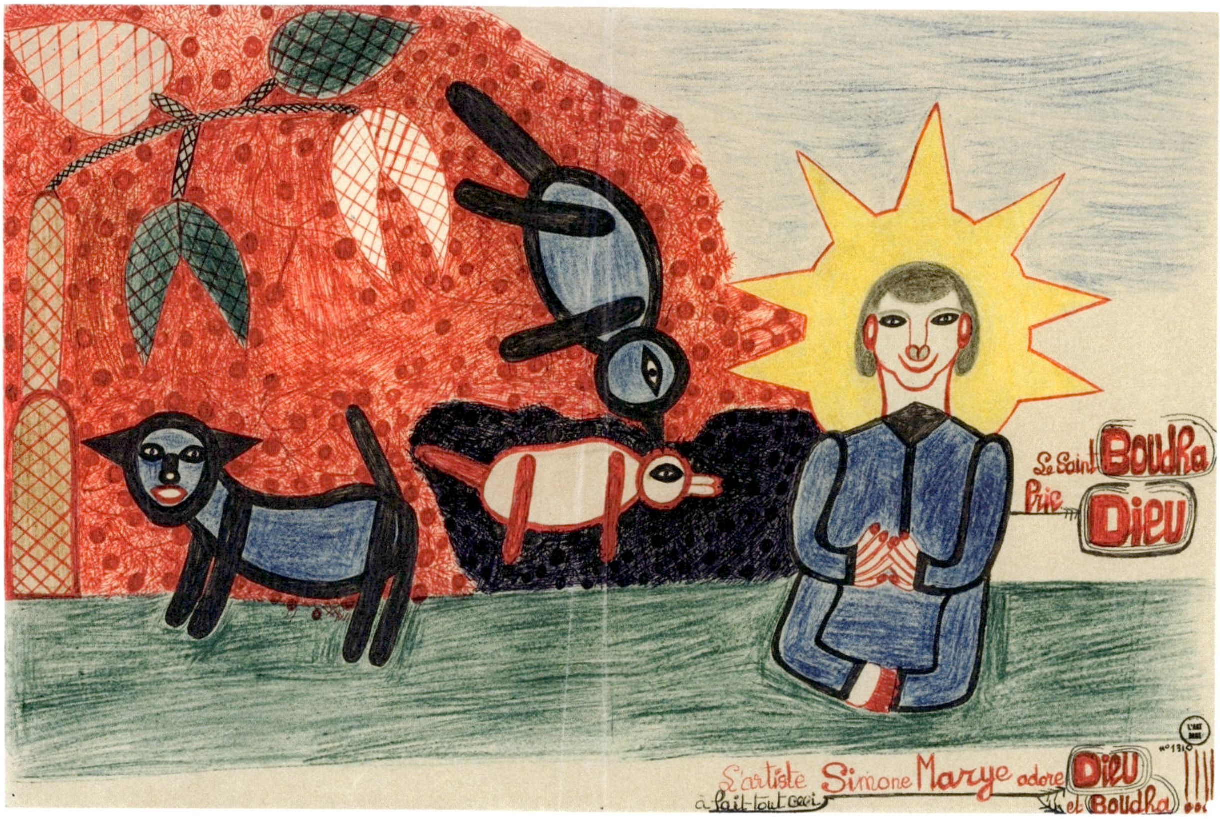

Simone Marye
Simone Marye adore Dieu et Boudha,
entre between 1959 et and 1961
mine de plomb, crayon de couleur
et stylo-bille sur papier graphite, coloured
pencil, and ballpoint pen on paper
27 x 42 cm
cab-1310

Simone Marye
Le saint (Bouddha),
entre between 1959 et and 1961
mine de plomb, crayon de couleur
et stylo-bille sur papier graphite, coloured
pencil, and ballpoint pen on paper
27 x 21 cm
cab-1262

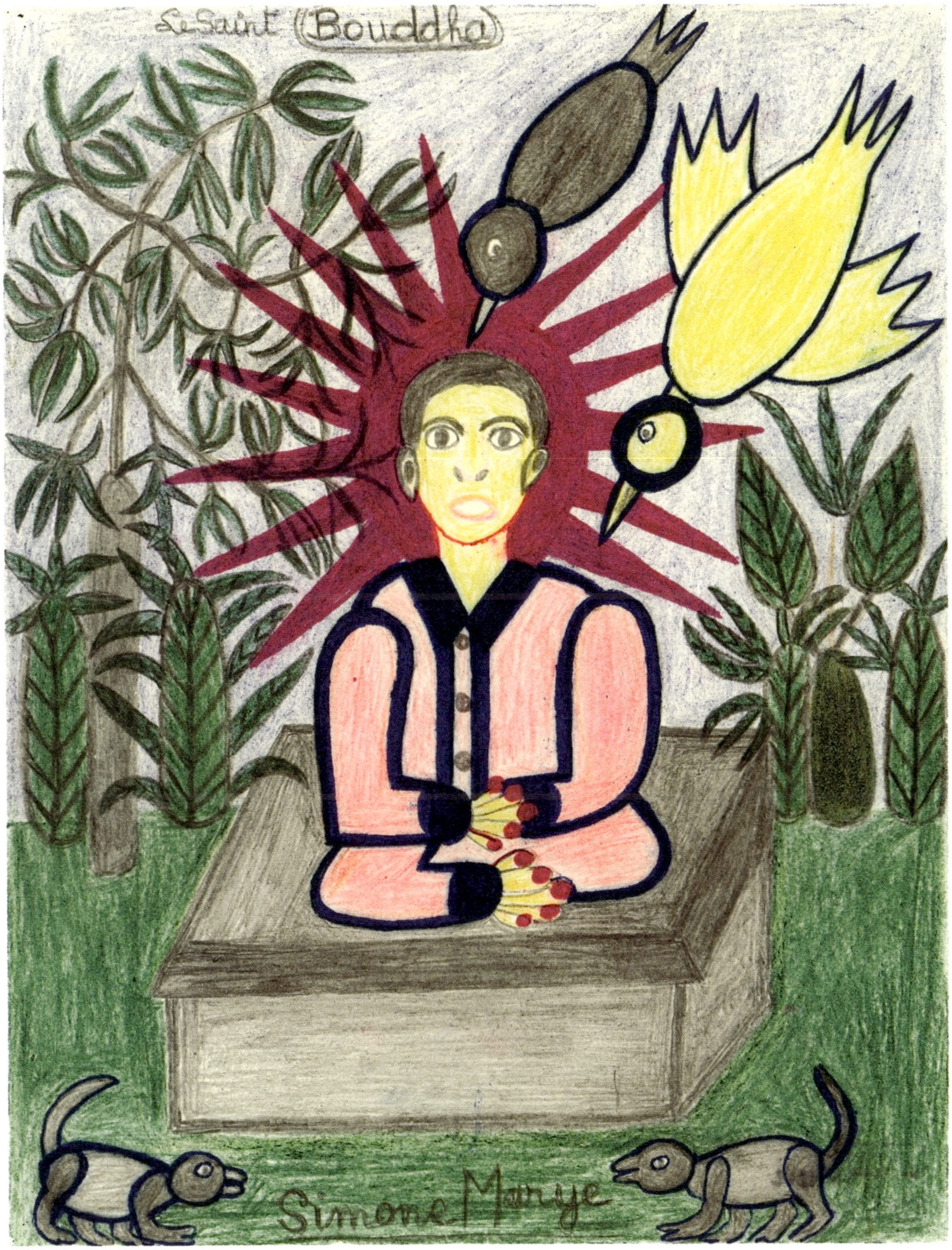
Le Saint (Bouddha)
Simone Marye

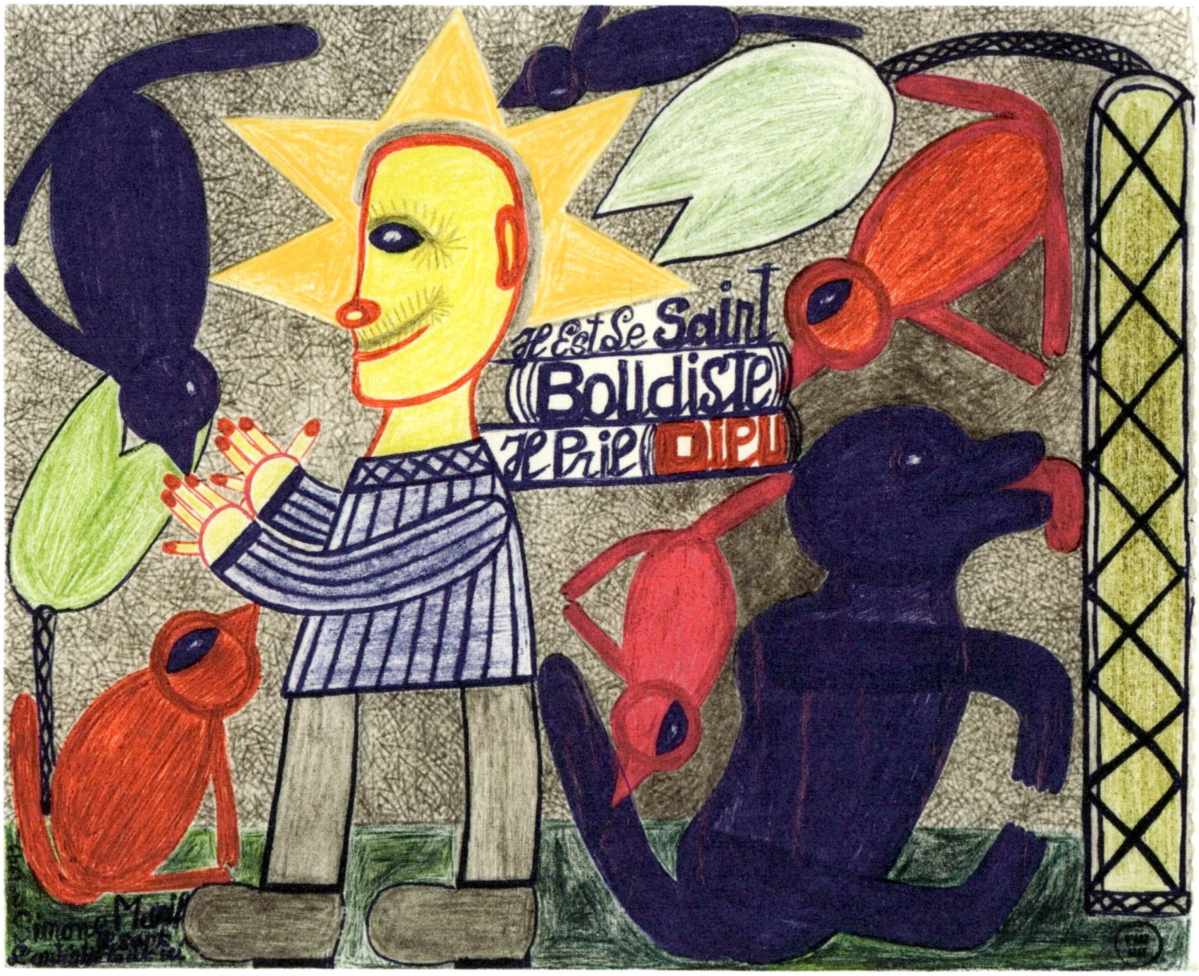

Simone Marye
sans titre untitled, entre between
1959 et and 1961
mine de plomb, crayon de couleur
et stylo-bille sur papier graphite, coloured
pencil, and ballpoint pen on paper
21 x 26,5 cm
cab-1293

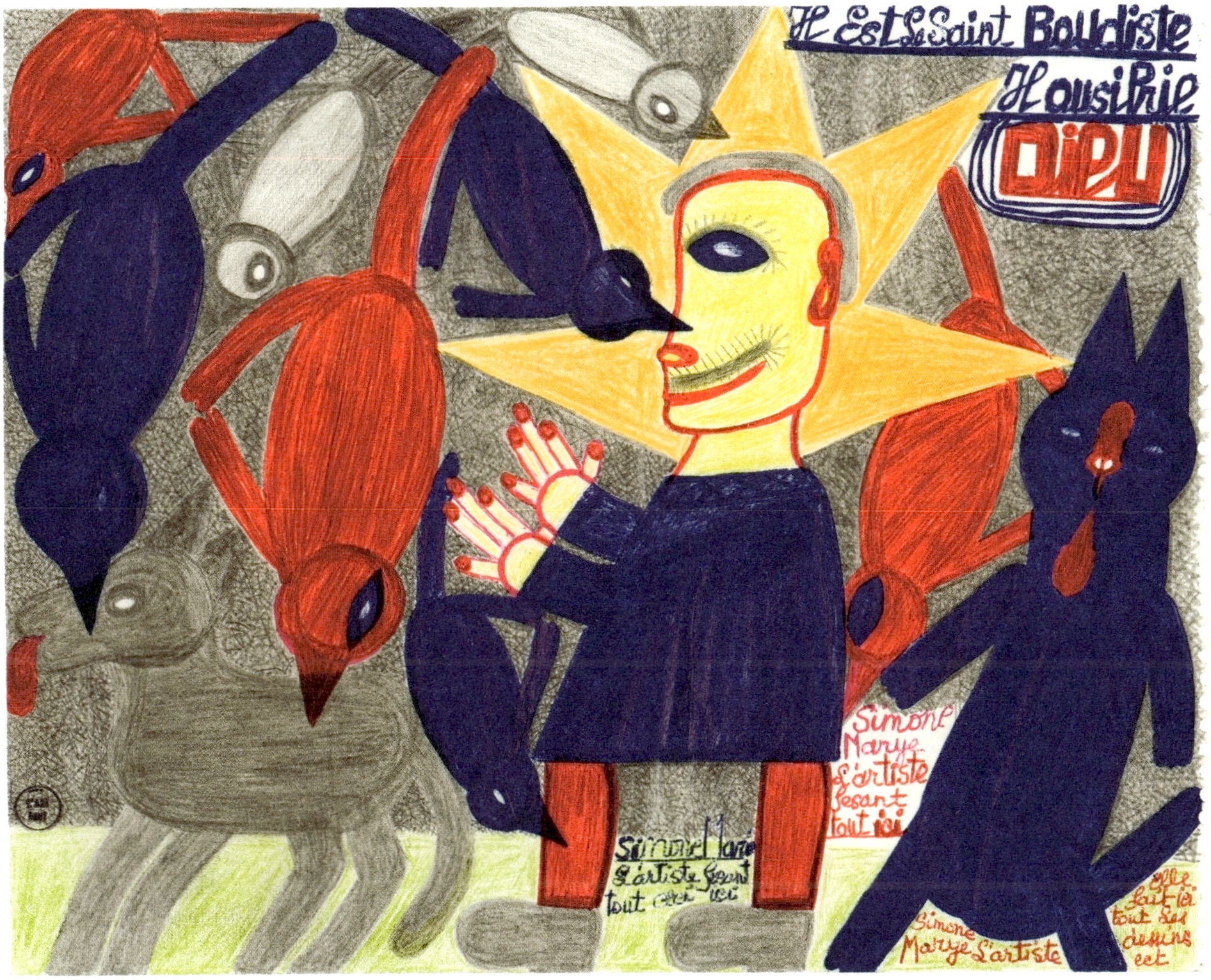

Simone Marye
sans titre untitled, entre between
1959 et and 1961
mine de plomb, crayon de couleur
et stylo-bille sur papier graphite, coloured
pencil, and ballpoint pen on paper
21 x 26,5 cm
cab-1294

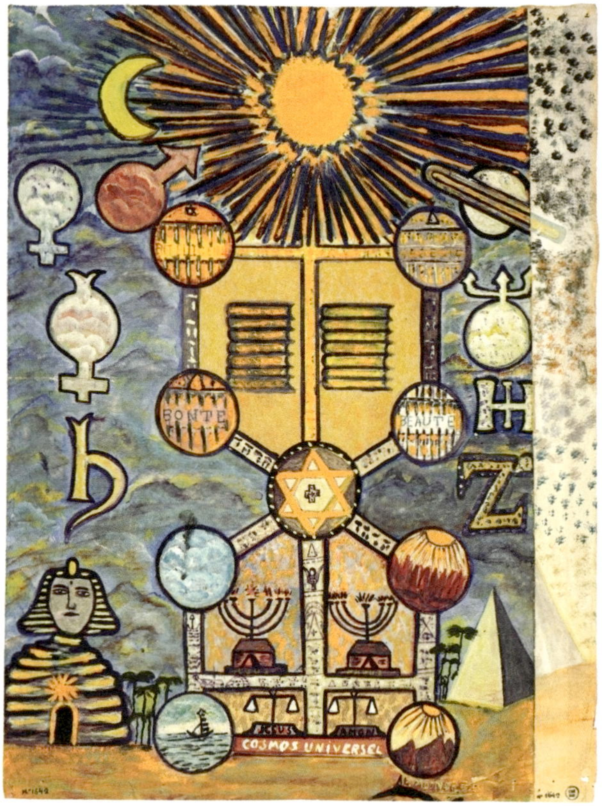

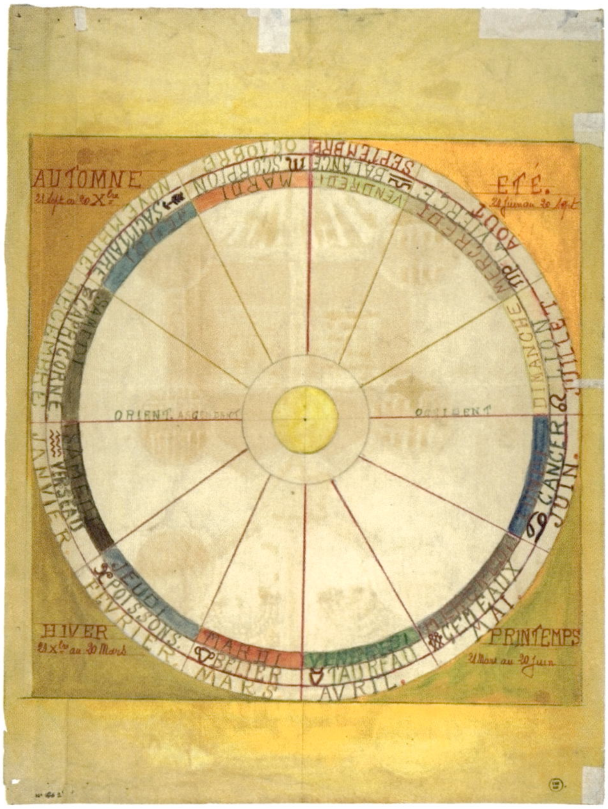

Joseph Moindre
Cosmos universel (recto),
sans titre untitled (verso),
entre between 1940 et and 1957
gouache sur papier gouache on paper
58 x 44,4 cm
cab-1642

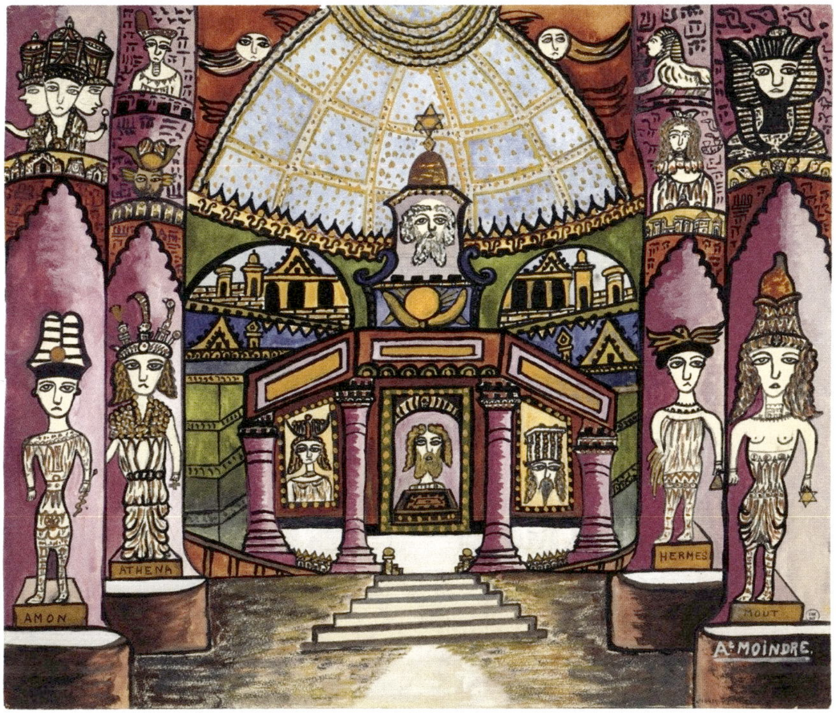

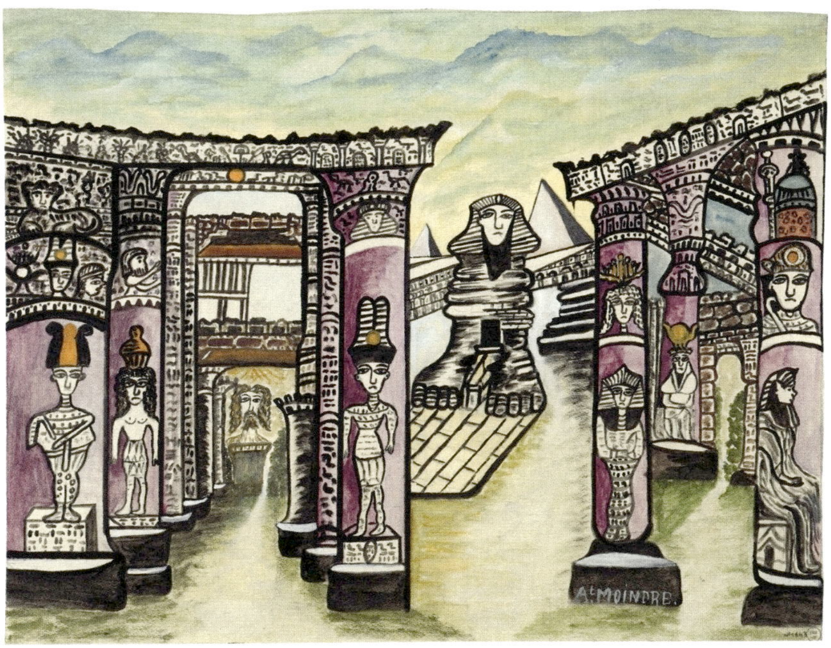

Joseph Moindre
sans titre untitled, entre between
1940 et and 1957
gouache sur papier gouache on paper
52,4 x 63 cm
cab-1641

Joseph Moindre
sans titre untitled, entre between
1940 et and 1957
gouache sur papier gouache on paper
42,2 x 56,4 cm
cab-1643

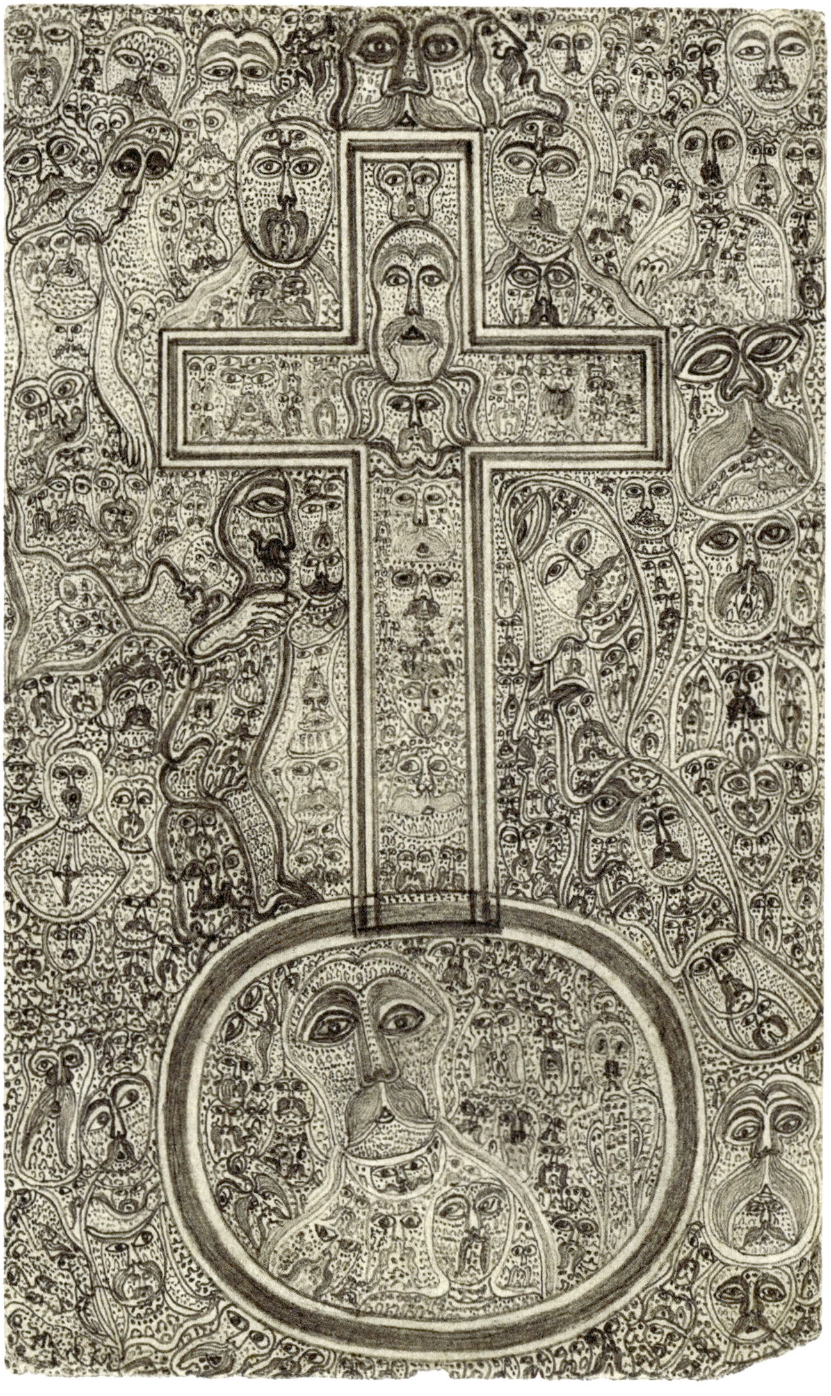

Edmund Monsiel
sans titre untitled, s.d. n.d.
mine de plomb sur papier
graphite on paper
16,1 x 10,2 cm
cab-4602

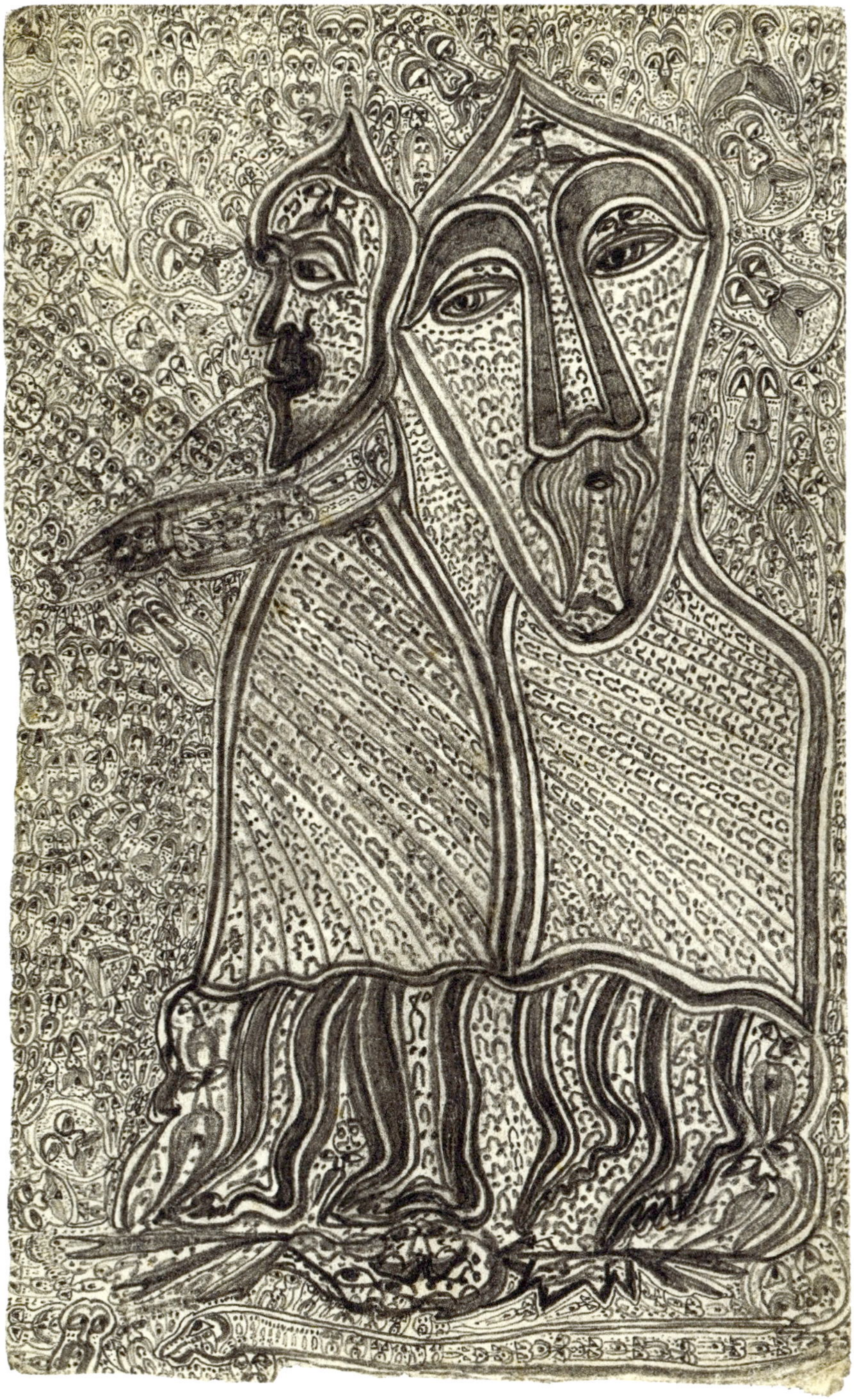

Edmund Monsiel
sans titre untitled, 1946
mine de plomb sur papier
graphite on paper
15,9 x 10 cm
cab-9888

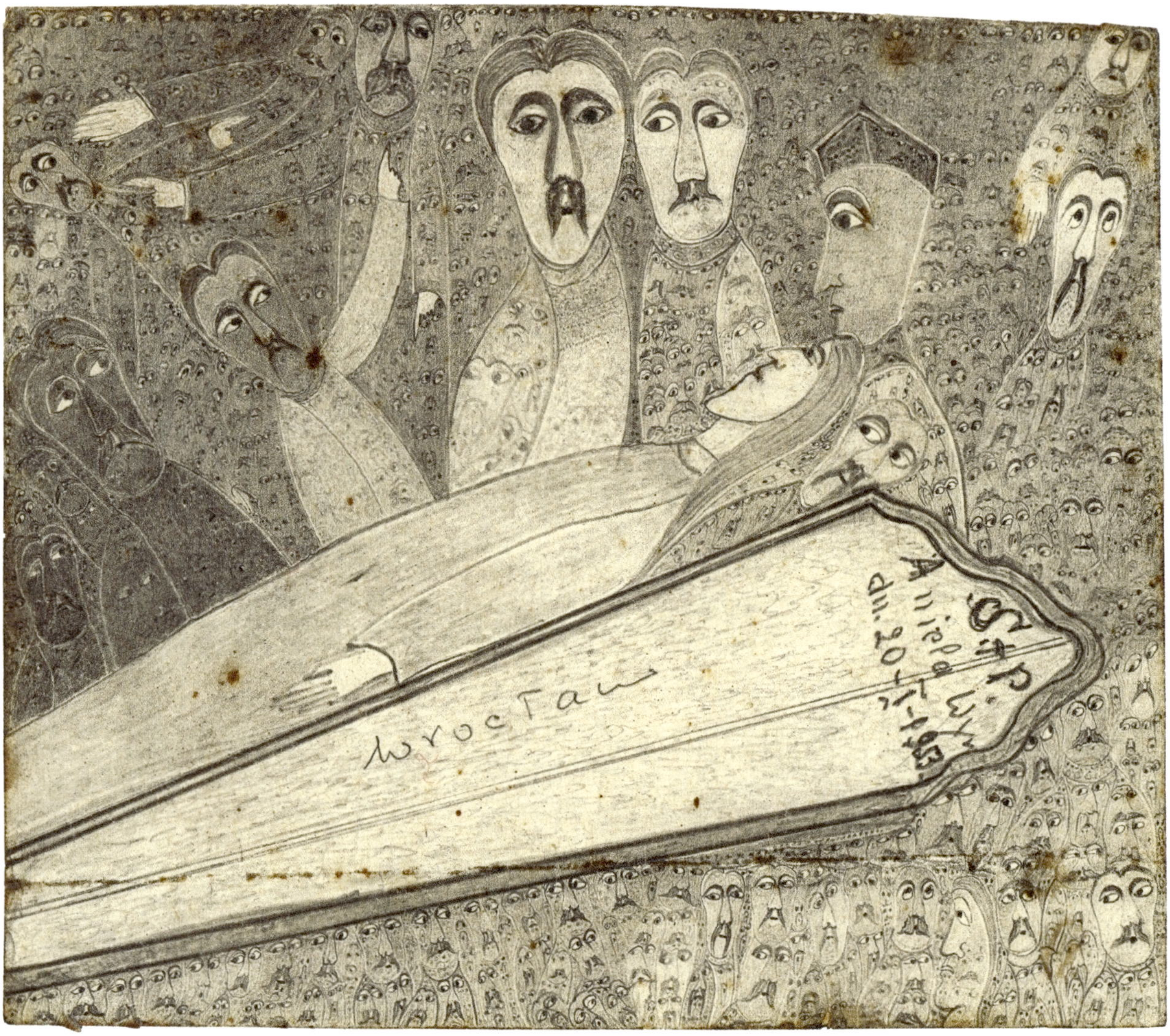

Edmund Monsiel
sans titre untitled, 1953
mine de plomb sur carton léger
graphite on light cardboard
12,5 x 14,5 cm
cab-4595

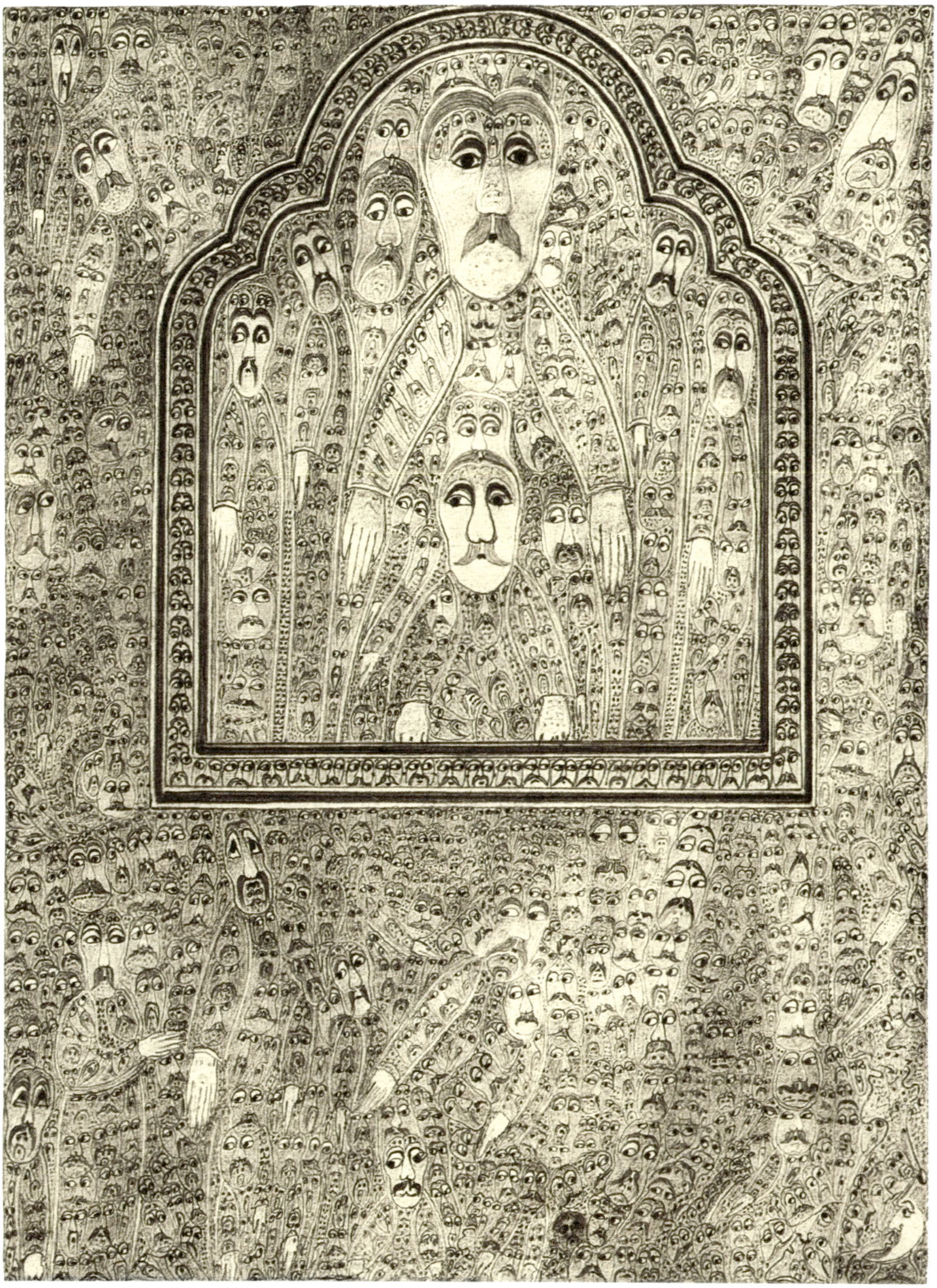

Edmund Monsiel
sans titre untitled, s.d. n.d.
mine de plomb sur papier
graphite on paper
17,7 x 13,2 cm
cab-4600

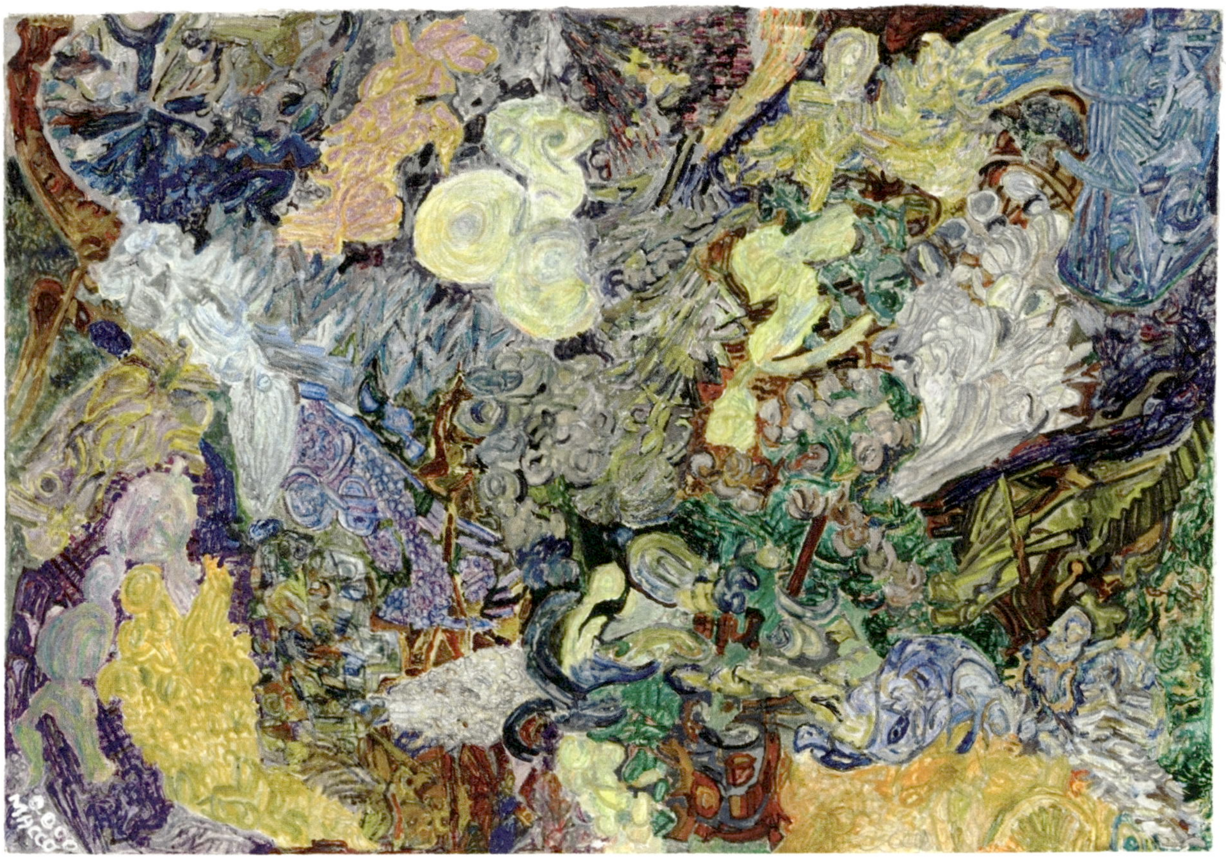

Marc Moret
sans titre untitled, 2000
gouache, aquarelle, crayon de couleur et vernis sur papier
gouache, watercolour, coloured pencil, and nail polish on paper
40 x 59,8 cm
cab-17059

Marc Moret
L'Eurasienne, entre between 1997 et and 1998
concrétion de verre pilé et tamisé, colle de peau, pigments et objets de récupération, sur bois chemisé de papier
concretion consisting of ground and sieved glass, rabbit-skin glue, pigments, and found objects on wood covered with paper
33 x 72 x 82,5 cm
cab-17056

Marc Moret
Extinction, entre between 1997 et and 1998
concrétion de verre pilé et tamisé, colle de peau, pigments et objets de récupération, sur bois chemisé de papier
concretion consisting of ground and sieved glass, rabbit-skin glue, pigments, and found objects on wood covered with paper
25 x 70 x 80,5 cm
cab-17055

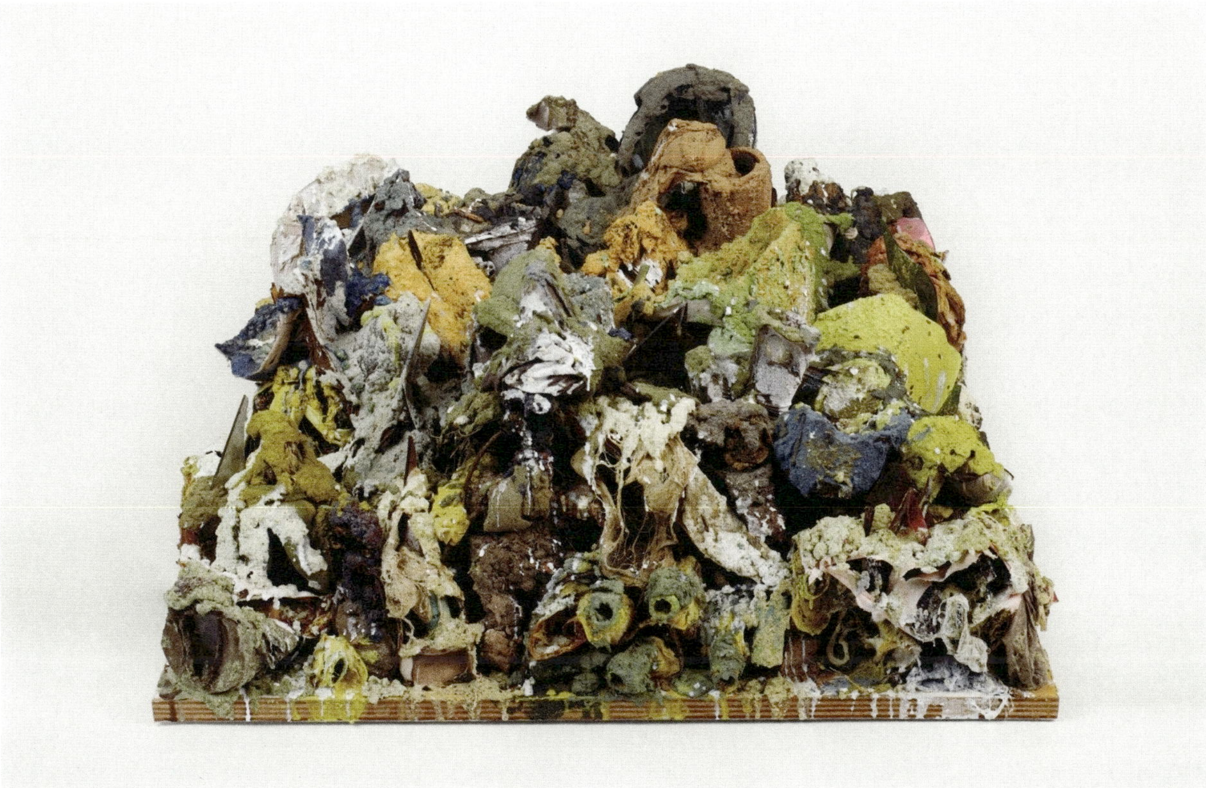

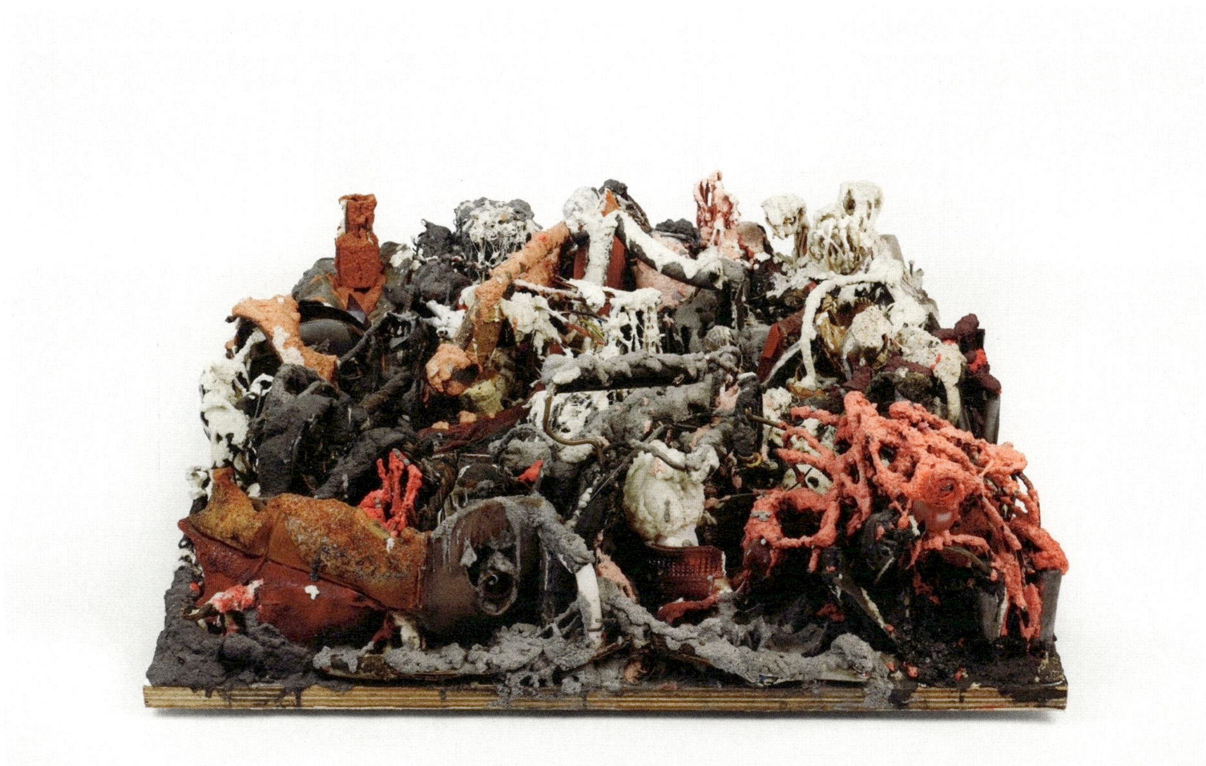

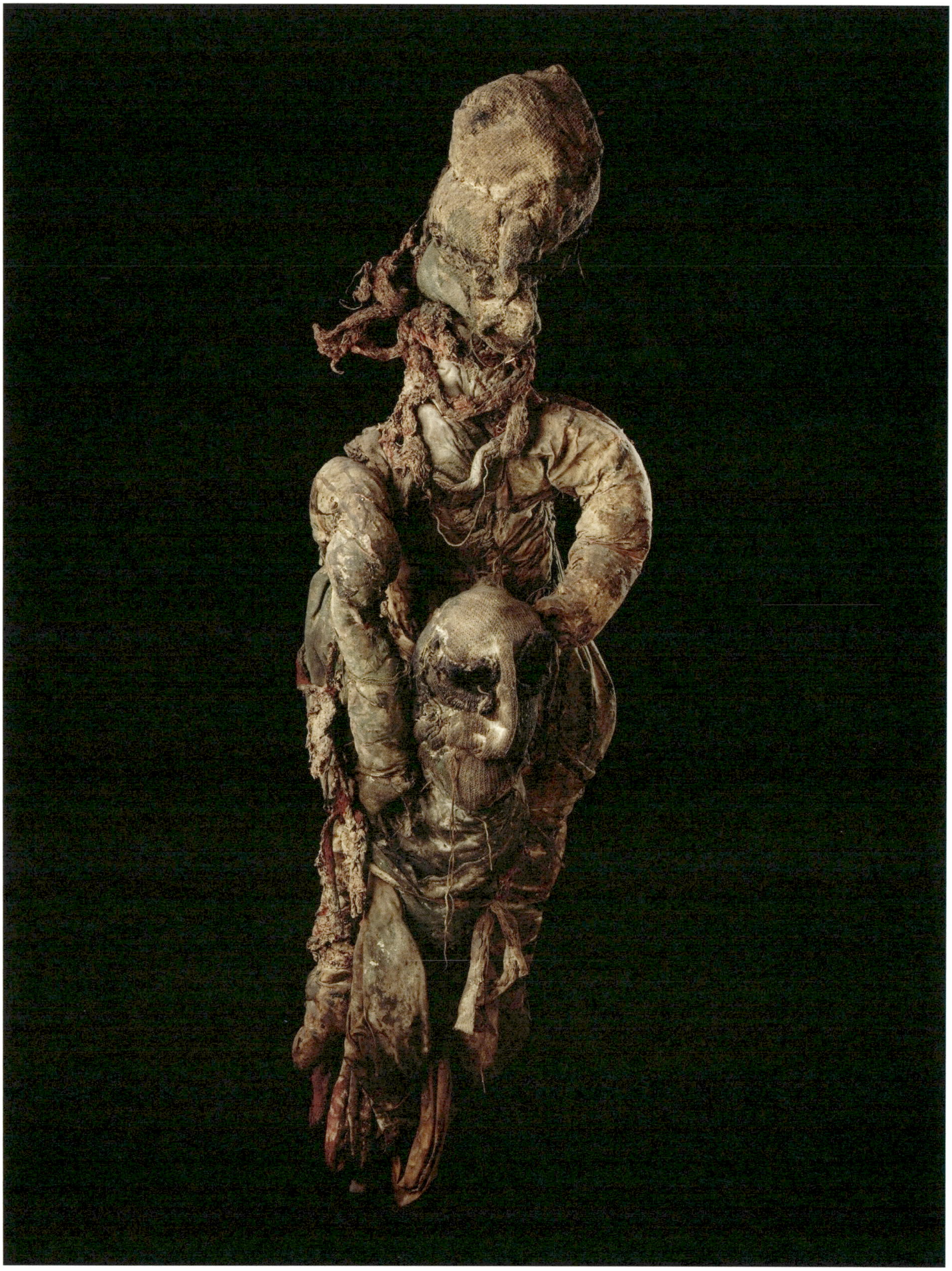

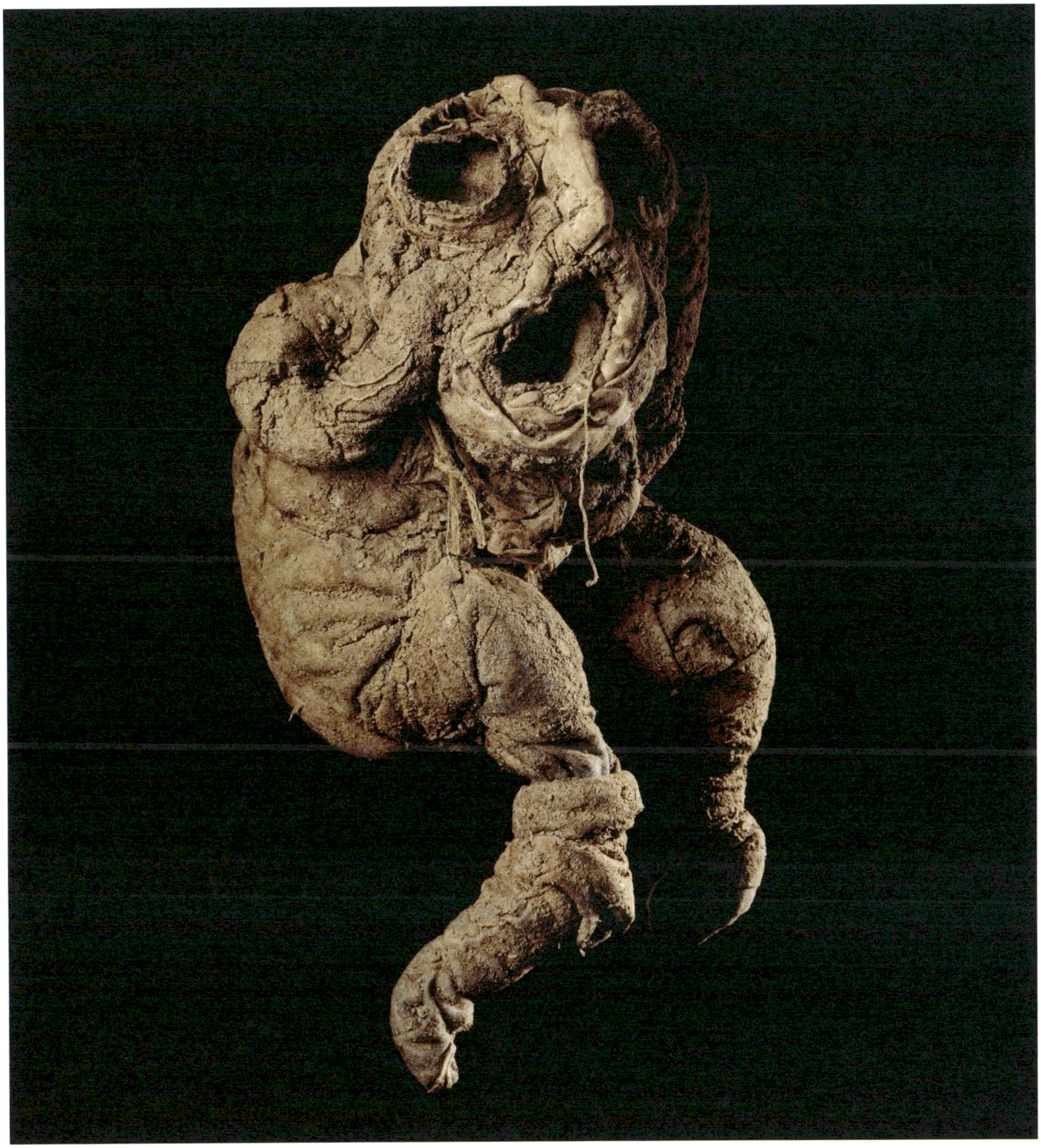

Michel Nedjar
sans titre untitled, entre between
1976 et and 1982
assemblage de tissu, tricot, ficelle, jute et matériaux divers, assemblage of fabric, needlework, string, jute, and miscellaneous materials
89 x 25 x 23 cm
cab-5181

Michel Nedjar
sans titre untitled, ca. 1981
assemblage matériaux divers : chiffons, ficelles, terre assemblage of miscellaneous materials: chiffon, string, soil
47 x 29 x 23 cm
cab-3051

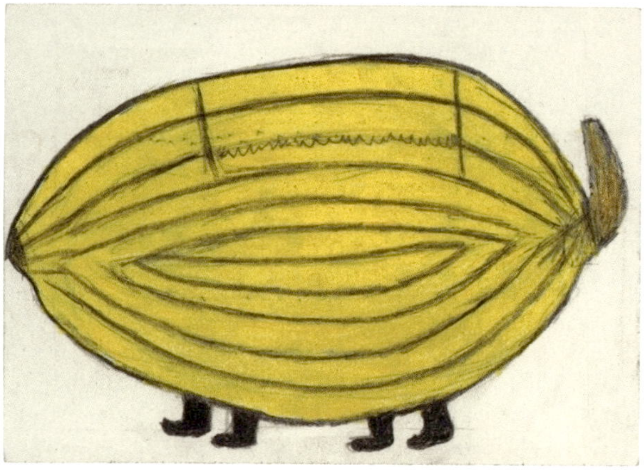

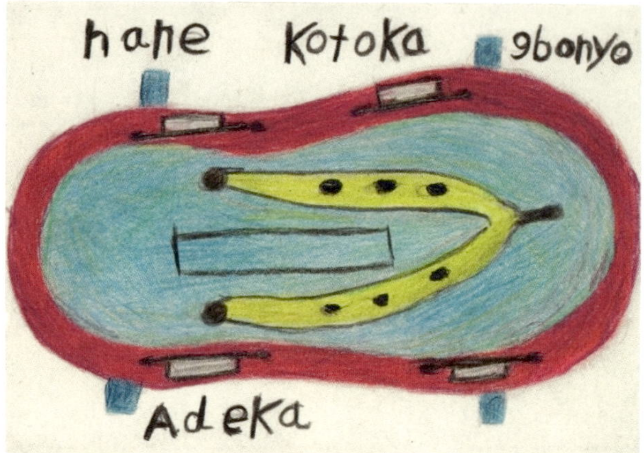

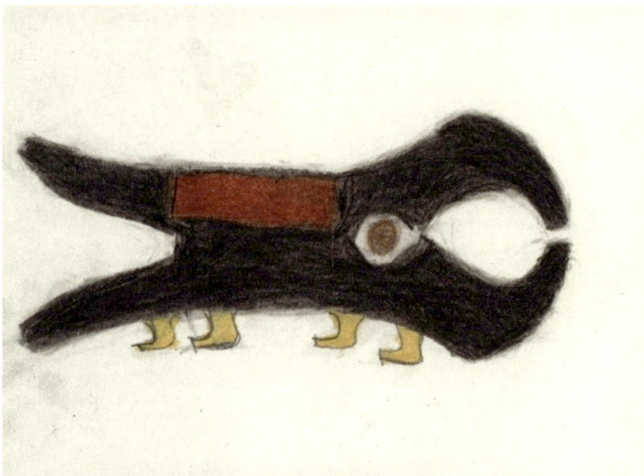

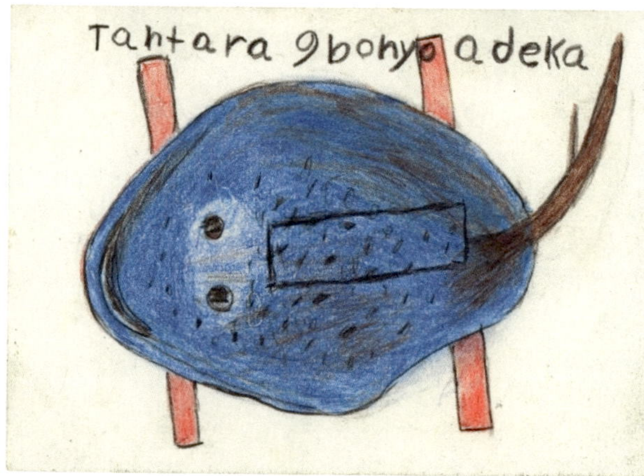

Ataa Oko
sans titre untitled, 2006
mine de plomb et crayon de couleur sur papier graphite and coloured pencil on paper
14,8 x 21 cm
cab-14564/15, cab-14564/13, cab-14564/14, cab-14564/8

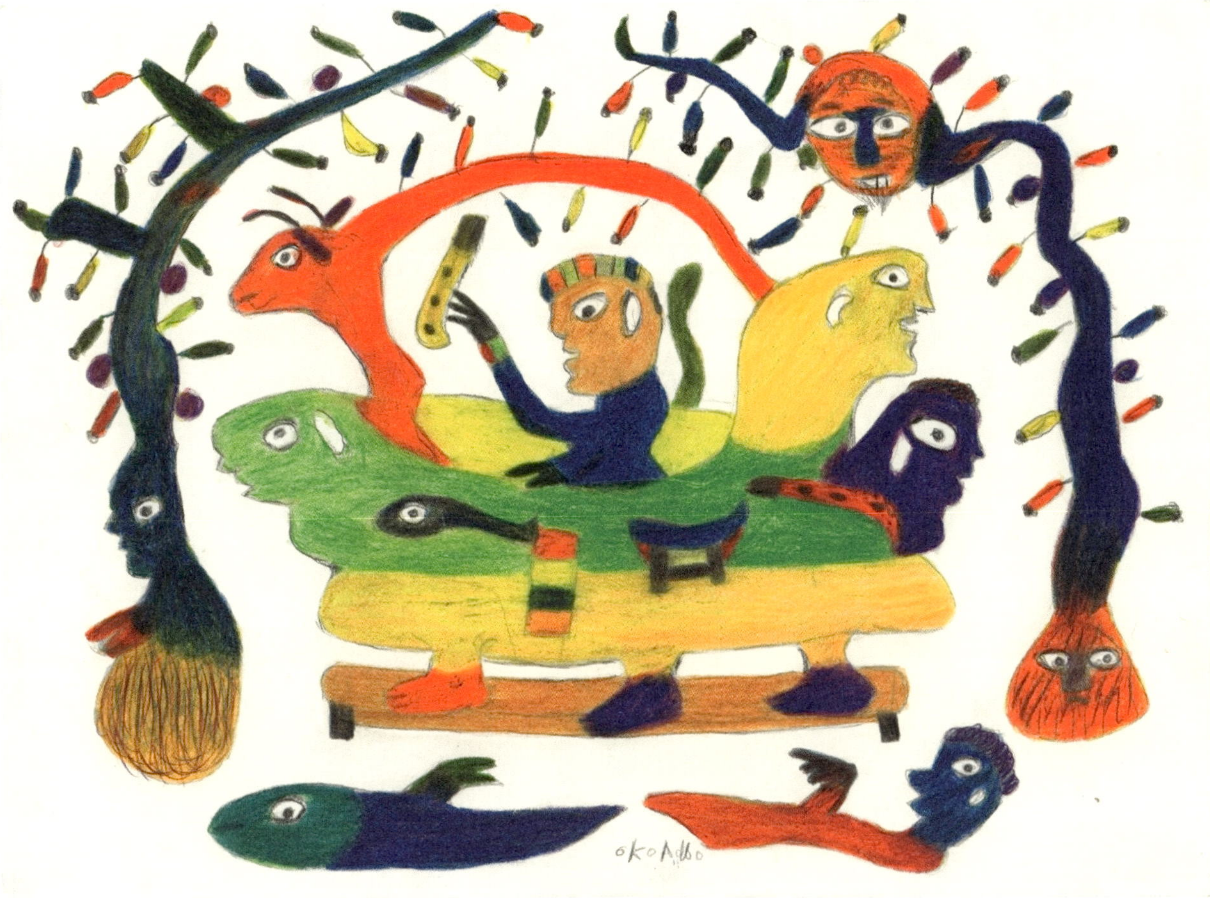

Ataa Oko
sans titre untitled, 2010
mine de plomb et crayon de couleur sur papier graphite and coloured pencil on paper
41,9 x 59 cm
cab-15404

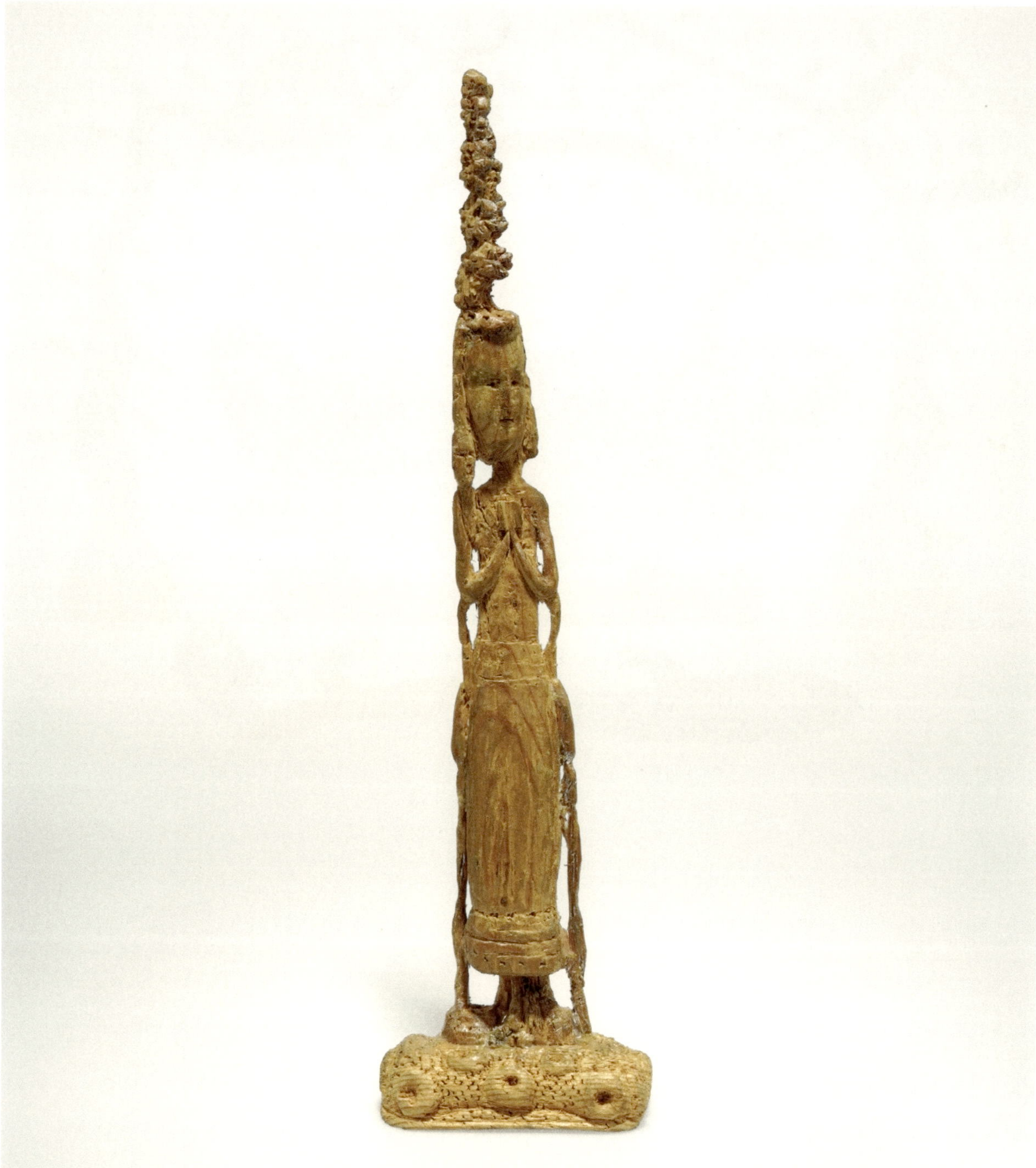

Michael Pankoks
sans titre untitled, entre between 1960
et and 1975
bois sculpté carved wood
35 x 9,2 x 5,2 cm
cab-8715

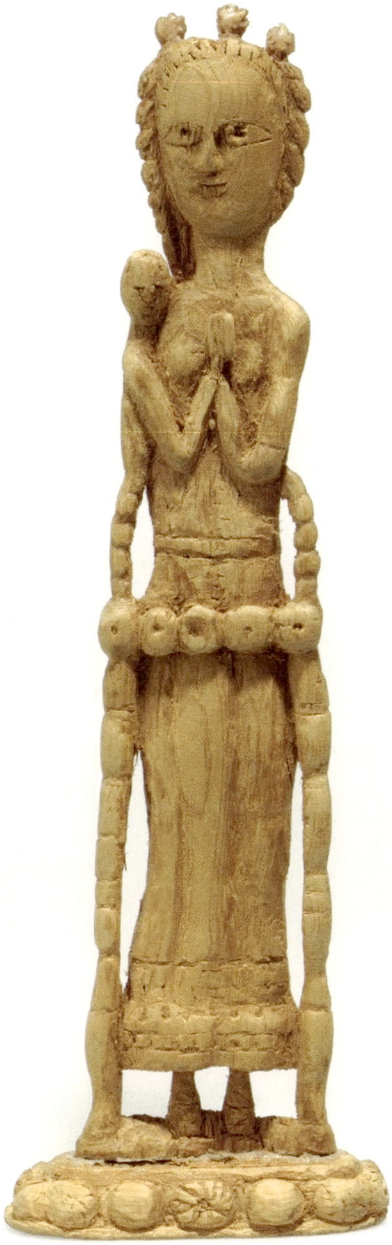

Michael Pankoks
sans titre untitled, entre between 1960
et and 1975
bois sculpté carved wood
34 x 11 x 4,5 cm
cab-8713

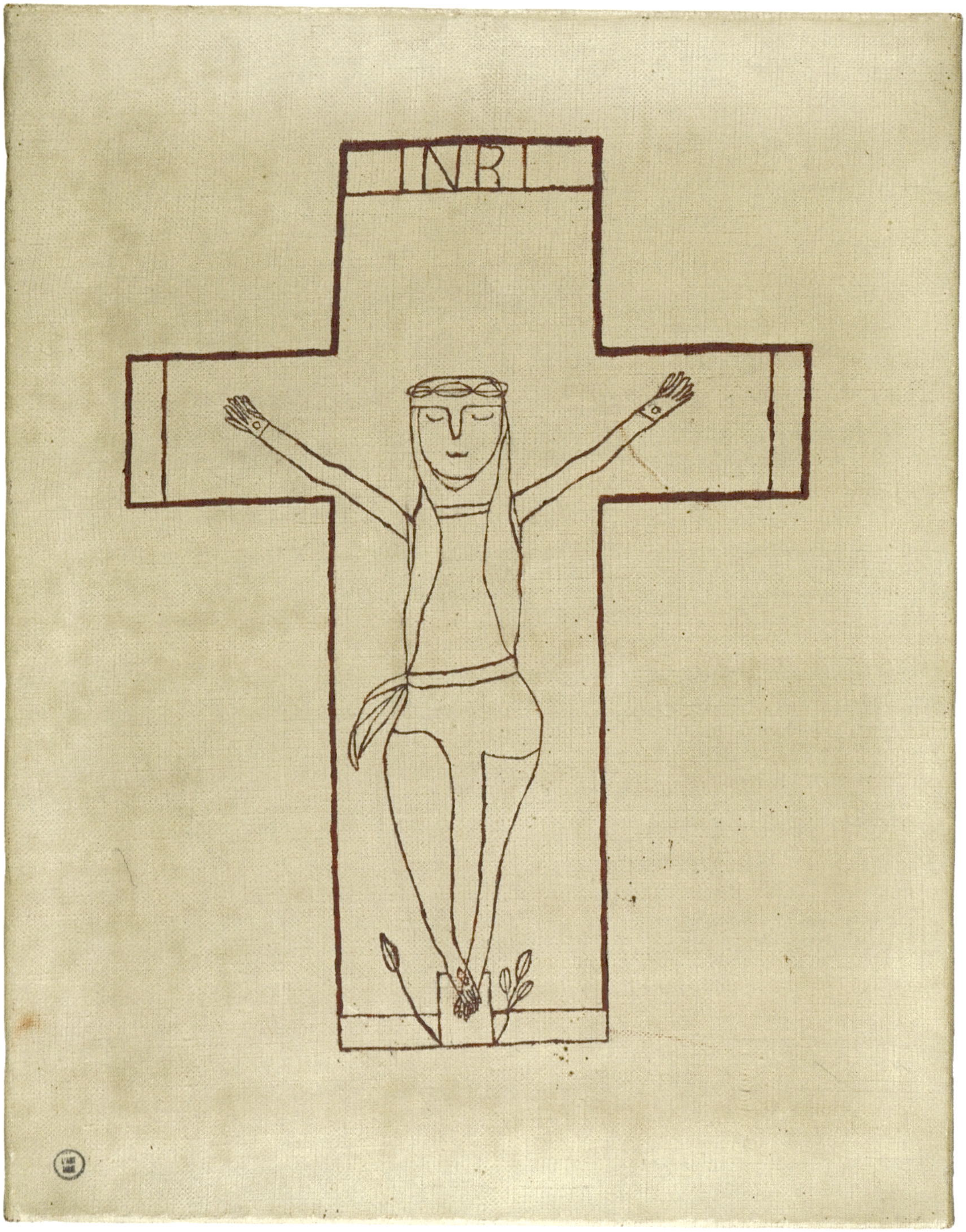

Laure Pigeon
sans titre untitled, ca. 1939
huile sur toile oil on canvas
41 x 33 cm
cab-1983

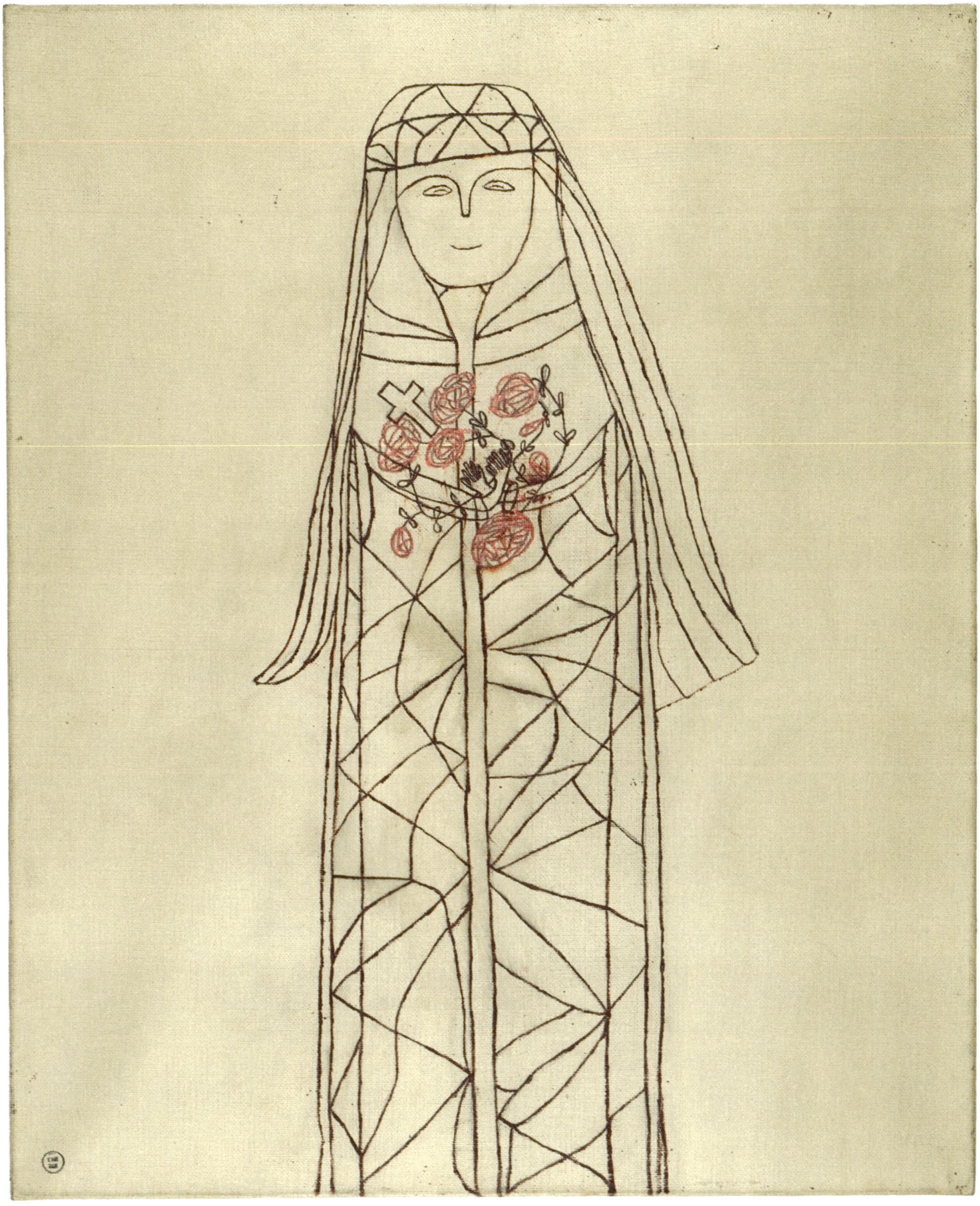

Laure Pigeon
sans titre untitled, ca. 1939
huile sur toile oil on canvas
55 x 45 cm
cab-1982

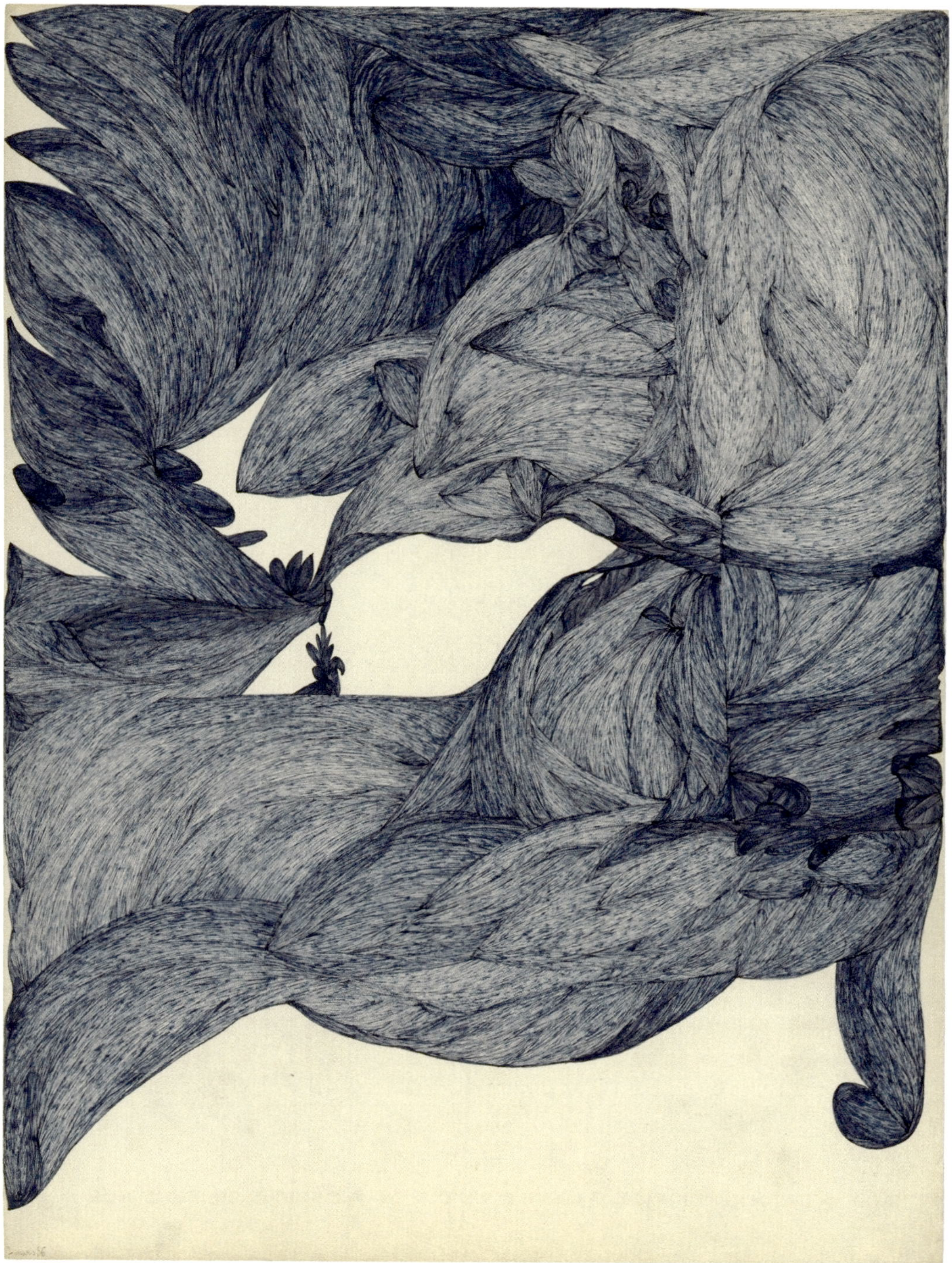

Laure Pigeon
7 mars 1956, 1956
encre sur papier ink on paper
65 x 50 cm
cab-1792

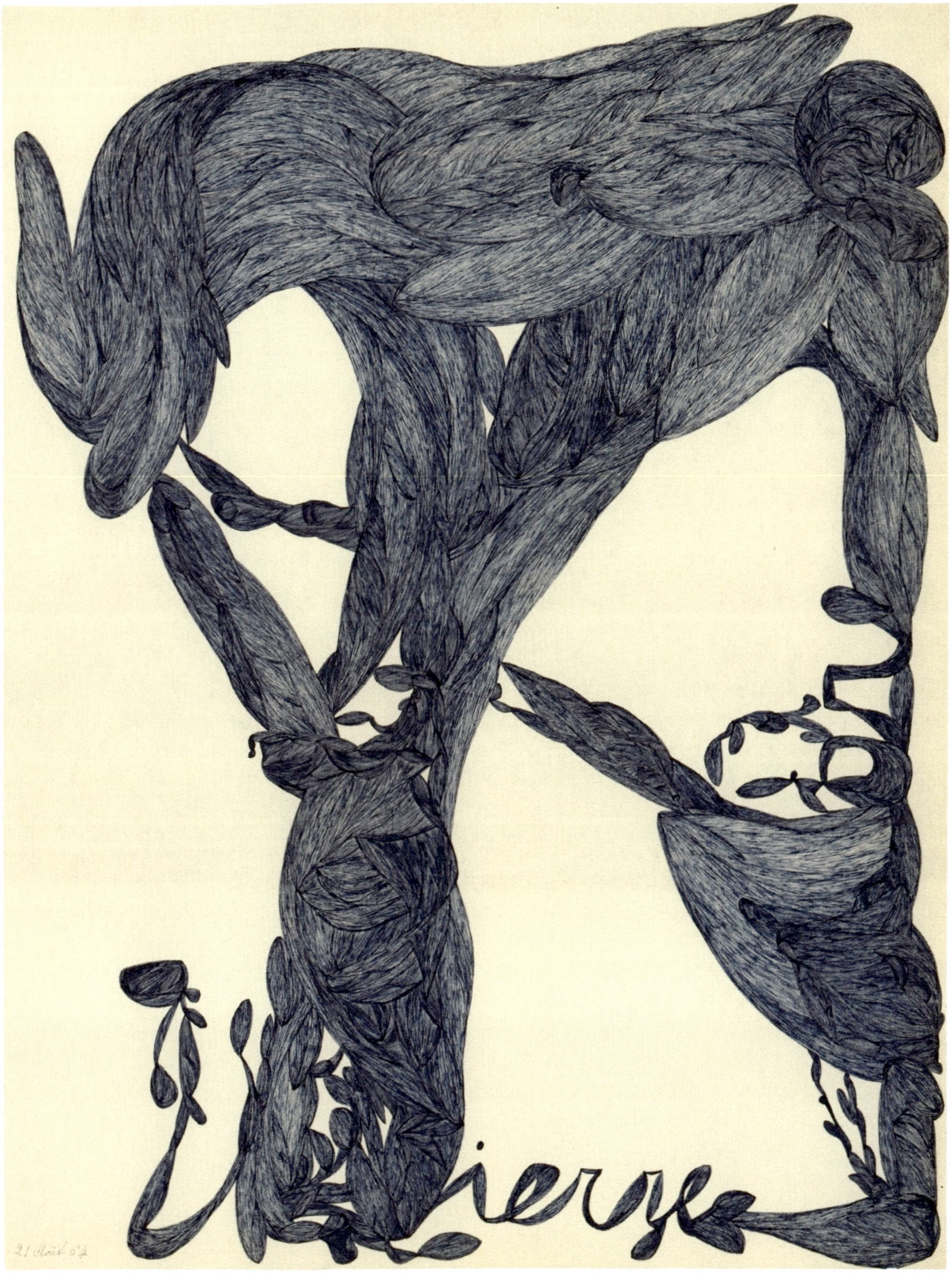

Laure Pigeon
Pierre, 1964
encre sur papier ink on paper
65 x 50 cm
cab-1920

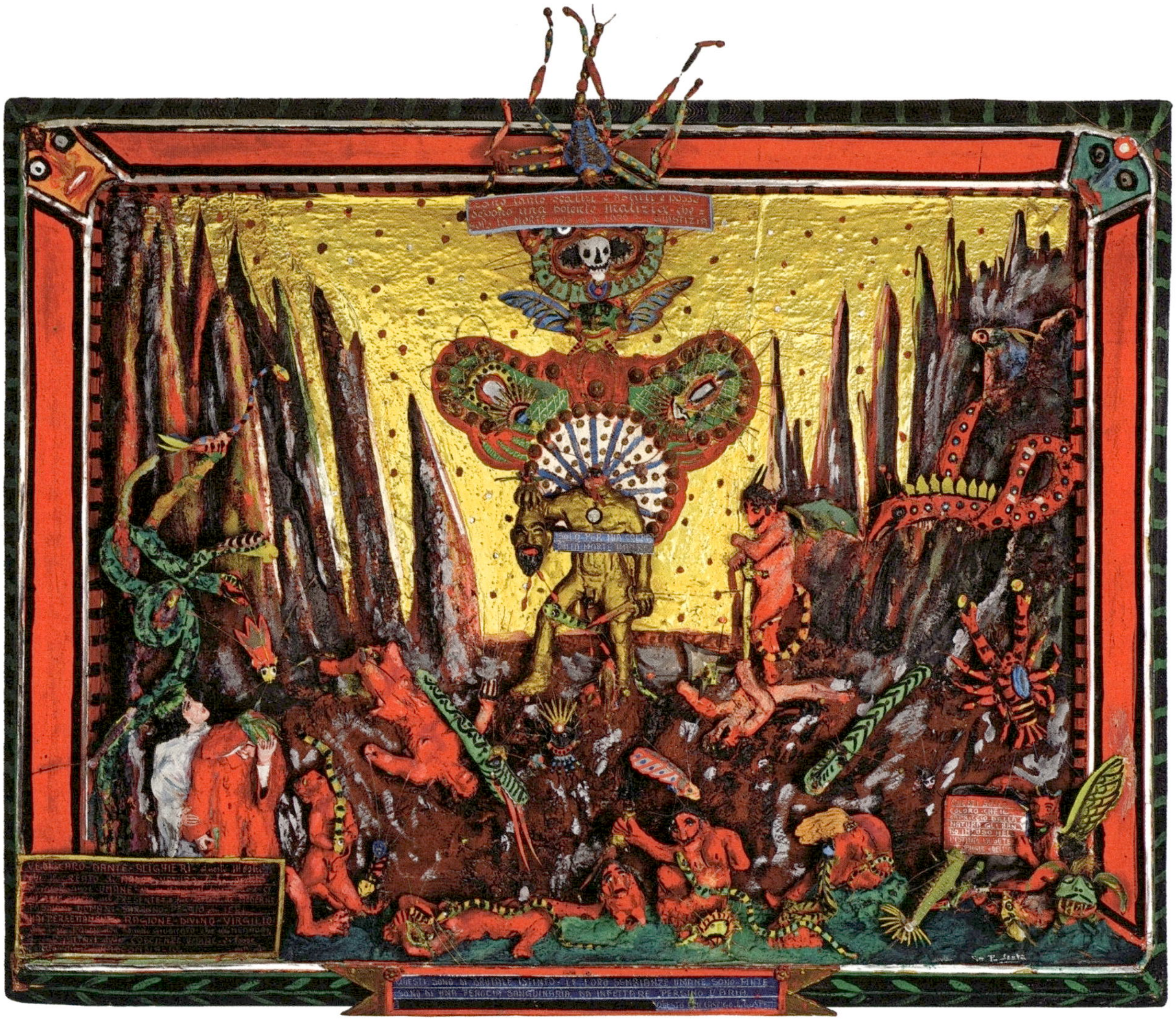

Giovanni Battista Podestà
L'inferno, s.d. n.d.
bois, mélange de sciure, colle et plâtre, peinture, papier wood, mixture of sawdust, glue, and plaster, paint, paper
85 x 103 cm
cab-1243bis

Giovanni Battista Podestà
sans titre untitled, s.d. n.d.
peinture sur toile paint on canvas
60 x 35 cm
cab-7493

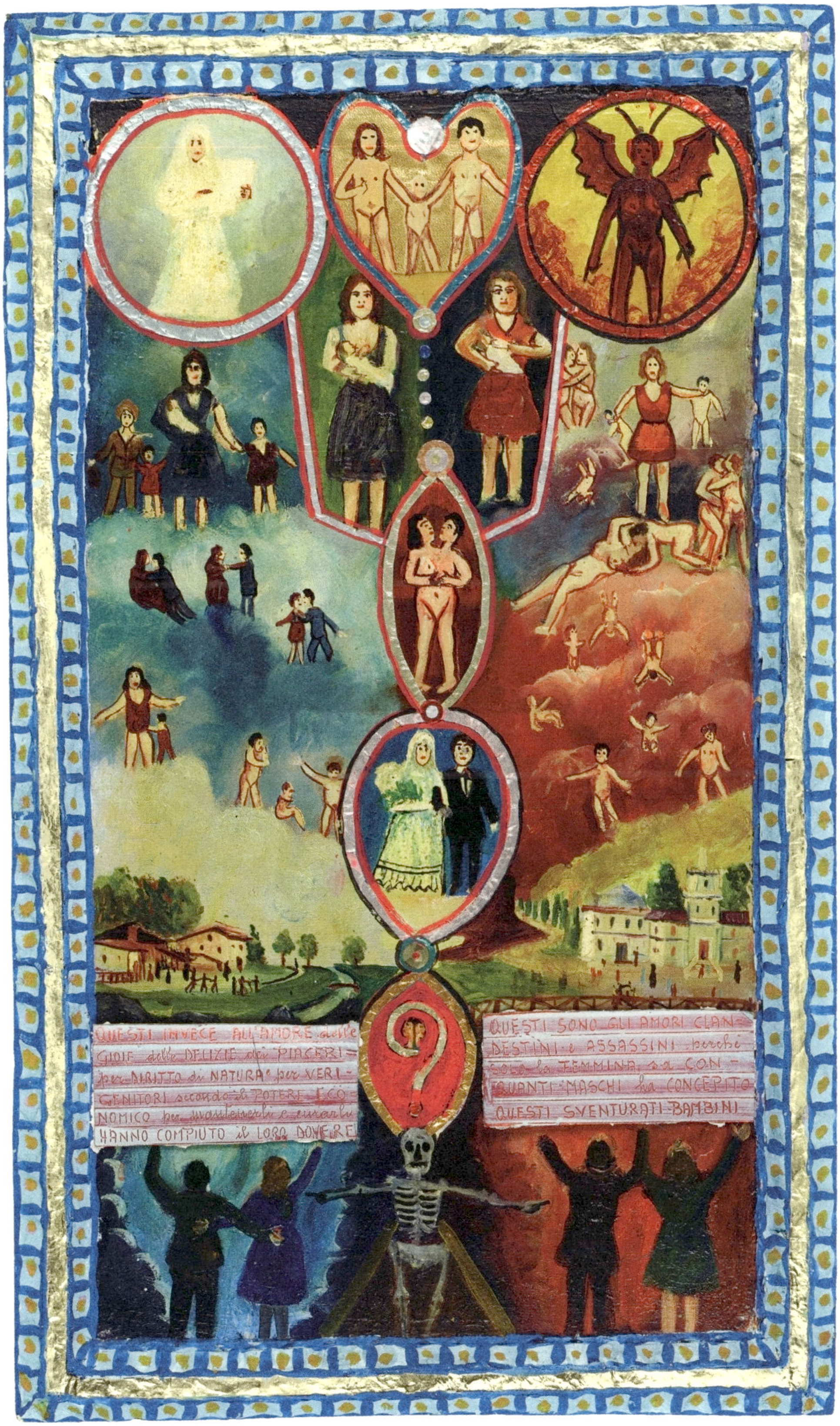
QUESTI INVECE ALL'AMORE delle
GIOIE delle DELIZIE dei PIACERI =
per DIRITTO di NATURA e per VERI-
GENITORI secondo il POTERE ECO-
NOMICO per mantenerli e curarli
HANNO COMPIUTO il LORO DOVERE
QUESTI SONO GLI AMORI CLAN-
DESTINI e ASSASSINI perché
SOLO la FEMMINA sa CON-
QUANTI MASCHI ha CONCEPITO
QUESTI SVENTURATI BAMBINI

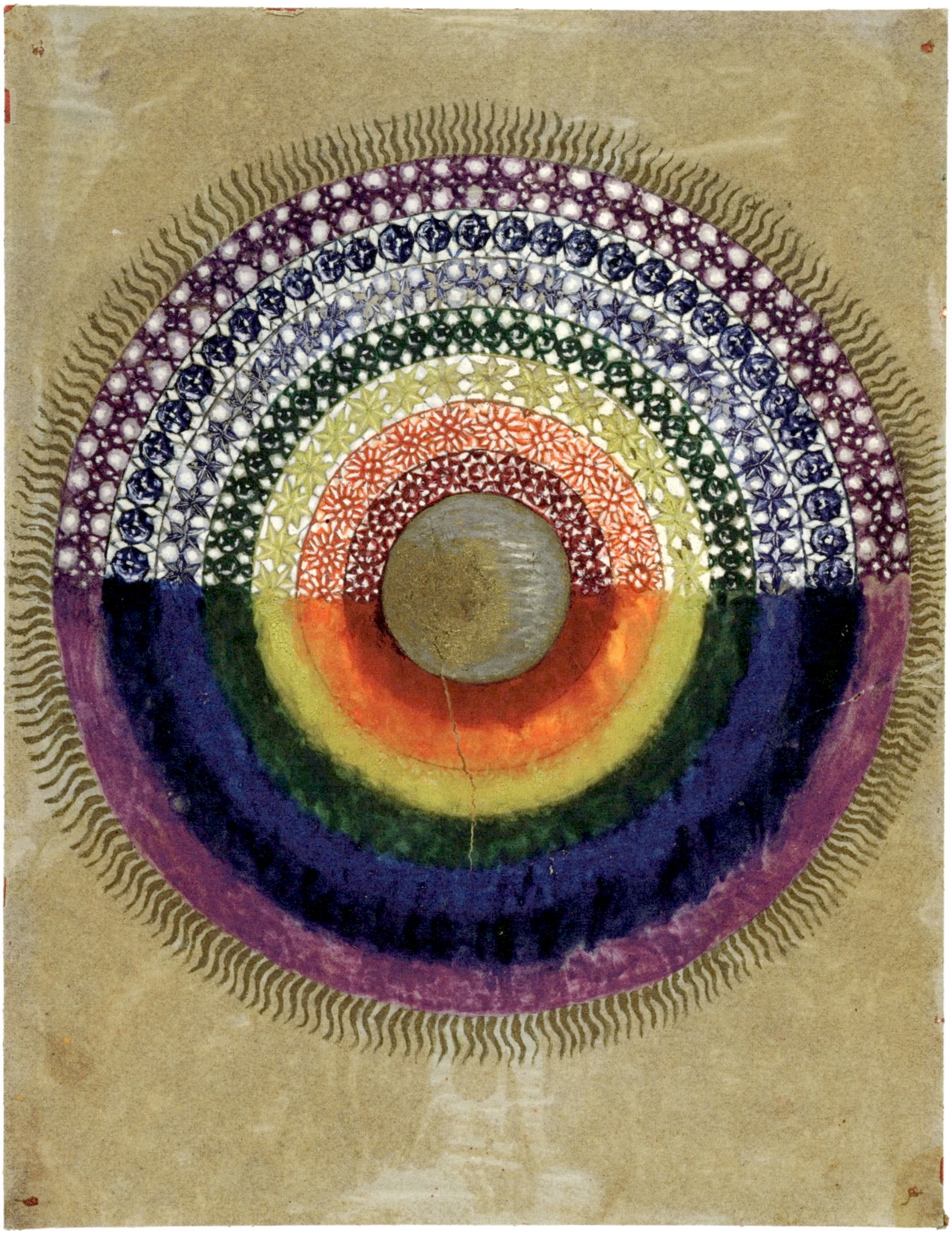

Catherine de Porada
L'union primordiale, entre between
1942 et and 1950
gouache sur papier gouache on paper
26 x 21 cm
ni-1263

Catherine de Porada
Les sept cadenas de la Bible, ca. 1942
gouache sur papier gouache on paper
65 x 50 cm
ni-1261

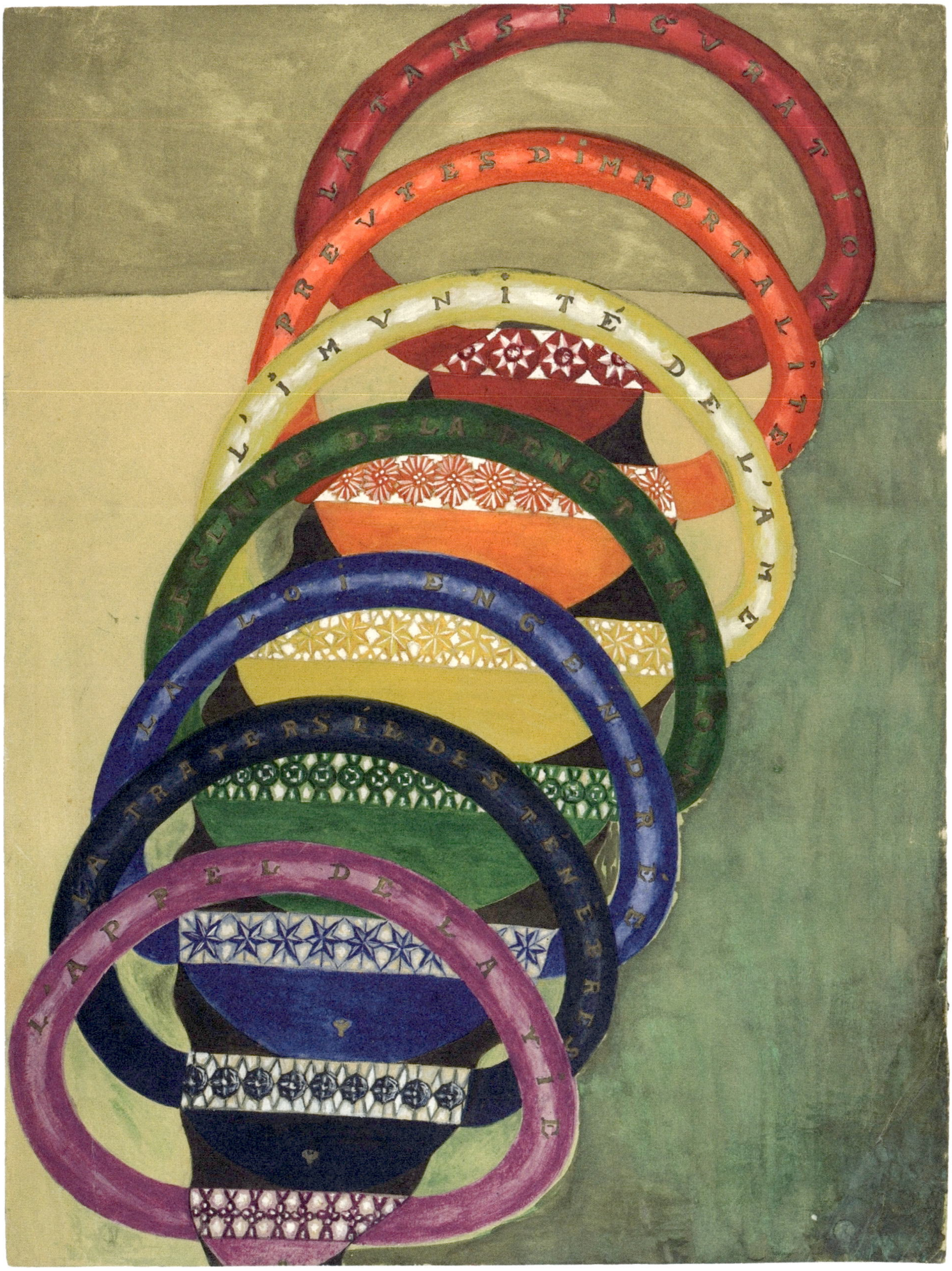
LA TANSFIGURATION
PREUVES D'IMMORTALITÉ
L'IMMUNITÉ DE L'ÂME
L'APPEL DE LA VIE

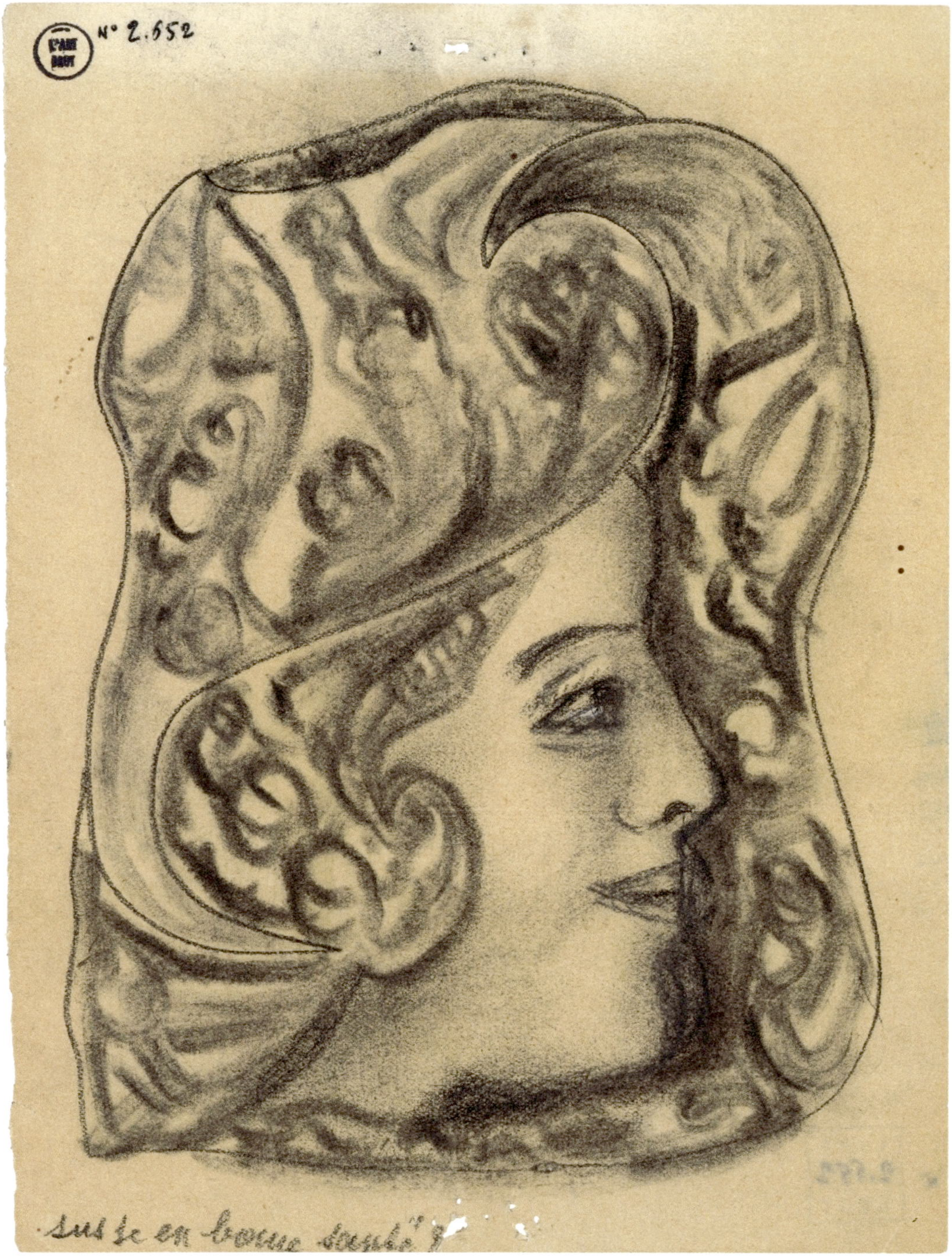

Jane Ruffié
Suis-je en bonne santé?, ca. 1939
crayon noir sur papier
black pencil on paper
22 x 17 cm
cab-2652

Jane Ruffié
sans titre untitled, ca. 1939
mine de plomb et crayon de couleur sur papier rose graphite and coloured pencil on pink paper
48 x 31,5 cm
cab-2647

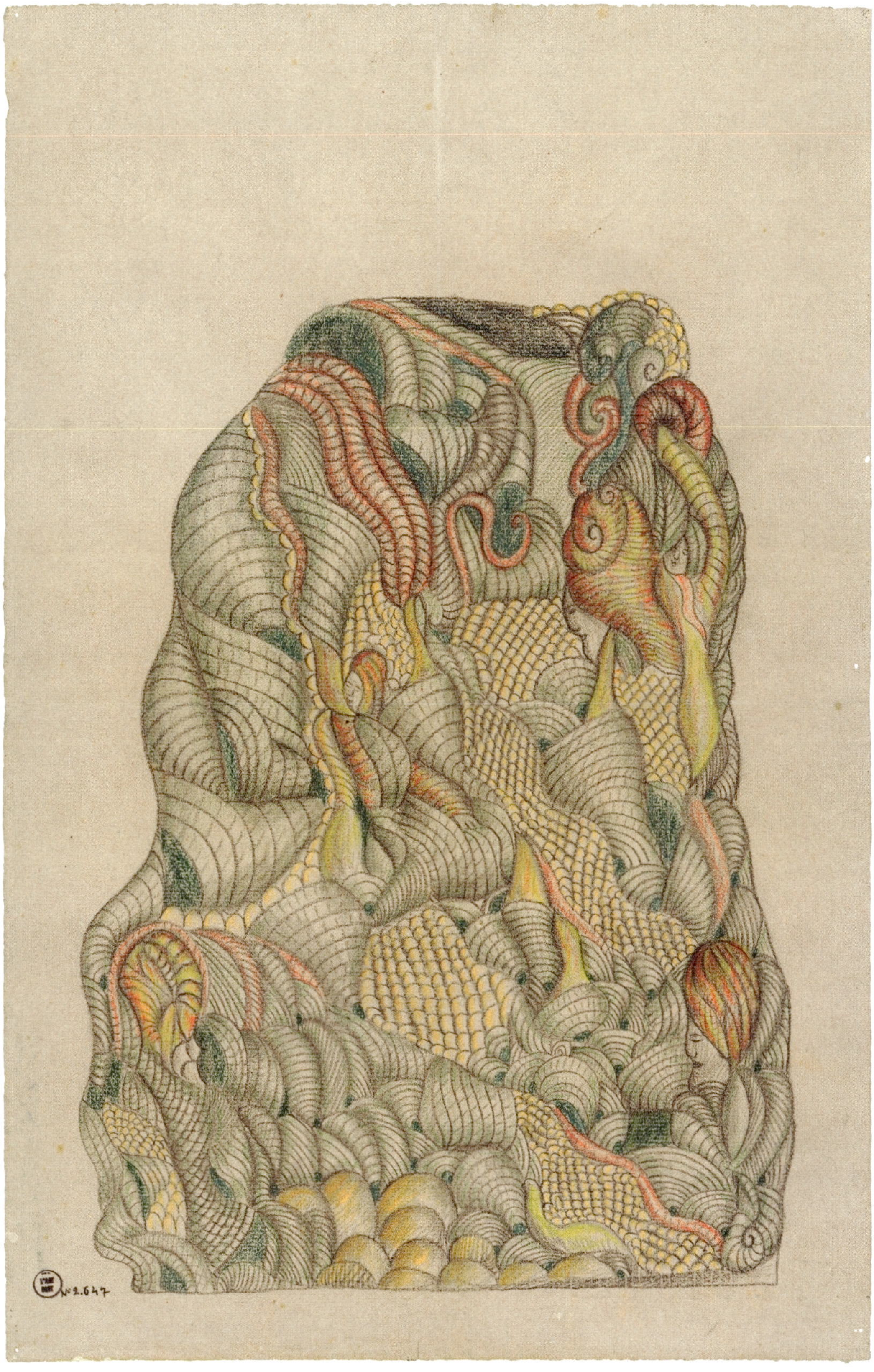

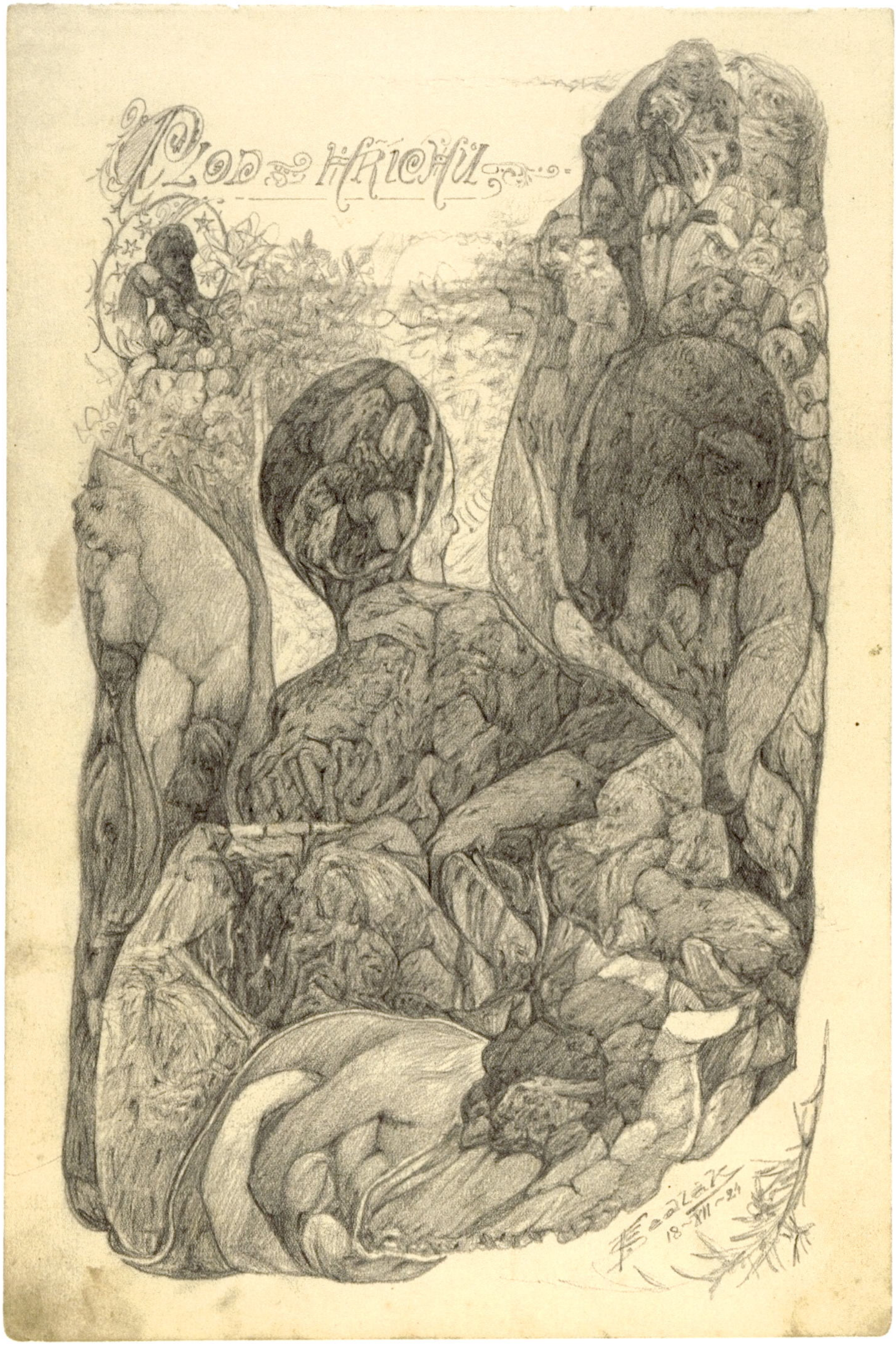

F. Sedlak
Fruit du péché, 1924
crayon sur papier pencil on paper
32 x 22 cm
ni-4001

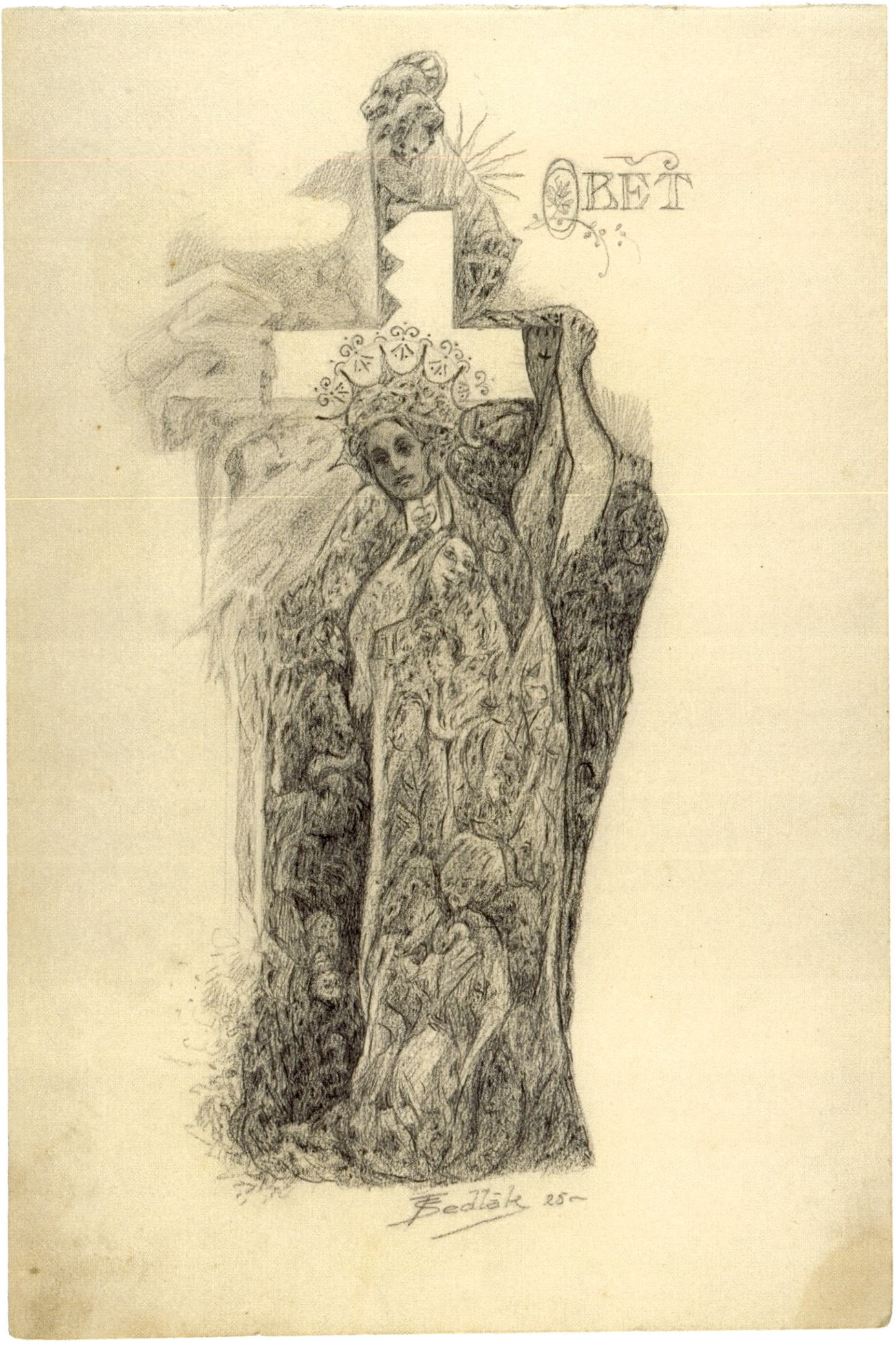

F. Sedlak
Victime, 1925
crayon sur papier pencil on paper
32 x 22 cm
ni-4014

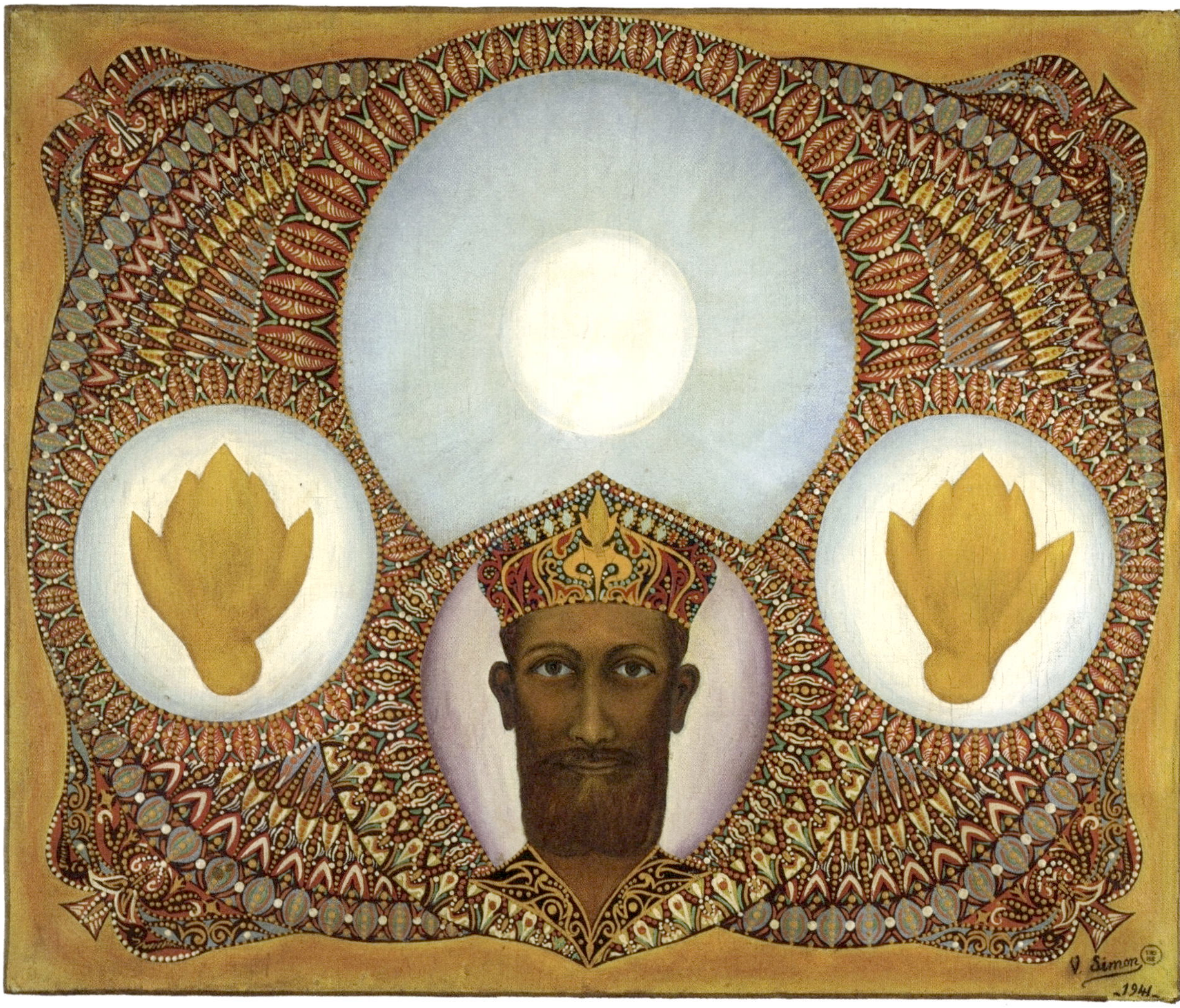

Victor Simon
Christ-Roi, 1941
huile sur toile oil on canvas
59 x 48 cm
ni-1394

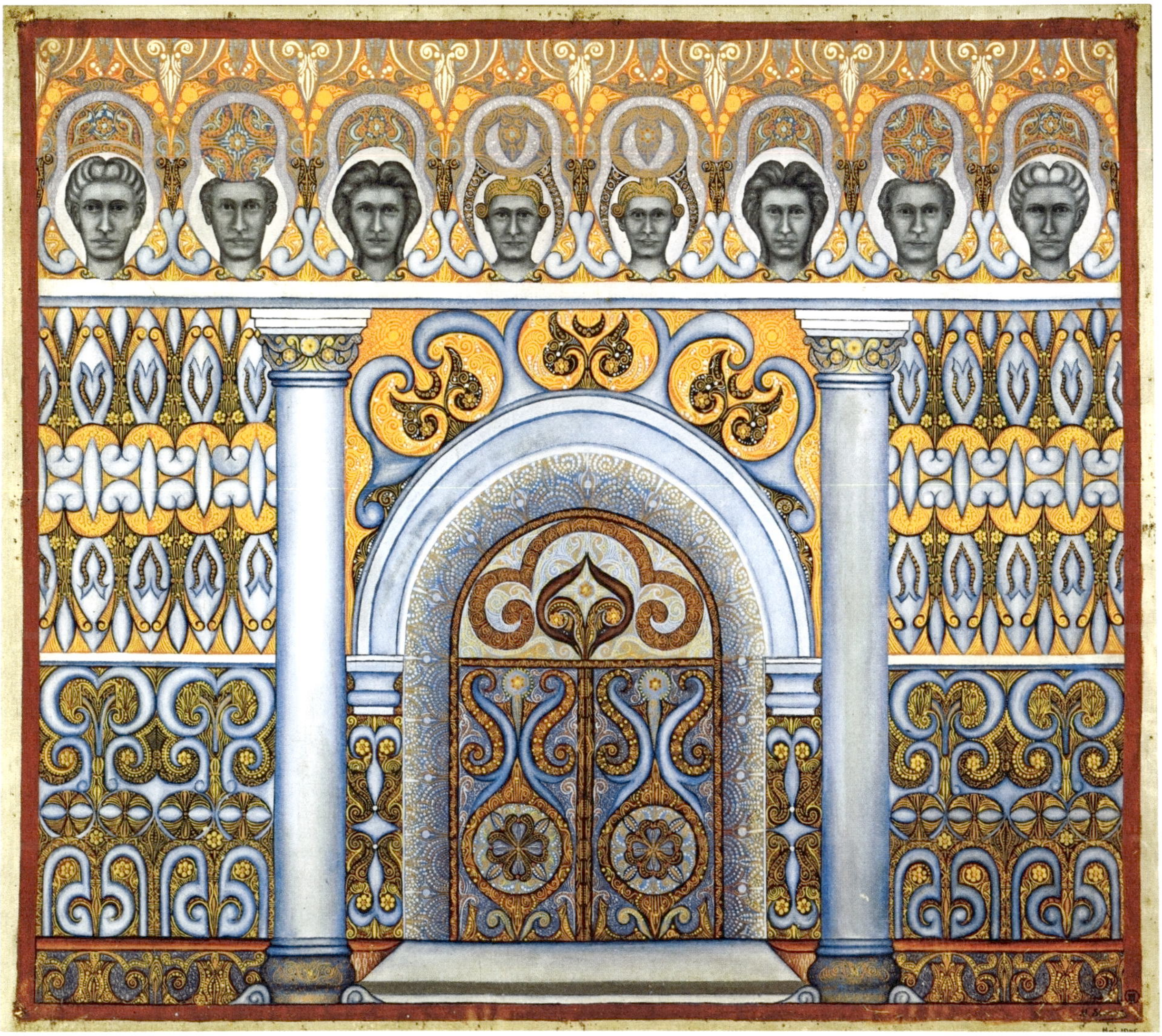

Victor Simon
La porte du temple, 1946
huile sur toile oil on canvas
81 x 71 cm
ni-1395

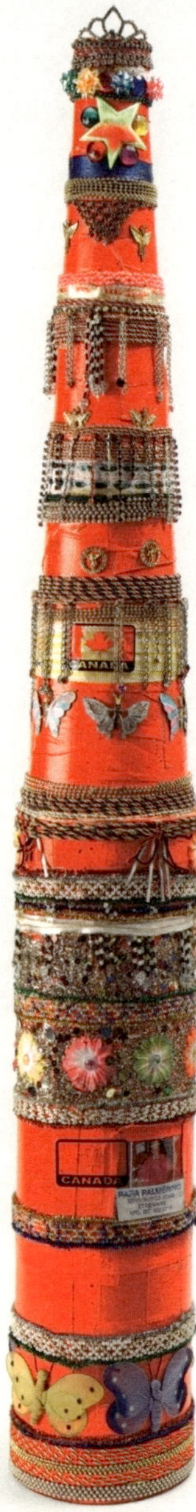

Palmerino Sorgente
sans titre untitled, entre between
1980 et and 2005
assemblage de matériaux divers :
carton, tissu, paillettes, bijoux
et photographie assemblage
of miscellaneous materials: cardboard,
fabric, sequins, jewellery, and photographs
135 x 17 x 17 cm, 119 x 38 x 38 cm
139 x 28 x 28 cm
cab-17013, cab-17011, cab-17012

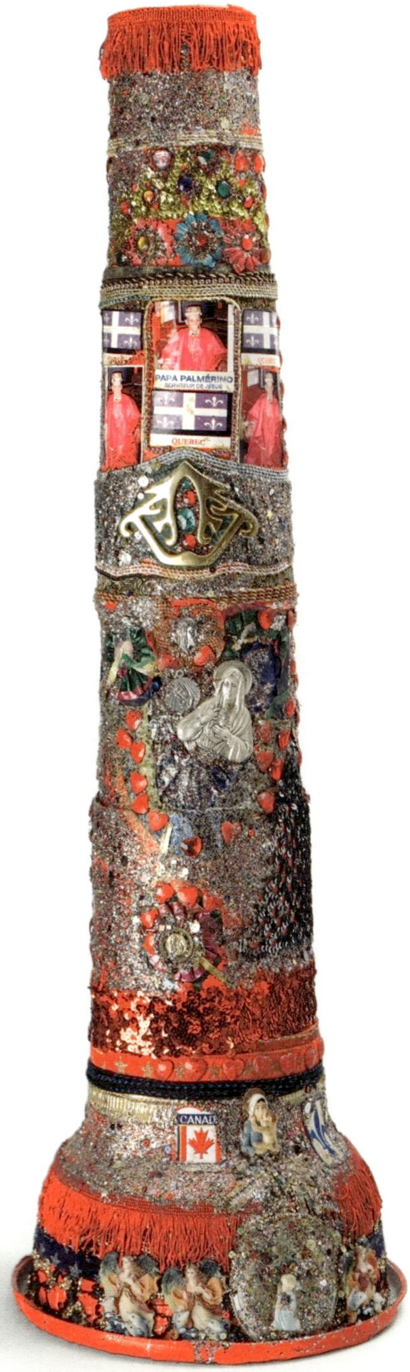
PAPA PALMERINO
QUEBEC
CANADA

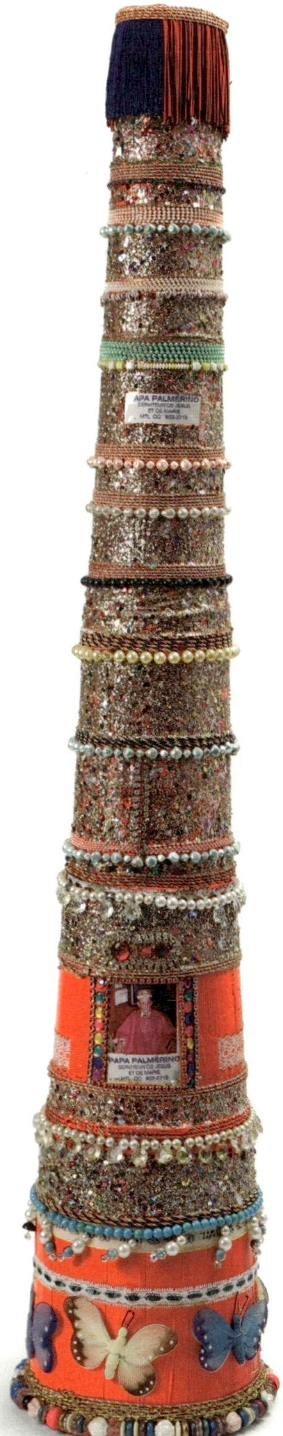
PAPA PALMERINO
PAPA PALMERINO

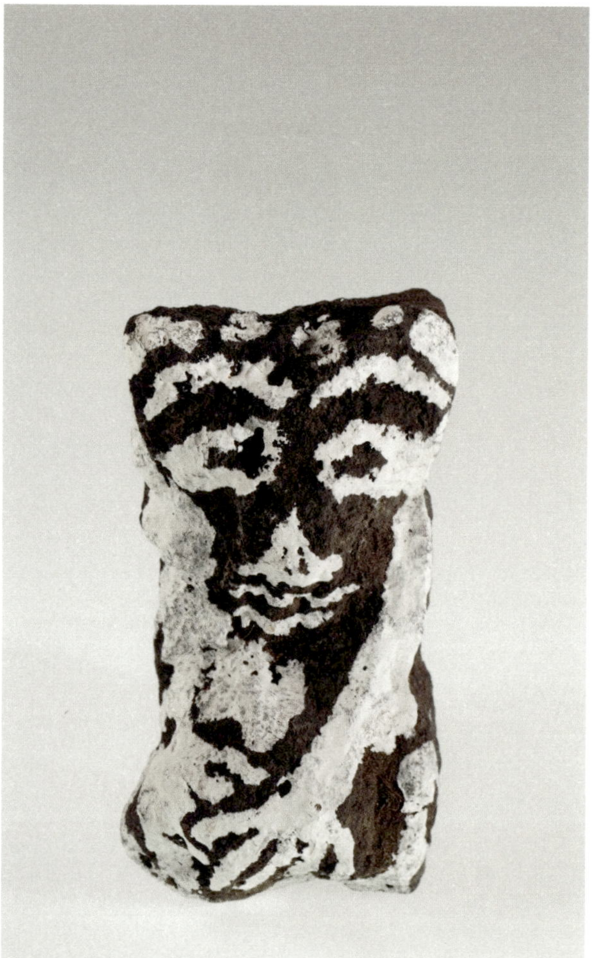 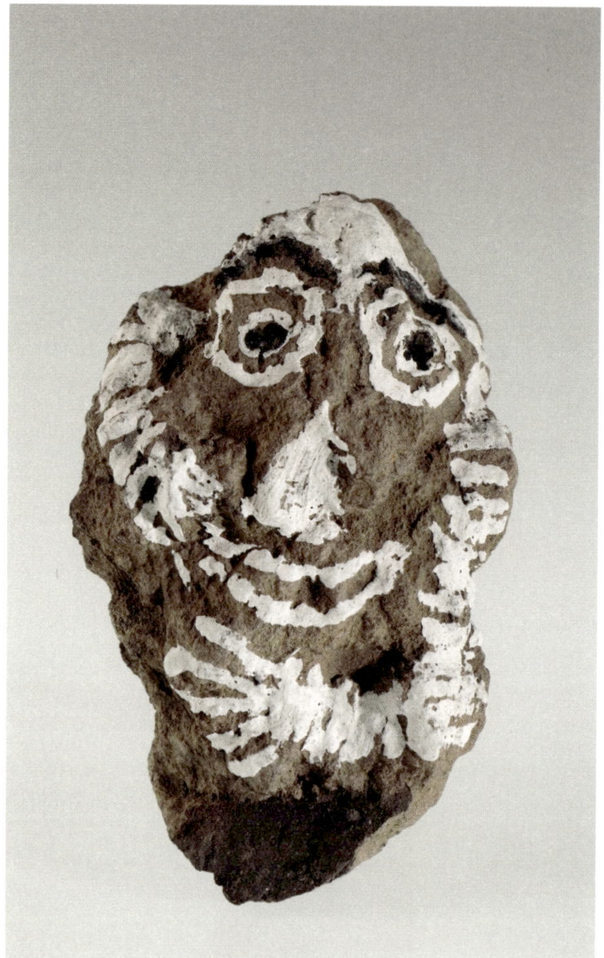

Ni Nyoman Tanjung
sans titre untitled, entre between
2003 et and 2006
peinture sur pierre paint on stone
dimensions diverses dimensions variable
cab-13940, cab-13939, cab-13938

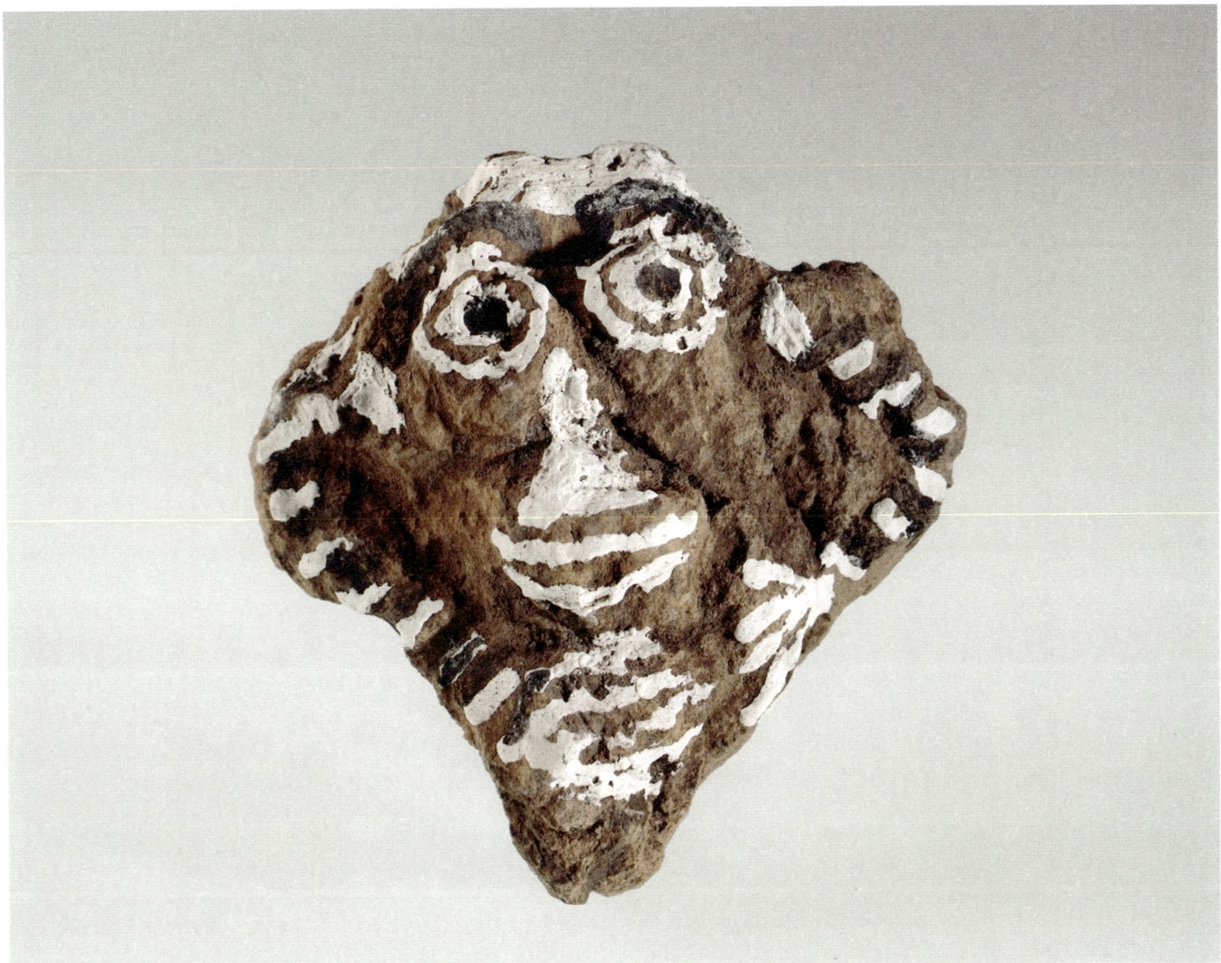

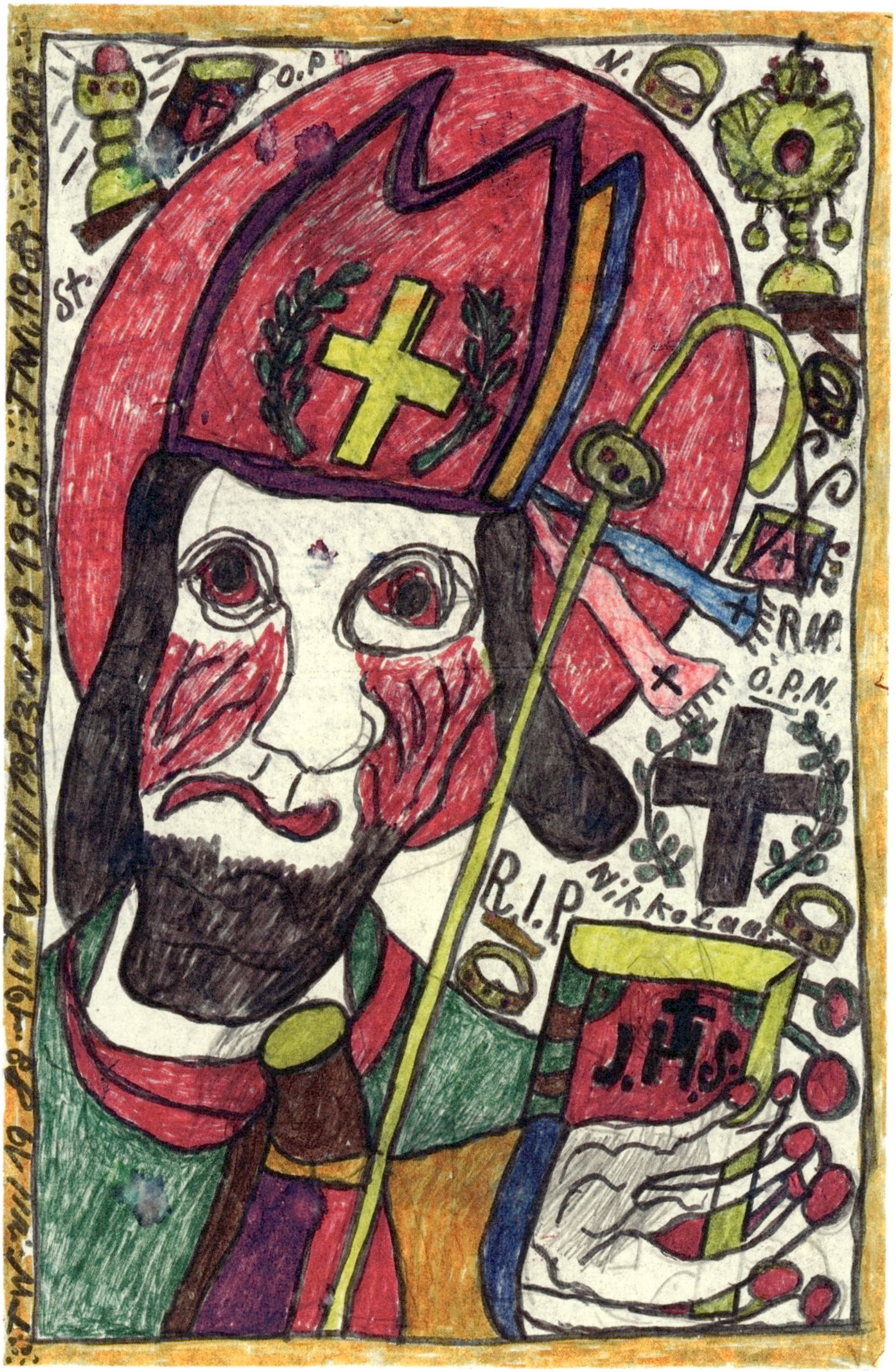

Theo [Theodor Wagemann]
sans titre untitled, 1983
feutre et crayon de couleur sur papier
felt-tip pen and coloured pencil on paper
37,5 x 25 cm
cab-7477

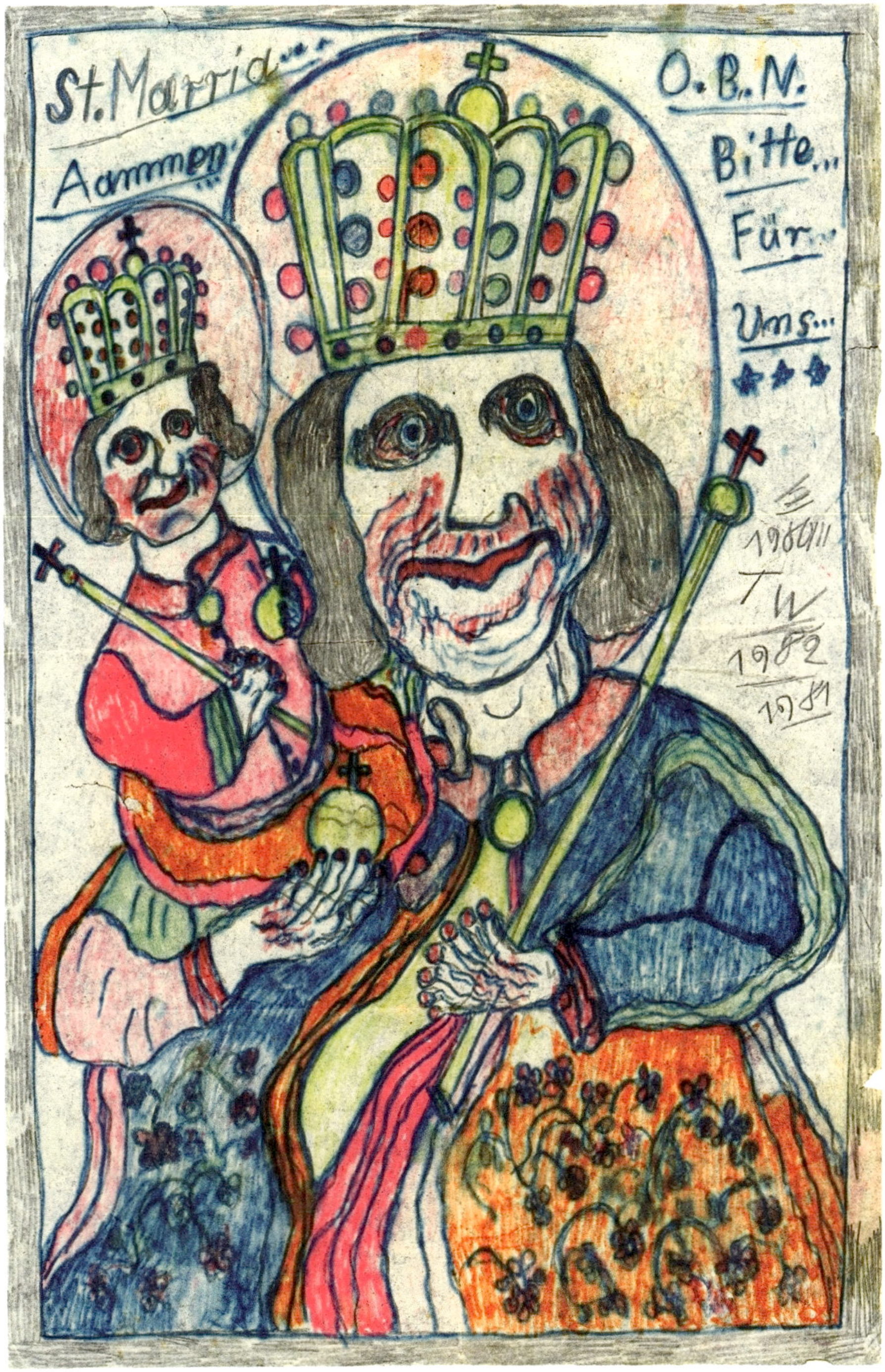

Theo [Theodor Wagemann]
St. Marria, 1982
feutre et crayon de couleur sur papier
felt-tip pen and coloured pencil on paper
37,5 x 25 cm
cab-7478

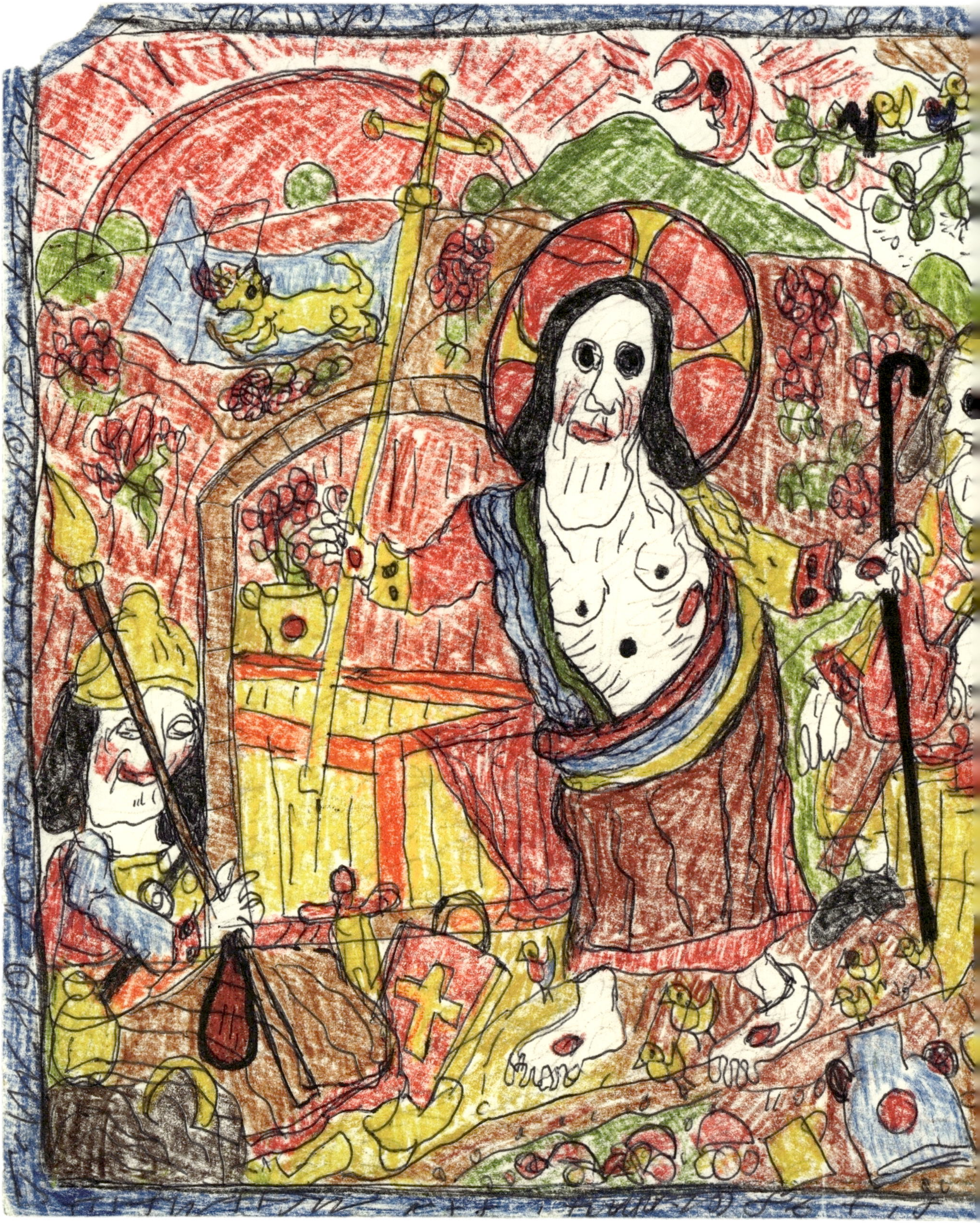

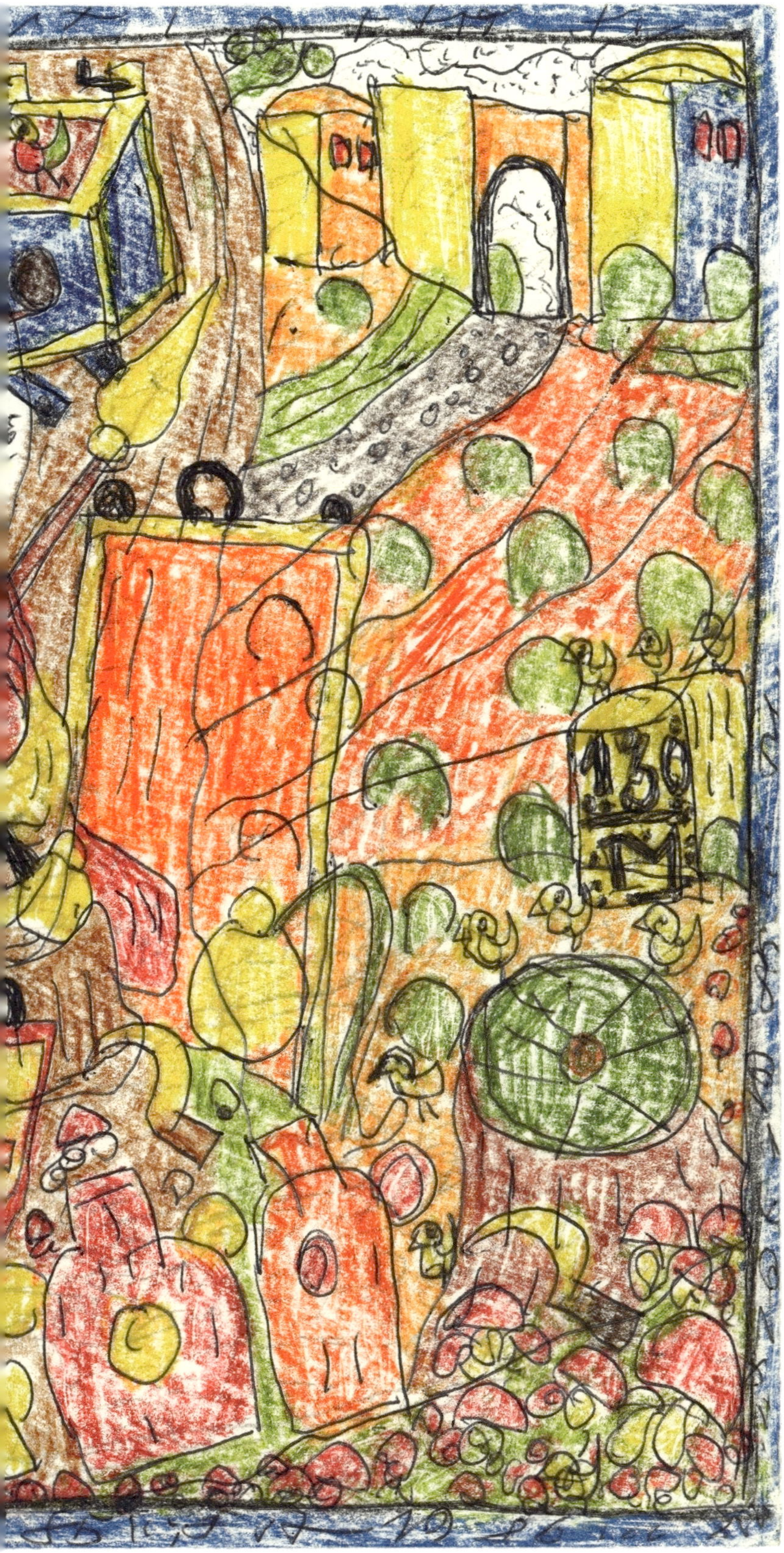

Theo [Theodor Wagemann]
sans titre untitled, 1986
stylo-bille et craie grasse sur papier
ballpoint pen and crayon on paper
21 x 29,8 cm
cab-7460

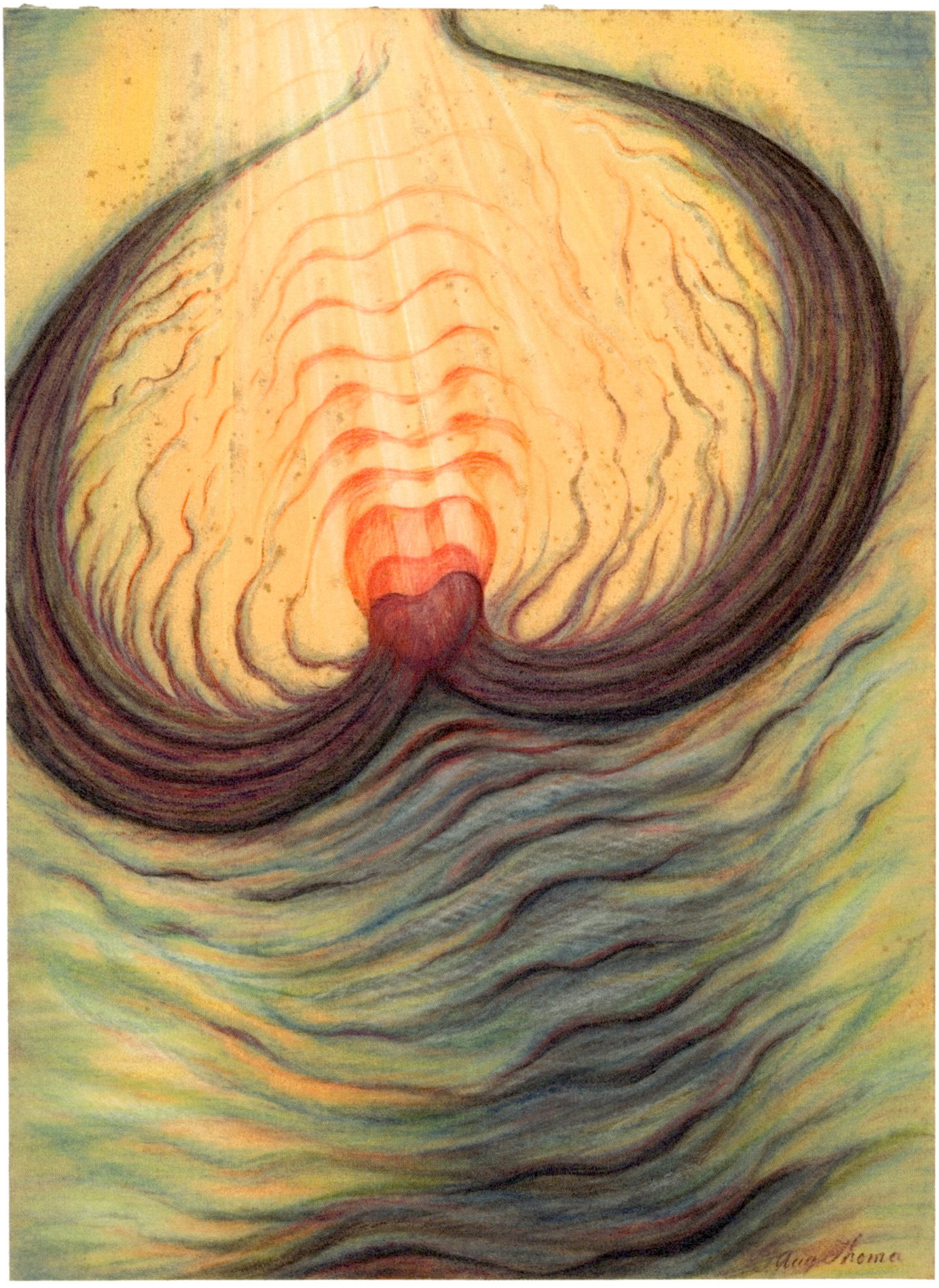

Johann Thoma
sans titre untitled, ca. 1930
pastel sur papier velours
pastel on velvet paper
50,3 x 37,7 cm
ni-6859

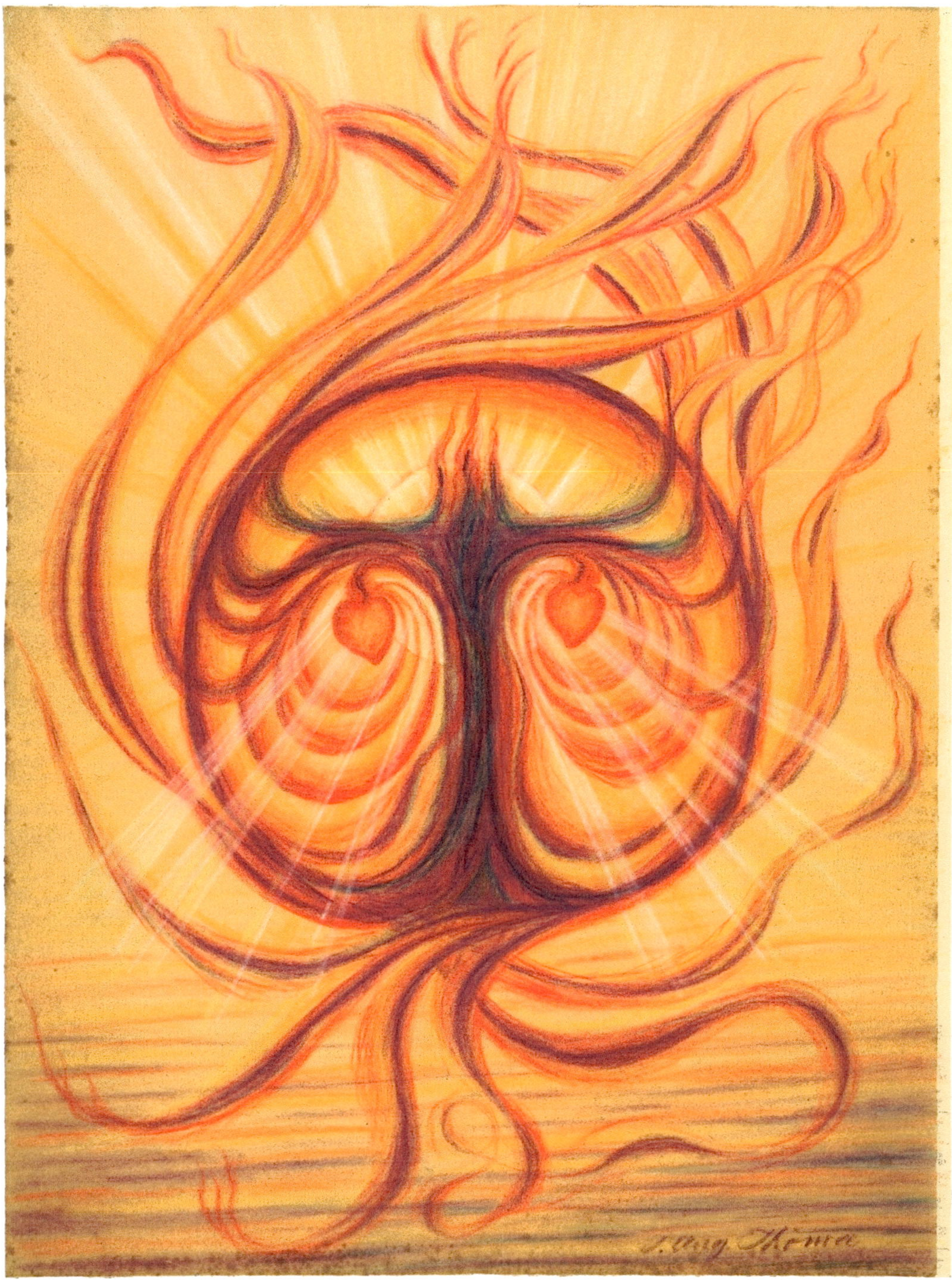

Johann Thoma
sans titre untitled, ca. 1930
pastel sur papier velours
pastel on velvet paper
50 x 38,4 cm
ni-7033

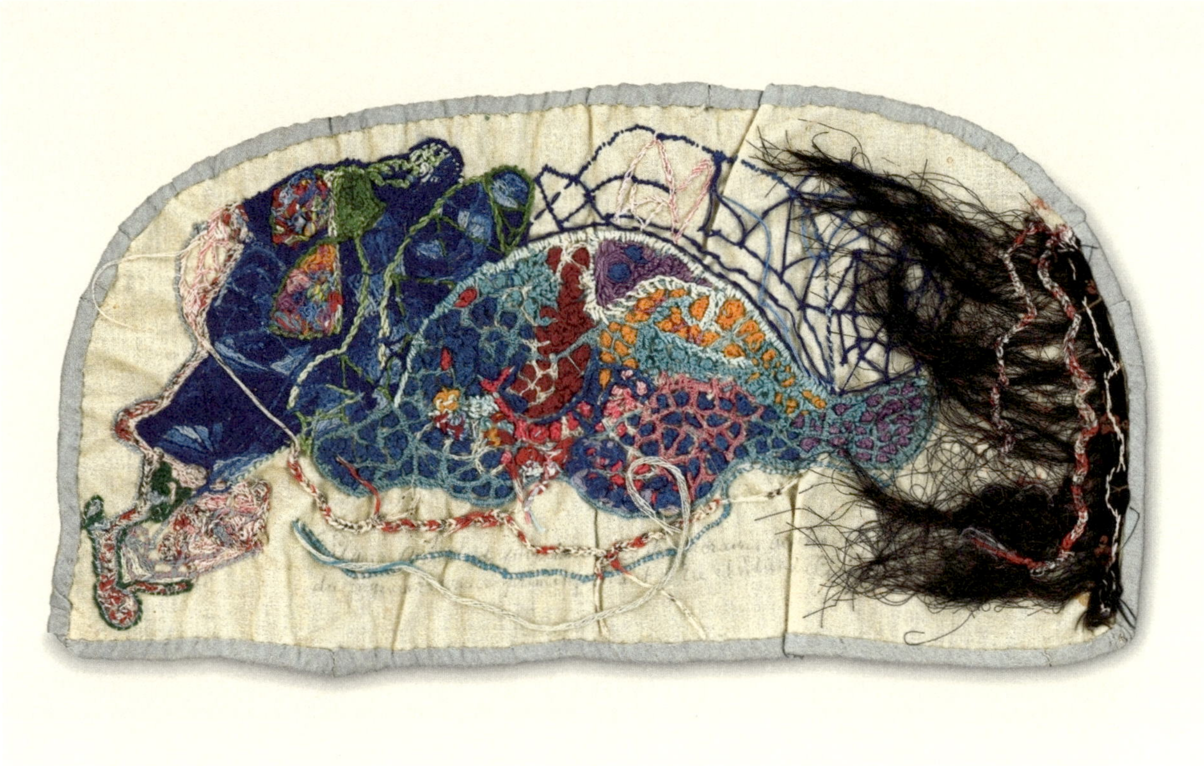

Jeanne Tripier
sans titre untitled, entre between
1935 et and 1939
coton, cheveux et mine de plomb sur toile
bordée de soie cotton, hair, and graphite
on silk-edged canvas
17 x 33,5 cm
cab-A659

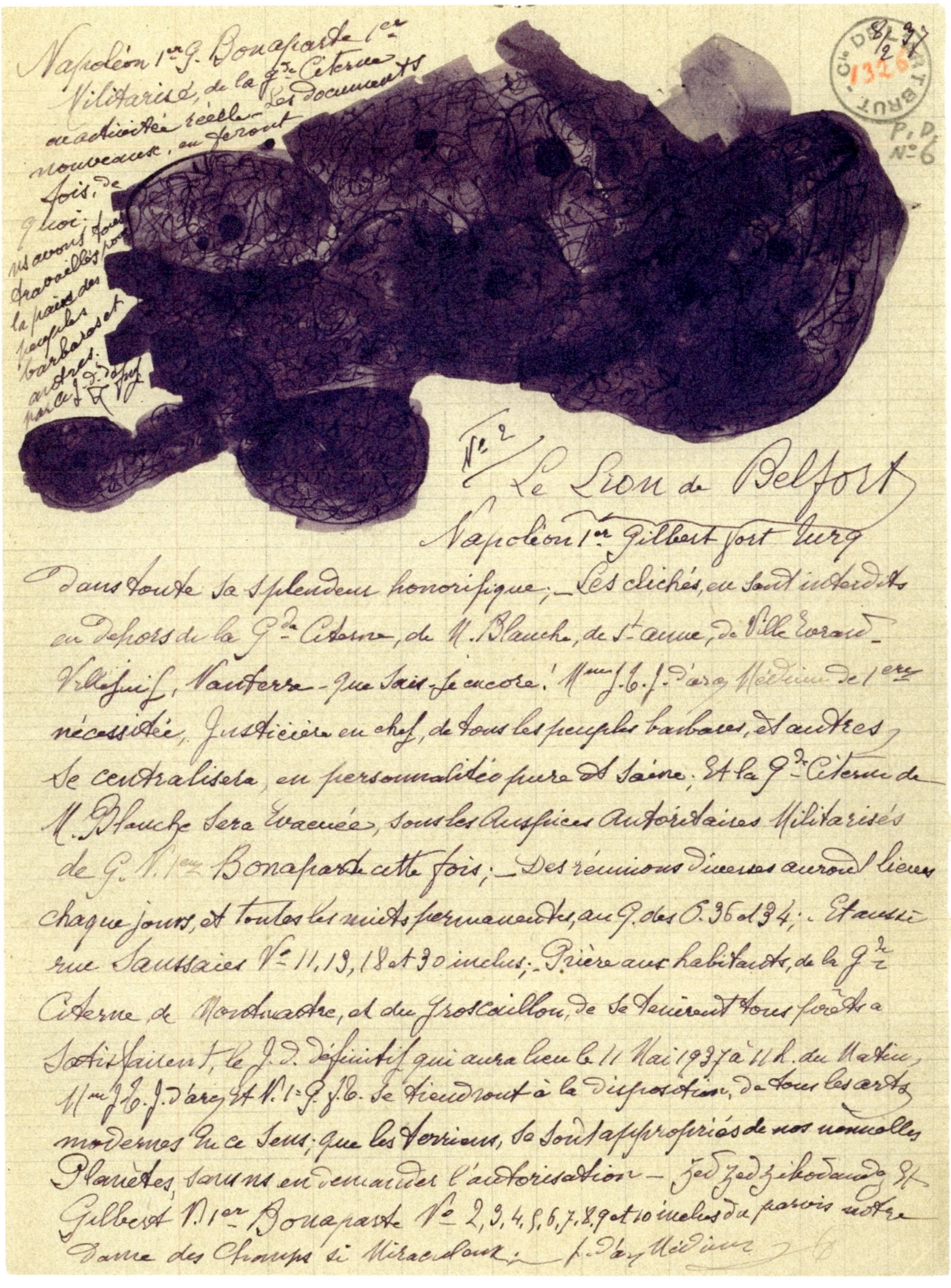

Jeanne Tripier
sans titre untitled, 1937
encre sur papier ink on paper
22 x 17 cm
cab-A633/11

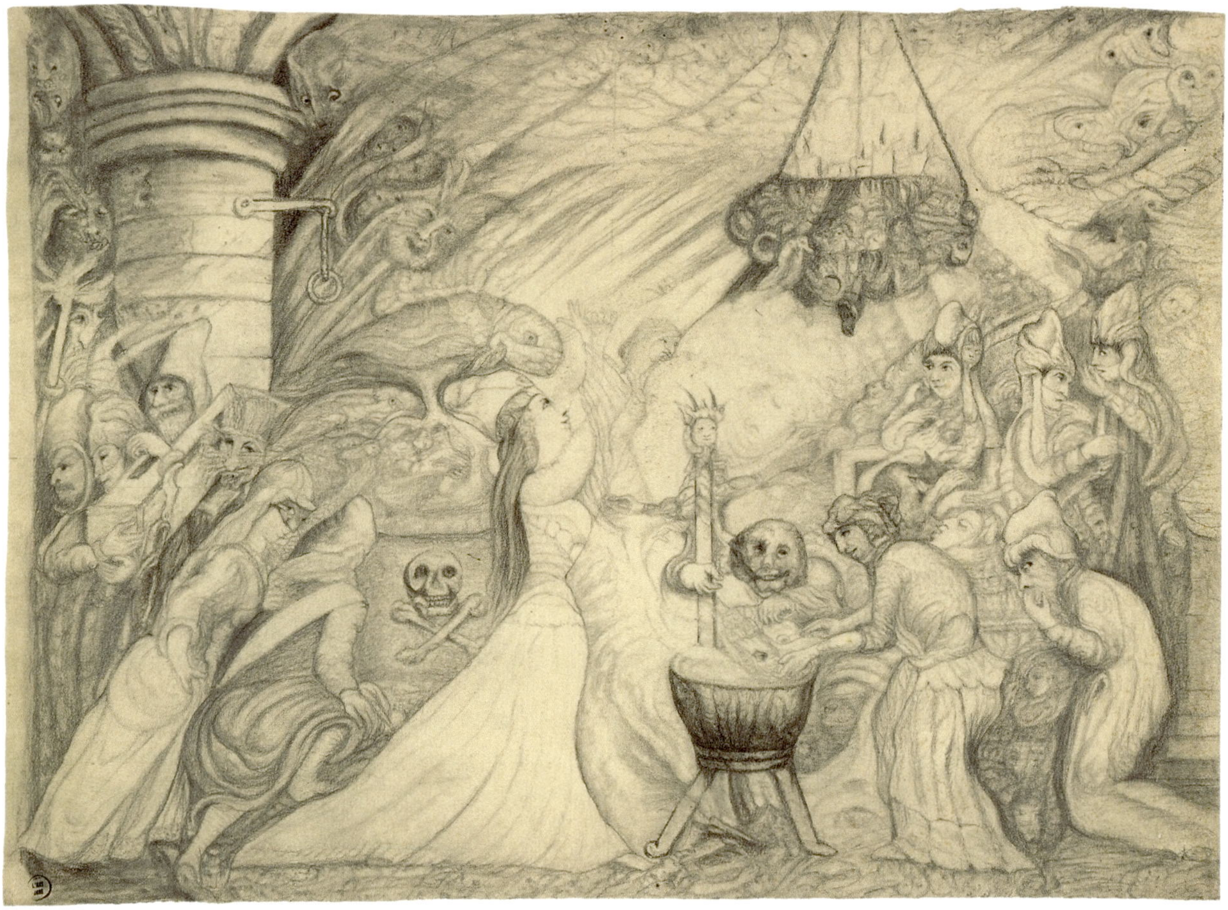

comte de Tromelin
sans titre untitled, entre between 1902 et and 1907
crayon noir sur papier
black pencil on paper
35,5 x 49,5 cm
cab-2292

comte de Tromelin
sans titre untitled, ca. 1903
crayon noir sur papier
black pencil on paper
32,5 x 24 cm
cab-2287

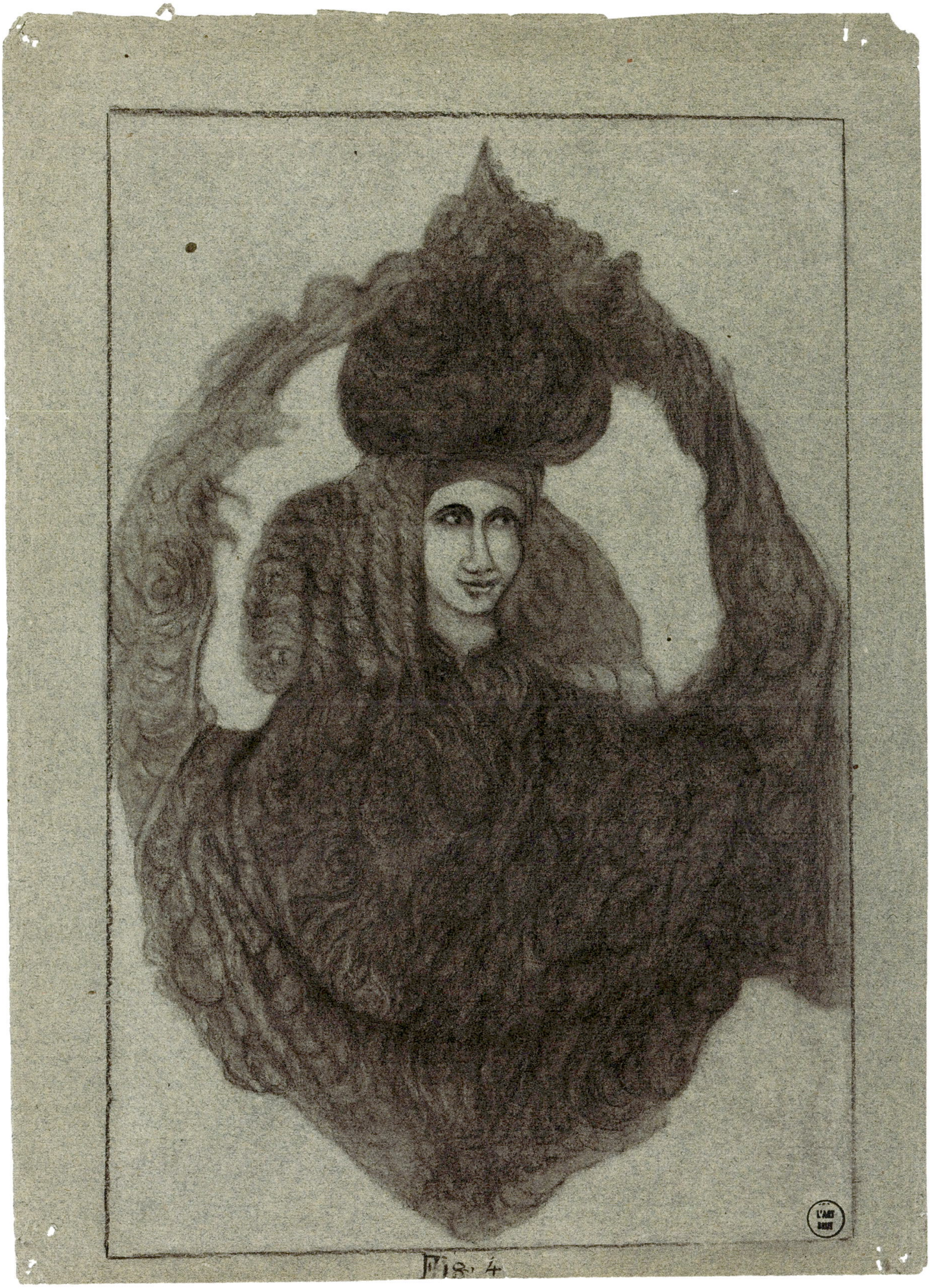
Fig. 4

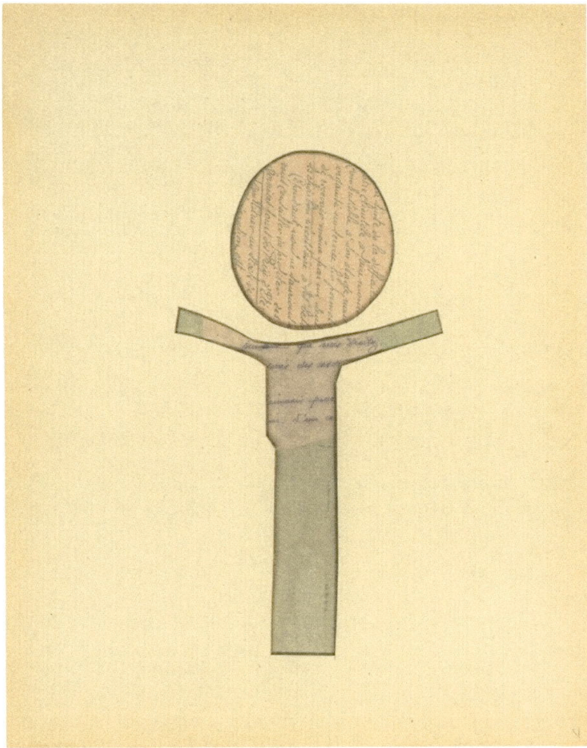

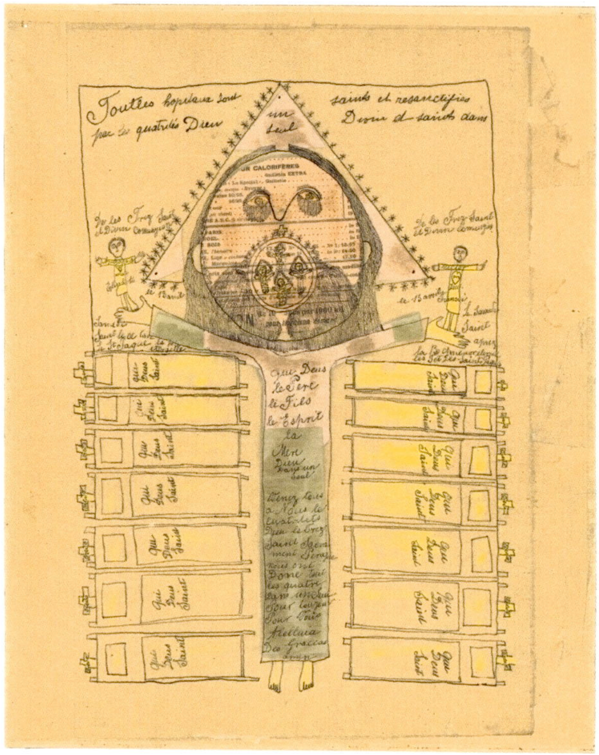

Victor-François
sans titre untitled, entre between
1900 et and 1915
encre de Chine, crayon de couleur
et collage sur papier India ink, coloured
pencil, and collage on paper
50 x 42 cm
cab-2257 (recto-verso)

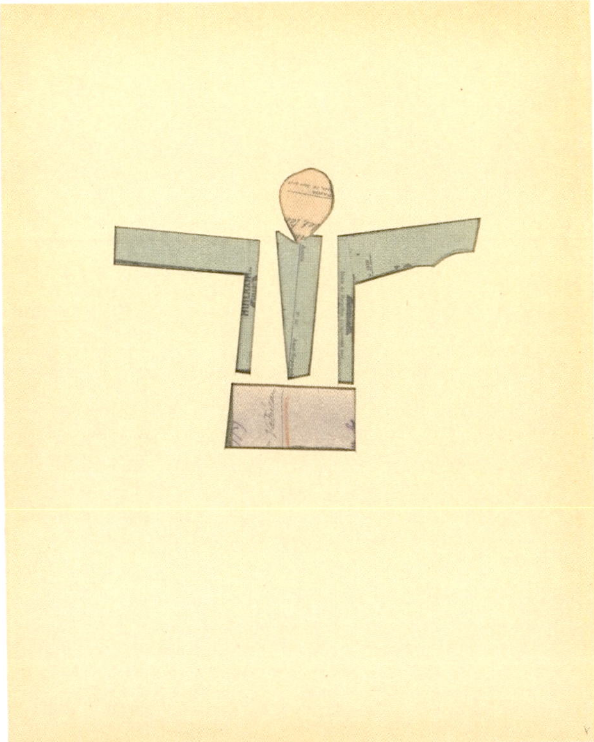

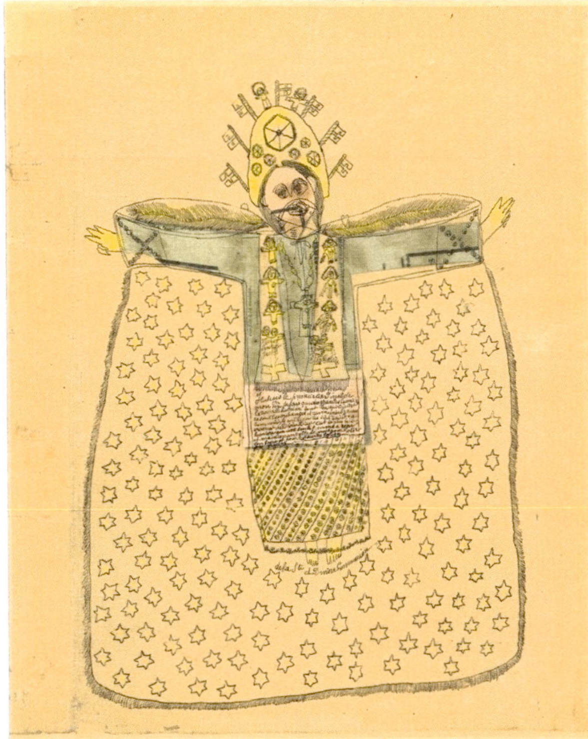

Victor-François
sans titre untitled, entre between
1900 et and 1915
encre de Chine et collage sur papier
India ink and collage on paper
50 x 39 cm
cab-2254 (recto-verso)

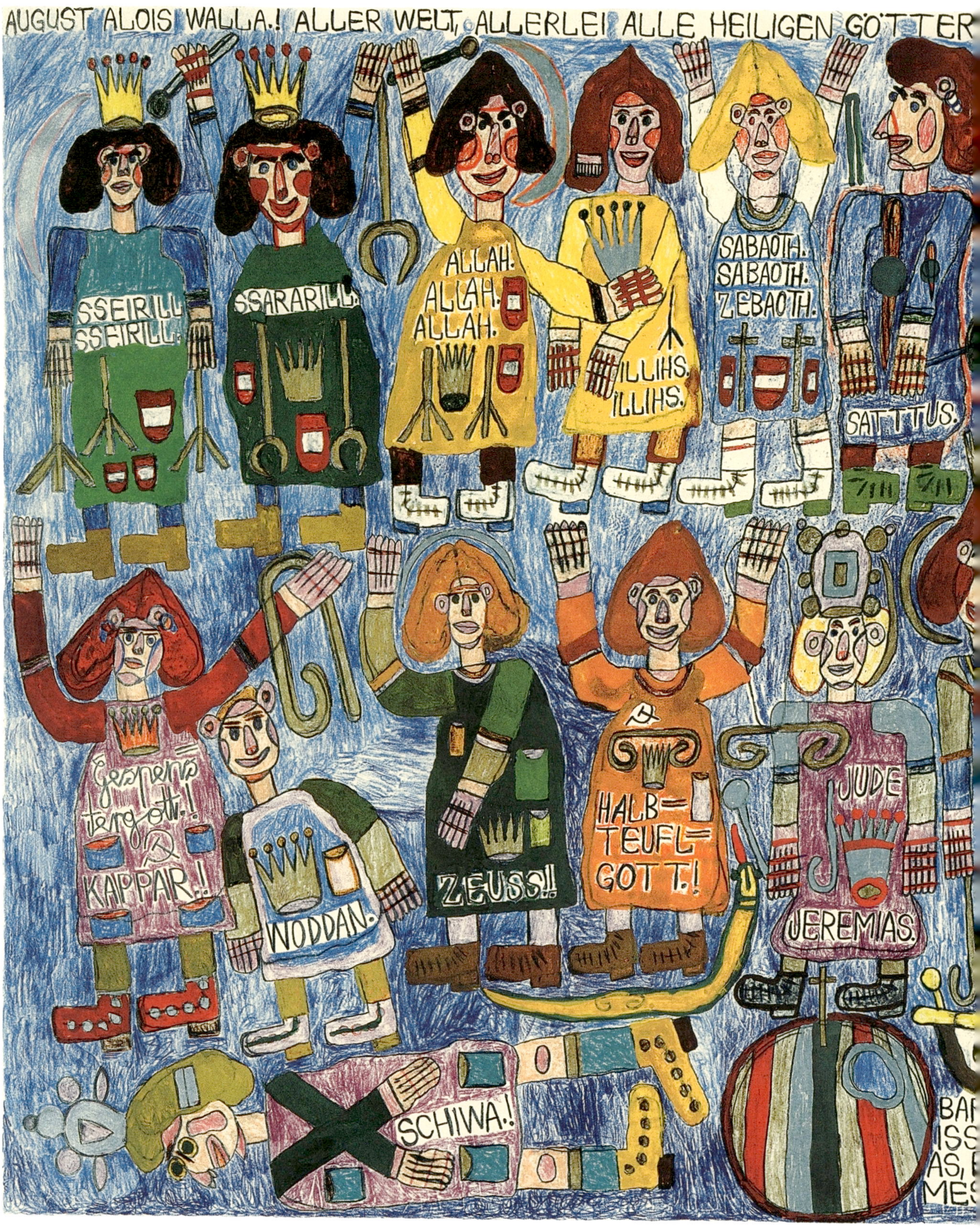
AUGUST ALOIS WALLA.! ALLER WELT, ALLERLEI ALLE HEILIGEN GÖTTER
ALLAH. ALLAH. ALLAH.
ILLIHS. ILLIHS.
SABAOTH. SABAOTH. ZEBAOTH.
SATTTUS.
KAPPAR.!
WODDAN.
ZEUSS.!
HALB= TEUFL= GOTT.!
JUDE
JEREMIAS.
SCHIWA.!

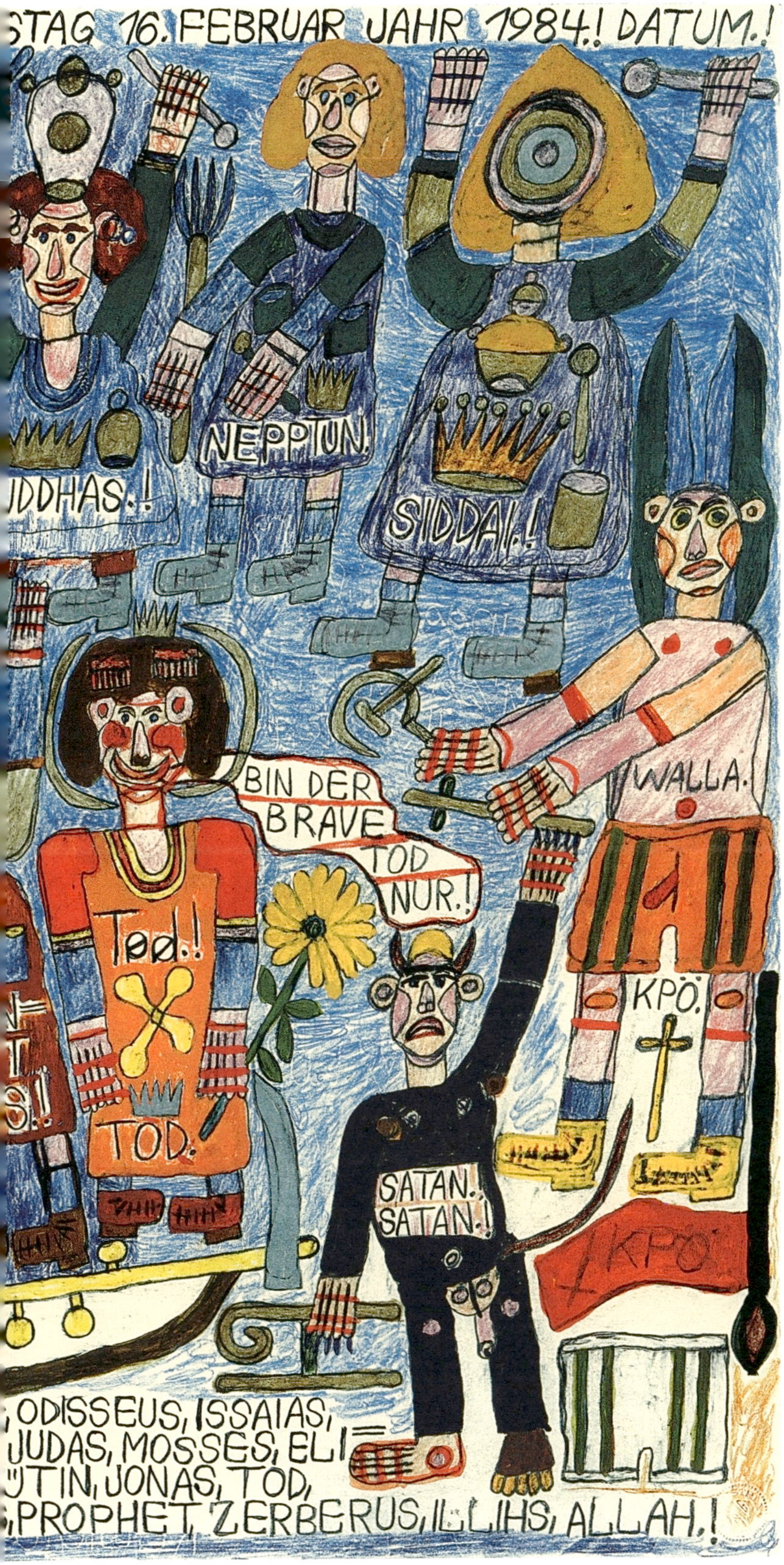

August Walla
Aller Welt, allerlei alle heiligen Götter, 1984
crayon de couleur et gouache sur papier
coloured pencil and gouache on paper
62,5 x 88 cm
cab-7653

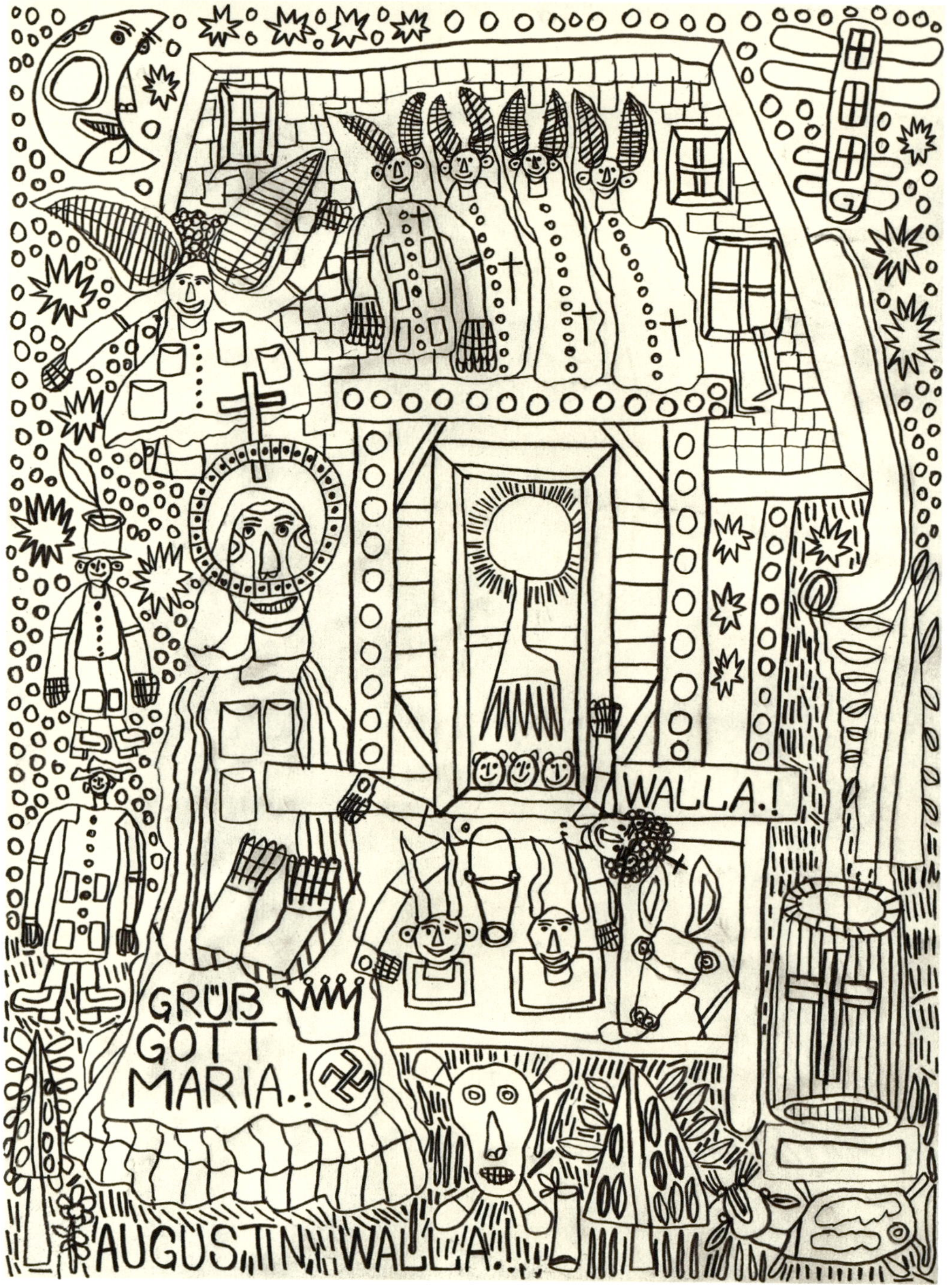

August Walla
Grüss Gott Maria. !, 1970
mine de plomb sur papier
graphite on paper
40 x 30 cm
cab-4835

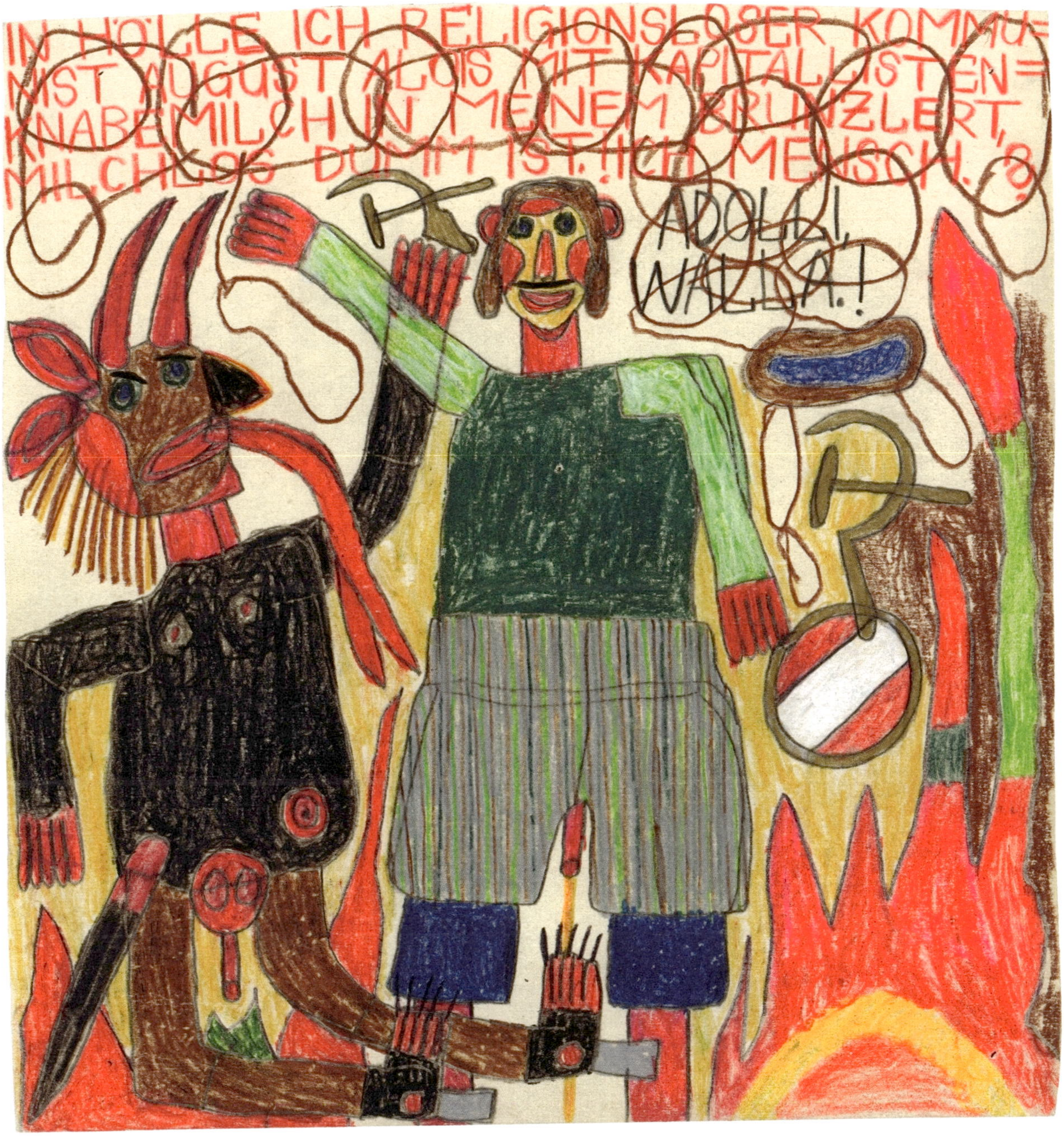

August Walla
In Hölle Ich..., 1982
mine de plomb, crayon de couleur
et craie grasse sur carton graphite,
coloured pencil, and crayon on paper
31,5 x 30,2 cm
cab-5131

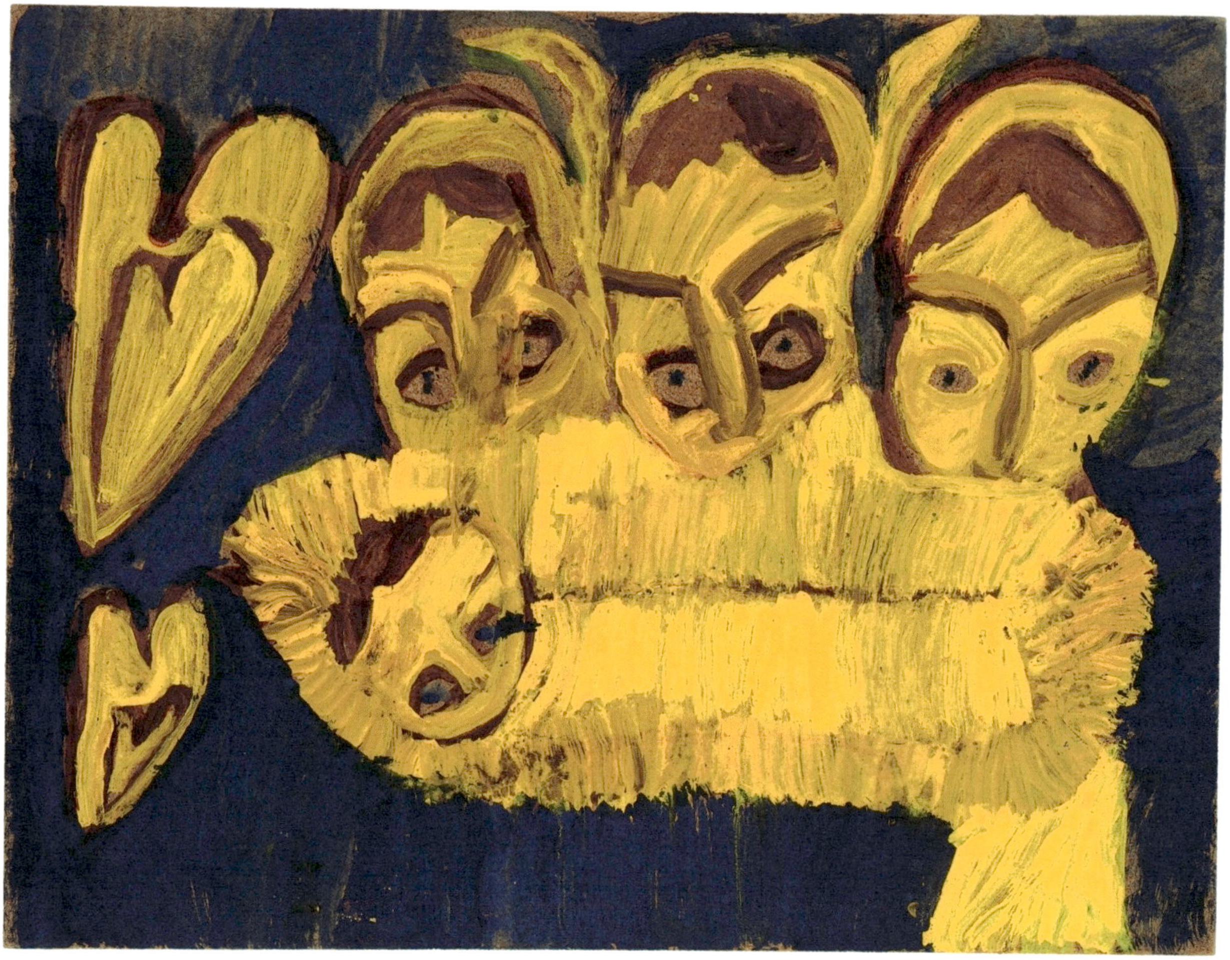

Maria Wnek
sans titre untitled, entre between
1990 et and 1996
gouache sur pavatex gouache on pavatex
20 x 40 cm
cab-10345

Maria Wnek
sans titre untitled, entre between
1990 et and 1996
peinture sur pavatex paint on pavatex
34,8 x 27 cm
cab-10342

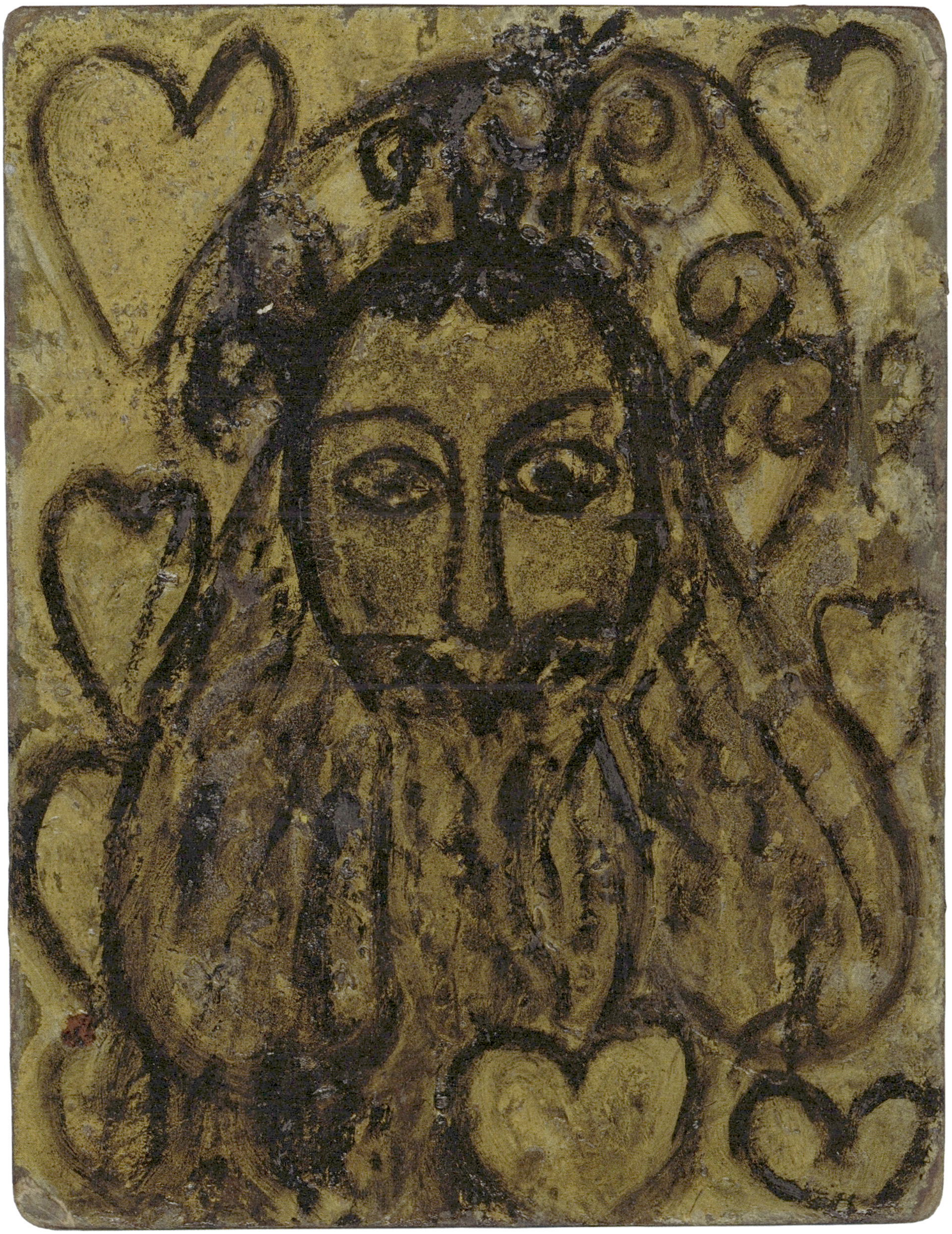

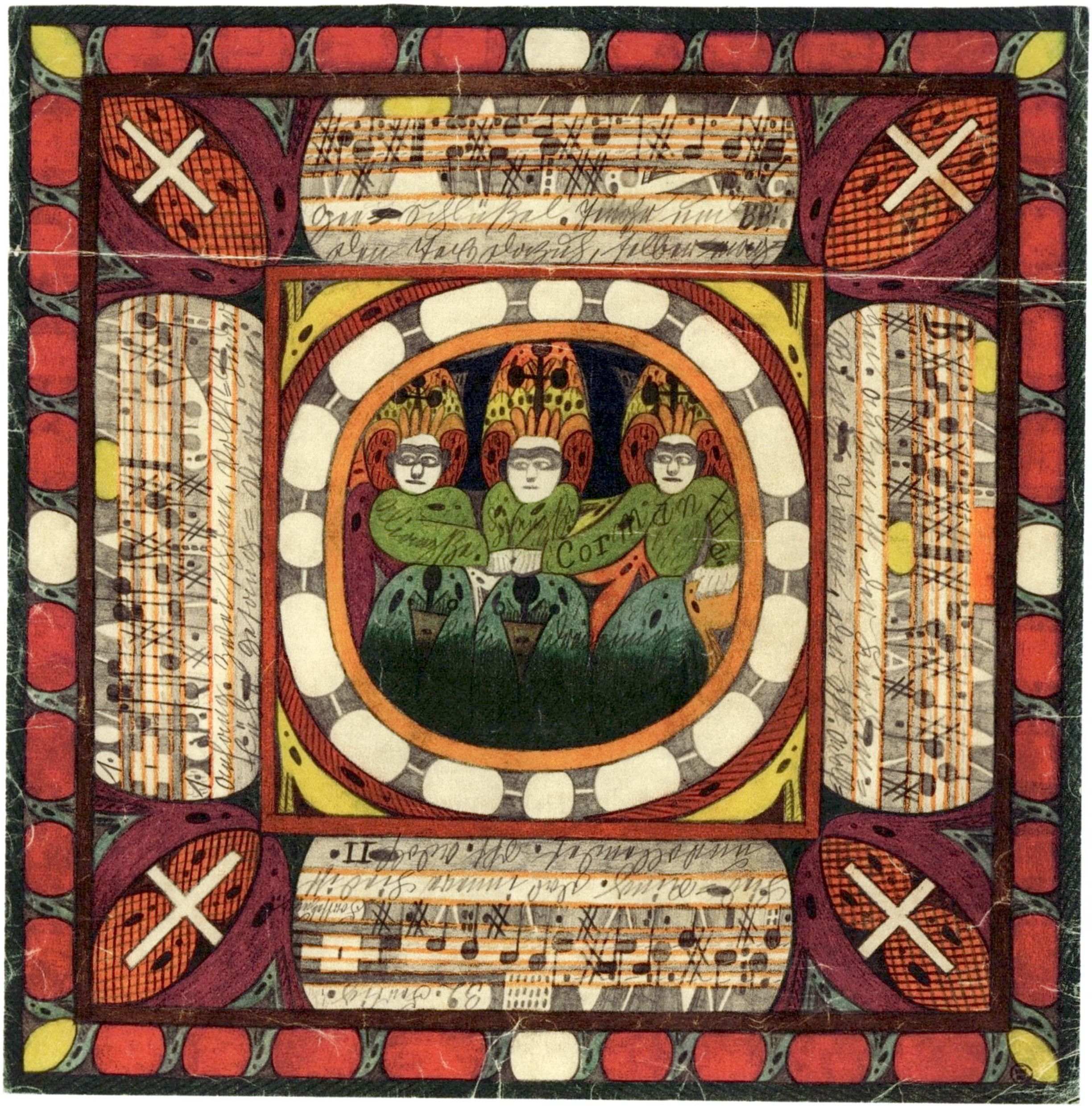

Adolf Wölfli
La sainte trinité dans la ville géante de Chant-Saint-Adolf, 1914
mine de plomb et crayon de couleur sur papier
graphite and coloured pencil on paper
51 x 51 cm
cab-969

Adolf Wölfli
Crucifixion de Jesus-Christ, 1914
mine de plomb et crayon de couleur sur papier graphite and coloured pencil on paper
100 x 72,5 cm
cab-922

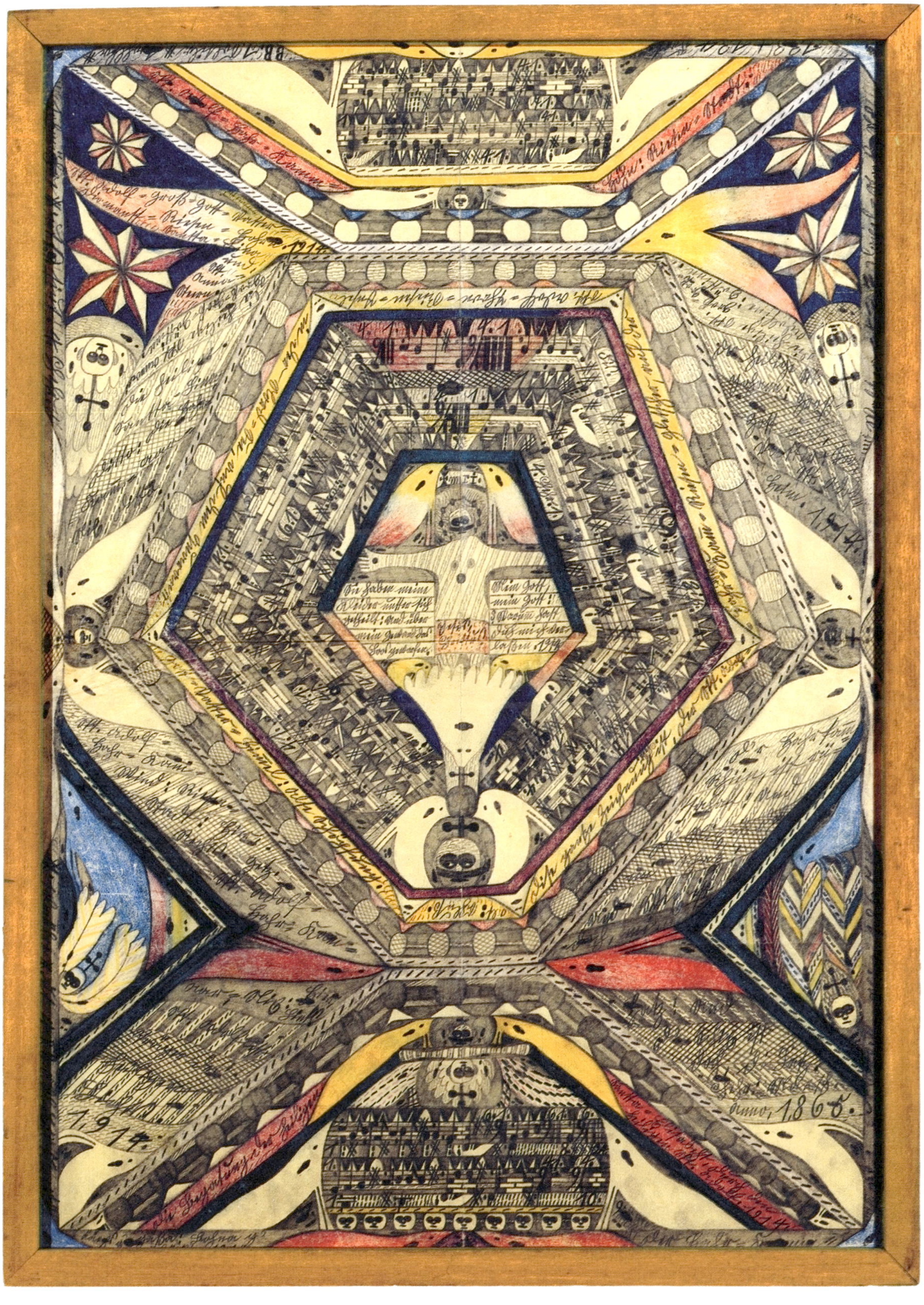

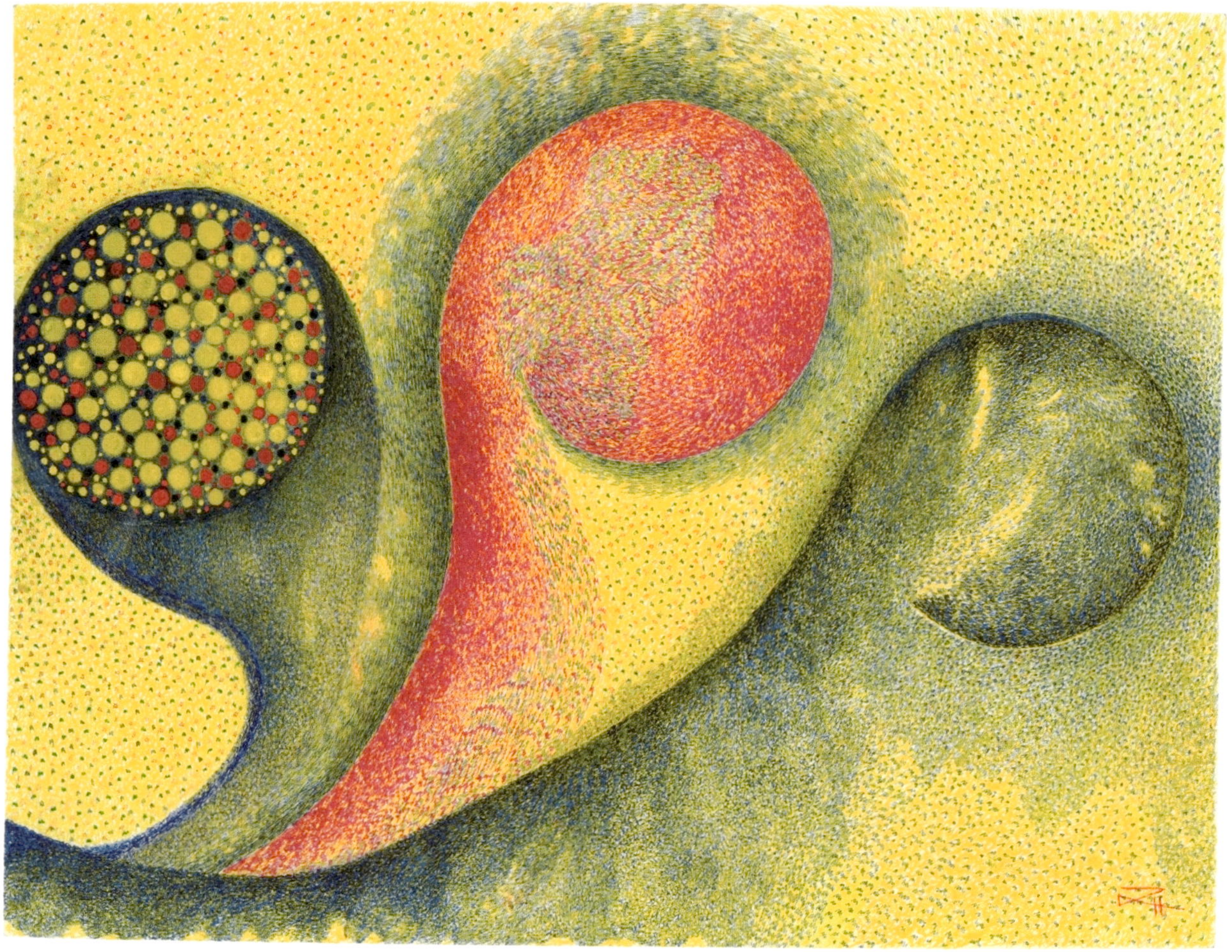

Henriette Zéphir
sans titre untitled, 1985
encre de Chine et aquarelle sur papier
India ink and watercolour on paper
38 x 56,5 cm
cab-16656

Henriette Zéphir
sans titre untitled, 1965
mine de plomb sur papier
graphite on paper
31 x 24 cm
cab-2552

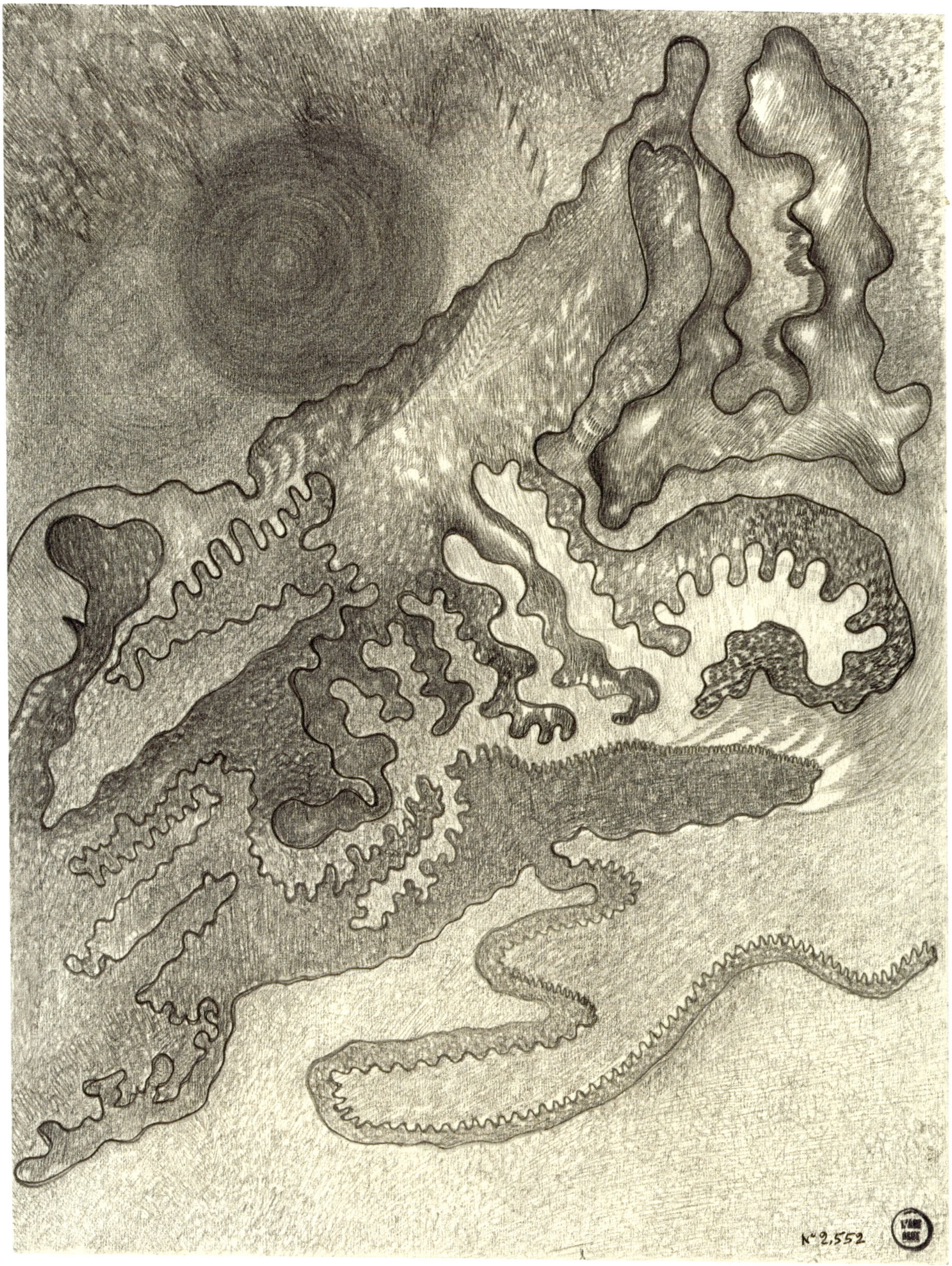
N° 2,552

Annexes

Biographies

Aloïse Corbaz, known simply as **Aloïse** (1886–1964), was born in Lausanne, Switzerland. She was thirteen when her mother died. She worked as a dressmaker but her dream was to become a singer. Following an unhappy love affair, she took up a number of positions as a governess in northern Germany. Employed at the court of William II in Potsdam, she became besotted with the emperor, with whom she had an imaginary love affair. But when war was declared, she was obliged to return to her native Lausanne, where she fell prey to bouts of anxiety and religious fervour that often took a pacifist turn. In the end her family had to have her confined to the asylum in Cery-sur-Lausanne in 1918. She was later moved to another institution, La Rosière, where she lived until her death, and it was not long before she began to draw and write. However, she pursued this activity in secret, using a graphite pencil and ink. When she had no alternative, she even used juice squeezed from petals, crushed leaves, and toothpaste. As a support, she sewed together pieces of wrapping paper with thread to obtain a large surface, or envelopes, bits of cardboard, and the backs of calendars. Aloïse created her own personal cosmogony peopled by princely figures and heroines, which she found in various publications — history books, art books, Bibles, novels, and so on. Recurrent themes in her work are Christmas and Easter festivities, whose rites and decorations are found throughout her oeuvre. She described the way she worked as a 'ricochet', in which, playing the role of the Earth, she was struck by a bright ray representing the disease's incursions, which she immediately diverted into the hereafter, transfigured into an astral body, an emanation of herself. By creating and developing this ghostly universe, Aloïse thus found the equilibrium that enabled her to exist by identifying with any creature, any world, rendering her day-to-day life atemporal and beyond the challenges of her internment and disease.

Noviadi Angkasapura (1979) was born in Jayapura, in the Indonesian part of the island of New Guinea. His parents are from Java and decided to move to this underpopulated area. When he was twenty-two, Noviadi Angkasapura had an encounter with a spirit, who urged him to draw, employing a phrase that included the concepts of 'patience' and 'peace'. For Angkasapura this was nothing short of a moral and spiritual awakening. The act of drawing became at once a prayer, a form of meditation, and a way of conveying messages from this spirit. In this equation, Angkasapura considers himself to be merely a messenger, a mediator between himself and this divine being, and he does not presume to understand or explain the content of his works. Strange, vaguely disquieting beings are scattered throughout his works, where internal and external forces meet: imaginary animals and anthropomorphic creatures with visible organs. Based though they are on various local figurative traditions, Javanese puppets and the Râmâyana, for example, his creations are never directly attributable to these sources and are, indeed, thoroughly original. He works with ballpoint pen, graphite pencil, and coloured pencil on small pieces of paper. Angkasapura now lives in Jakarta and is able to provide for his family by drawing.
Neuve Invention Collection*

Charles Boussion (1925–2021), aka 'Cako', was born in Biarritz, France. His father was a newspaper editor and his mother was a homemaker and busy socialite. After his parents' divorce, Charles was looked after by an uncle and went to live in Montpellier. However, he was only five when his parents separated, and the experience left him deeply scarred. He joined the Resistance during the German occupation and at the same time became heavily involved in the 'Zazou' movement, whose members were enthusiasts of swing and indulged in eccentric behaviour. These unsavoury associations were enough to have him brought in one night by the Vichy police. Just after the war, he married Bernadette, with whom he had a daughter. Following his business studies, he became a salesman for a perfume company and spent almost thirty years crisscrossing mainland France and Corsica. All this travelling gave him plenty of opportunity to visit churches. By the time he was fifty, Boussion had grown tired and was fed up with having to make long trips away from his family. As if this was not enough, he was injured in an accident and had to give up work altogether, causing him to sink into a deep bout of depression. Hoping to find relief, he took up painting, using the equipment his wife gave him. Working mostly at night, Boussion developed his own figurative world based on the traditional icon and Byzantine painting as a whole, from which he borrowed certain iconographic features. He used all kinds of felt-tip pens and markers to create his teeming decorations redolent of Moorish jewellery or medieval illumination, as found for instance around portraits of Tsars, Byzantine Christs, or beautiful Asian women. One of his favourite themes was the Virgin and Child, using his wife or daughter as models. He often photocopied his drawings so he could retouch them later. For Boussion, decoration was not simply an adjunct to or an embellishment of the central theme. He devoted to it a special and highly personal attention that could be compared to prayer.

Little is known about **Marie Bouttier** (1839–1921), known as Madame Bouttier. She was born in Lyon, France, into a family of canut silk workers and was drafted into her father's workshop as a silk weaver. In 1862 she married André Bouttier, a weaver himself, and gave birth to their only child, a daughter, the following year. Marie Bouttier developed a strong interest in the occult and became an active member of a group of spiritualists in Lyon led by Alphonse Bouvier, the editor of a magazine specialising in the subject. At the age of sixty, in a state of trance, she began to make automatic drawings with a pencil. Her works depict strange creatures of indistinct shape in which plant motifs intermingle and the foliage seems to turn into insects, fish, or larvae.

Fleury-Joseph Crépin (1875–1948) was born in Hénin-Liétard, in northern France. In his youth, Crépin sometimes played the clarinet at his local dance hall and even won music prizes in various competitions. After obtaining his school certificate in 1888, he had a number of jobs and worked with his father before opening his own hardware store after the First World War. In 1931, an acquaintance introduced him to spiritualism and he began to patronise the mediums of Douai. He then turned his attention to dowsing, working with his hands and using his watch as a pendulum, which led him to discover his gift as a healer. Refusing to accept any payment, he would welcome the sick into his home and even performed long-distance treatments through the aid of photographs or a lock of hair. In 1938, at the age of sixty-three, Crépin was copying some music when his hand suddenly ceased to obey him and began to draw mysterious architecture and starry skies. Convinced he was being guided by his guardian angels, he then embarked on a full-blown artistic endeavour. His subsequent oil-on-canvas paintings are all carefully numbered and dated. Depicting the temples seen in his dreams, the central feature of these works is their concern with symmetry and the unique technique he developed, which involved dripping thick paint onto the background colour fields and in this way achieving a three-dimensional effect. During this process, the artist felt he could hear music that was inseparable from the painting he was working on. Crépin then became convinced the Second World War would come to an end when he finished his three-hundredth painting, and indeed this work bears the date 7 May 1945.

Antonio Dalla Valle (1939–2020) was born in Roncio, in the province of Trento, in northern Italy. Brought up heavy-handedly by his distant and ageing parents, Dalla Valle found it hard to mix with children of his own age. His school years were largely spent writing and drawing alone and in silence; he showed no interest at all in collective pursuits. Later, he worked as a labourer on building sites before leaving to try his luck as a bricklayer in Germany. He became enormously homesick and felt lost in an alien environment, to the extent that when he returned in 1962, Dalla Valle had to be committed to a psychiatric hospital. It soon became hard for him to get on with the staff and it was only through his writing that he was able to express himself properly. In 1997, Dalla Valle was moved to a hospital near Cremona, where he attended the creative workshop. He started gradually covering pieces of paper or cardboard with writing and mysterious symbols. Once cut out, he would put them into transparent plastic containers or carefully made plexiglass boxes. These works were then tied up with string or adhesive tape, an operation that was designed to decorate and to hide at one and the same time. His sculptures are imbued with mystery and look like magic boxes whose contents are known only to the artist. Once a work was finished, Dalla Valle would take it with him wherever he went as part of a ritual, before abandoning or destroying it as soon as he decided its power or purpose had run its course. He would even use his own body as a medium, wrapping his left foot in a strip of cloth every day and covering his wrists with the numerous watches he collected and wore as symbolic lucky charms.

Fernand Desmoulin (1853–1914) was born in Javerlhac, in the Dordogne, in France, where his parents kept a dry goods and grocery store. His father left the family soon after Fernand's birth, at which point he and his mother moved to Angoulême. He grew up and obtained his baccalaureate high school diploma in this town. In 1870 he moved to Paris to study medicine, but switched to the fine arts two years later. By the 1880s Desmoulin's drawings and watercolours were earning him a considerable reputation and he found himself welcome in the leading literary and artistic circles. His talent as an etcher in particular led him to illustrate several novels, notably those by Alphonse Daudet and Victor Hugo. He also made a name for himself as a portrait artist, and he became the official artist of several celebrities of the period. However, domestically he suffered enormously through the death of his first wife in 1894 and an ill-fated love affair with a married woman a few years later, at which point he plunged into a profound state of depression. After taking part in a 'table-turning' session with friends, he experienced an irrepressible need to perform automatic writing and drawing. Letting his hand wander uncontrolled over a blank sheet of paper, Desmoulin abandoned the canons of academic art altogether and launched himself into the realms of spiritualism, in which he relinquished all control. He would work in the dark and, as his hand swept across the sheet, faces, often upside down, would loom out of the dense network of lines and spirals, as if imprisoned in a silkworm's cocoon. Desmoulin made hundreds of these drawings guided by the hereafter, mainly in pencil or charcoal, until he felt 'abandoned by supernatural forces' in 1902.
Neuve Invention Collection*

Janko Domsic (1915–1983) was born in Malunje, Croatia. He seems to have completed only elementary school, and the circumstances surrounding his arrival in France are not clear. He probably spent some time in jail before finding work as a labourer on a new railway line at Pont-sur-Yonne in 1935. He then moved to Paris, where he lived in a poky apartment on the sixth floor of a run-down block of flats where he was to remain for the rest of his life. This was when Domsic began to develop his artistic inclinations, drawing on pieces of cardboard with coloured pencils, felt-tip pens, and green, blue, and red ballpoints, mainly in the capital's vibrant bars. These drawings depict human figures rendered with geometric shapes, so much so that they are made with the aid of a ruler and compass and are combined with symbols and phrases in French, Croatian, or German. Without taking any account of syntax, this jumble of words throws together scraps of personal life, excerpts from Nazi songs, and scatological preoccupations, but refers particularly to religious and mystical ideas. The words 'Jesus', 'God', or 'Bog', in Croatian, appear several times in his drawings. The moral code of freemasonry is another common theme through symbols such as three dots, various abbreviations, pentagrams, or swastikas. Domsic's figures sometimes feature man as part of the microcosm, Christ, or an angel with outspread wings, but they always convey a sense of mystery. Whatever the nature of the figure, Domsic is sure to identify with it.

Philippe Ducollet-Michaëlef (1962) was born in Paris, France. He grew up in a happy family environment, with very affectionate parents and a sister and brother who were both far older than him. He began to show signs of mental instability during his adolescence and especially when he was an adult. As a child he spent a lot of time lining up his toys and putting them in order, an activity that gradually became almost compulsive. When he was around twenty he often visited museums and began to take an interest in ancient painting and in collecting art books. He read voraciously and widely. After winning a place at the school of decorative arts, he was forced to turn it down following a series of panic attacks that left him in a state of deep depression accompanied by migraines and insomnia. His brother's sudden death in 1989 distressed him tremendously, and he created a huge collage in his memory. This is when he began to fill school exercise books with miscellaneous drawings, until in 2006 he found his favourite subject: the figure of the 'Virgin – the Mother Goddess'. Philippe drew inspiration from an old memory of a Cretan idol depicting the 'Snake Goddess' that he saw in his father's library. He gradually merged this figure with that of the Virgin, giving rise to a curious blend of the religious and the sexual, where the themes of birth and death are set in close juxtaposition. Ducollet-Michaëlef's compositions, in pencil or ink, are extremely repetitive and represent a way of defending himself from his chronic anxiety and agitation. By concentrating on their variations and shared features, he uses all these carefully arranged figures of the Virgin as a bulwark he can rely on to underpin his psychological equilibrium. If he feels some detail has not come out right, he looks through his exercise books for the right 'fragment', which he proceeds to cut out and stick over the old one.
Neuve Invention Collection*

Elijah (1953) was born in Alderton, Jamaica. She was raised in a Christian family and her mother was a priestess in a church. After completing her elementary schooling, she attended the town's high school and later found employment in an office. During the course of a long and serious illness, the nature of which her doctors were unable to establish, she claims God appeared before her and told her to get baptised, which she hurried to do. Guided by God, she then became a healer and priestess and moved into an economically depressed neighbourhood of Kingston, where every Sunday she holds a service in the church next to the house. She is married with seven children and has brought up several more. As the head of her local community, she divides her time between educating the orphans she is raising, looking after the sick, and painting. In her art too she has been inspired by God, who gave her the power to depict things of the spirit. She began by painting the corrugated iron walls of her house. Her pictures of angels, saints, and prophets are supposed to ward off violence and aggression, and thus have a magical protective power in the tense atmosphere of the run-down area. Elijah has since moved on to canvases, where she continues to portray Biblical subjects from both the Old and New Testament. However, other influences typical of the intense religious life of this poor neighbourhood in Jamaica, such as the African animist tradition and Rastafarianism, seem to sneak into her work in unexpected ways. The themes of Elijah's paintings are highlighted by handwritten inscriptions that draw out the narrative aspects of her work.

Minnie Evans (1892–1987) was born in Long Creek, North Carolina, USA. Soon after her birth, Evans moved to Wilmington with her mother, who was only fourteen at the time, to live with her grandmother and great-grandmother. They brought her up together and told her all about her ancestors in Trinidad and Tobago, who had arrived in North Carolina as slaves. She began to have bouts of recurring dreams and mystical visions that often stopped her sleeping. After spending only a short time in school, Minnie started working at a mussel farm to help the family. In 1908 she met her future husband there and they had three children. In 1948 she found work at the 'Airlie Garden' park, where she sold entrance tickets. She enjoyed her work and remained at the park until 1974, when her poor health obliged her to give up work altogether. At the age of forty-three Evans made her first two drawings one Good Friday, in answer to divine instructions, according to her. And she continued thereafter to produce drawings and oil paintings, explaining that this new activity relieved the stress caused by her dreams and visions. For her, art used as a means of meeting religious requirements became the physical embodiment of belief. Her works are brightly coloured, just like her visions, and provide a pictorial universe in which Biblical themes, motifs taken from nature, and wide-eyed exotic creatures all sit cheek-by-jowl according to a principle of symmetry. Using images from her dreams as symbols and metaphors, Evans found her own way of celebrating her understanding of the miracle of existence.

Jill Galliéni (1948) was born in the United States. She started to make cloth dolls when she was still very young, and at around thirty she began a long series of graphic works: prayers to St Rita, the patron saint of lost causes. These prayers represent an artistic development that has lasted more than twenty years and are the outward sign of Jill Galliéni's permanent questioning of her spirituality, as well as being a way out of the problems and issues that bedevil her life. The continuous line of her felt-tip pen drawings make her incantations visible. She traces endless series of interlacing letters, like crochet, from which there sometimes emerge recognisably figurative motifs and in other cases abstract ones. Galliéni employs this alternative to writing as a form of protection, as well as a way of keeping the content of her interactions with St Rita secret. She turns to the saint for help on behalf of those near and dear to her, or to ask for her intercession to end some armed conflict in the world, or just simply for herself. As her hand travels across the sheet of paper it performs an act of prayer. Galliéni continued this procedure tirelessly until one day she decided her prayers should no longer be turned into art objects and she has now ceased drawing altogether.
Neuve Invention Collection*

Madge Gill (1882–1961) was born in a suburb of London, in the UK. She was brought up by her mother and aunt, before being sent to an orphanage and eventually travelling to Canada, where she worked on a farm for three years. She returned to London at the age of nineteen and found employment as a healthcare worker in a hospital. In around 1901, her aunt introduced her to spiritualism and astrology. Four years later she married, and during the course of the marriage she had three sons as well as a stillborn baby girl. Her second son died in the Spanish Flu epidemic of 1918. Madge Gill then fell extremely ill herself and was left blind in her left eye. During her illness, she was seized by sudden artistic inspiration and began to draw, embroider, and write automatically, creating an extremely rich and varied body of work. Working at night by the light of an oil lamp, she said she was guided by a spirit she named 'Myrninerest', which looked at closely reveals its role: my inner rest. She made a large number of works with the recurring motif of a female figure with big round eyes and a hat, surrounded by geometric shapes, swirls, and coils. Some pictures are purely abstract and evoke a more tranquil world, revealing extraordinary similarities with the work of other spirit artists. She drew her creations in India ink or ballpoint pen on a cardboard or calico support, which could sometimes be dozens of metres long. She would occasionally take a break from her large-scale works to fill numberless postcards with little drawings. On the back, she would often add inscriptions complementing her images, then ritualistically sign them 'Myrninerest'. These scribbles are based on Scripture and explore many aspects of spirituality, although they also delve into her knowledge of the occult sciences. In 1936, Gill started organising séances and building horoscopes based on astrological calculations whose prophecies gained her a certain notoriety.

Jules Godi (1902–1986) was born in Italy and worked on building sites until his retirement, when he went to live near Draguignan, in the Var region of France. He was also a dowser: he would be asked to detect underground water and find missing persons or lost objects. In 1959, his family was killed when a dam burst, and this disaster was probably the trigger that released his creative urges. Once he had retired, Godi painted under the guidance of his pendulum, as spirit artists do. Following his instrument's directions, he would cover the paper with a series of dots, sometimes corresponding to the configuration of the stars. He would communicate with 'occult forces', linking up the dots, and then filling in the areas thus formed with different colour felt-tip pens. Not surprisingly, the pendulum's metronomic movement gave rise to the feature that characterises all Godi's work: a sense of diagonal movement, from bottom right to top left. Falling between abstract and figurative art, these pictures depict patterns of foliage, heaps of houses, roofs, or jagged blocks of stone, reminiscent of the place where his family was tragically killed. His vivid landscapes, often dotted with wayside crosses or cemeteries, suggest both the Stations of the Cross and necropolises. In all these works, the sheet is entirely covered with geometrical areas of colour.
Neuve Invention Collection*

Guo Fengyi (1942–2010) was born in Xi'an, in the Chinese province of Shanxi. She obtained her high school diploma in 1962 and found work as a technician in a rubber and solvent factory. However, severe bouts of arthritis forced her to give up her career at the age of thirty-nine, by then a mother of four. In the hope of alleviating her symptoms and strengthening her immune system, she turned to Qi Gong, a form of traditional Chinese medicine. Among other things, this discipline involves serious and profound introspection, and, in 1989, while Guo Fengyi was concentrating in this way, she found she started experiencing visions, which she rushed to articulate by drawing them, hoping in this way to re-establish the proper balance between mind and body. The phenomenon continued, and as a result she produced large numbers of drawings, first on the backs of pages from calendars, then later on rice paper, some up to five metres in height. When working on these very large works, the paper would be unrolled as in a scroll and she would paint with no initial design in mind, simply making it up as she went along and therefore never seeing the finished work until the very end. In order to achieve the correct state of mind, she would dress entirely in red, the Chinese colour of serenity and happiness, meditate, and let herself be inspired by Buddha, she claimed. She worked mainly with India ink and brushes. Her subjects lurk in a no-man's world where human figures and vegetation intermingle, formed by a multitude of delicate lines like threads in a tapestry. The figures often enclose one another, like a mise en abyme of a human being and his multiple identities. Dominated by the theme of man's link with nature, Guo Fengyi's visions represent a plunge into traditional Chinese cosmology and popular culture, crossed with symbols associated with medicine, astrology, historical myths, and deities. Having discovered her gift as a medium, the artist also used her powers to heal the sick and predict the future.

Frantz Jacques, aka **Guyodo** (1973), was born in a small house off the Grand Rue, the main commercial street of Port-au-Prince, Haiti, and still lives and works in the same rooms where he grew up with his grandmother, parents, six sisters, and four brothers. Like many other children, after attending several years of primary school he began to make wooden tourist souvenirs. He also enjoyed football, playing professionally until he was twenty-five. Later, he helped to found the Atis Rezistans art group, whose members make art from discarded materials found in an industrial area. Some of these works are monumental social and political statements denouncing the extreme poverty in which many families are forced to live. Guyodo gradually began to ease away from the group, preferring to work alone as a self-taught artist, drawing with a ballpoint pen on found materials like the backs of calendars and cornflake boxes, as well as making sculptures from pieces of old car chassis, electric wires, and even human bones. Among his favourite themes are figures representing various voodoo gods and spirits. Guyodo has opened a workshop in his neighbourhood, where he tries to get children and teenagers interested in art. An accidental fire that broke out in 2020 destroyed more than two thousand of his works.
Neuve Invention Collection*

Werner Hertig (1908–1985) was born in Winterthur, Switzerland. After an apprenticeship as a machine operator, he worked for many years in the field of research and development for various companies. In 1959, he moved to Lausanne, where he took over a medical syringe factory. Finding pieces of Roman tiles on his land in Crissier, he started to dig and discovered the foundations of an ancient farmhouse. After that he began using a pendulum to look for hidden objects or sources of water, finding several more Roman remains in the process. Impressed by the results, Hertig took to dowsing in a serious way from 1976, combining it with the study of cosmic rays and those from the earth's core. In order to do this, he placed a sheet of tracing paper over a map of the area or a ground plan that had a pre-established grid system. He then let himself be guided by the movements of the divining rod in his right hand as it vibrated under the effect of the terrestrial rays. He recorded these oscillations by turning them into lines traced on the transparent paper, showing lines of power, areas of vibration, or watercourses. While the divining system served to collect information, Hertig's efforts were aimed at identifying the epicentre of the disturbance and advise those who were affected by it to use a particular room for a different purpose, for example. In his final years, Hertig dedicated his time to trying to discover if and by what means it was possible to block rays that cause disease. The idea was to develop an instrument that would eliminate harmful rays. As part of this scheme, he started producing little wooden rings that he would place at specific points or use as pendants to protect the body and living area from the effects of harmful energy.
Neuve Invention Collection*

Augustin Lesage (1876–1954) was born in Saint-Pierre-les-Auchel, in the Pas-de-Calais region of France. His was a mining family, and sure enough he was down the mine himself at the age of fourteen. In 1911 he heard a voice at the bottom of a tunnel telling him he would be a painter one day. He gave these voices no heed at first, not wanting to be taken for a madman, but a few months later he attended spiritualist sittings where he heard several messages that seemed to confirm the earlier announcement. From then on he concentrated on making drawings 'dictated' by the dead, especially his younger sister, who had died at the age of three. Soon after, his spirits prompted Lesage to drop drawing and take up oil painting instead. His first canvas showed he was not shy: measuring nine square metres, it took him from 1912 to 1913 to complete. He took a break from painting the following year but resumed again in 1916, finally leaving his job as a miner seven years later in order to devote himself exclusively to art until his death. He became ever more involved in the spiritualist milieu, where he met other artists and painted in public at a sitting held at the Metapsychical Institute of Paris. Lesage claimed he never knew what he would paint before beginning and had no sense of an overall composition. Each colour was added where it was necessary according to his voices' instructions. The actual process of painting unerringly followed the same routine, laying lines of various kinds from the top down, in which he arranged words and figures, as if in a spiritual progress. The titles of the canvases, the inscriptions, and the figures portrayed (Greek, Egyptian, Christian, Buddhist deities) all confirm that, directly or indirectly, these religions are the ultimate source of Lesage's inspiration.

Raphaël Lonné (1910–1989) was born in the Landes area, in southwestern France, to a family of sharecroppers. He was a sensitive child and suffered from poor health, especially asthma. He left school at the age of twelve to work the land to help his family. Later on, he was successively a tram conductor, a concierge, a handyman at a hospital, and then, after the Second World War, a postman. At the same time he took an interest in music and poetry, which made him the butt of his colleagues' jokes. His reading introduced him to the theories of Allan Kardec, especially his thoughts on reincarnation, which captivated him. Then, in 1950, during an improvised spiritualist meeting at a friend's house, he made his first drawings. Surprised by the results, he came to believe he was gifted with supernatural powers and was a natural medium. He felt his hand was guided by spirits and that he wasn't the author of his own works. From then on, he devoted all his free time to this new activity, which he carried out in his kitchen and required absolute silence. Starting always from the top left-hand corner of the sheet, Lonné's first works depict human figures, landscapes, birds, or easily recognisable animals. Using a rigorous, microscopic, meticulously detailed technique, his spontaneous creations are covered in curves and delicate arabesques, whose fine lines gradually evolved towards abstraction. The difference between two works is sometimes tiny, but it is nonetheless there and is no less important for being hard to see. Lonné worked in a trance using pencil, ballpoint pens, oil paints or water, India ink, and felt-tip pens, and he always painstakingly dated each work.

Simone Marye (1890–1961) was born in Paris into a well-off, sophisticated family of doctors. She spent part of her childhood in South America, until her father's death forced the family to return to France. Marye was already working at the age of thirteen: firstly by finding a way to get hired by a fashion house, then teaching French in a school in England, and finally running dance classes. At the outbreak of the First World War, she joined the Red Cross and cooked for soldiers in transit, refugees, and the poor. A few years later she entered the antiques business, before becoming creative herself as a sculptress. Academic in nature, her bronze works depict a variety of animals and were displayed in numerous exhibitions. In the doldrums by 1933, she moved to Cairo in an attempt to relaunch her career. Sensing the approach of war, she returned to France to help in the war effort. Thereafter, Marye declined into a condition of loneliness and destitution. At the end of a period of pitiful vagrancy she was finally admitted to a psychiatric hospital at the age of sixty-seven. This was where she resumed her artistic activity, this time making small, naïve drawings in which animals and human figures jostle for pre-eminence in forms that become increasingly symbolic. Converting to Buddhism and praying with fervour, Simone took to expressing her religious imagination with enthusiasm. Her drawings began to be filled with impressively haloed saints, with arms outstretched or hands held together, surrounded by lush vegetation and mystical creatures. The words 'Il ou elle prie Dieu' (He or she prays to God), which are added to most of her compositions, reinforce the considerable importance of prayer in Marye's world.

Joseph Moindre (1888–1965) was born in a small village in the Seine-Maritime region of France. For six years he worked as a business real estate broker in Paris, at which point he sold his practice and continued working as an agent. He was attracted by religion and liked visiting churches in Paris during his walks. At the same time, he was critical of the practices and dogmas of the Catholic Church and decided on a civil ceremony for his funeral and his wife's. A friend later introduced him to spiritualism and he developed a passion for the myths of ancient Egypt, a civilisation whose esoteric mystery held a great fascination in occult circles. He read a great number of books and reviews on the subject and began to fancy he was a real Egyptologist. In 1939 he began to keep a journal in which he recorded all his most intimate thoughts, as well as all the exchanges he had with the hereafter, including one with Moses, in which Moindre asks for help in his 'mission'. In addition to his writing, in 1940 he also started painting small pictures in gouache on scrap paper. On the backs he painted scenes from the Bible, pyramids, and Egyptian temples adorned by anthropomorphic figures, while on the fronts, as if to disguise his works' true meaning, he depicted more down-to-earth scenes, such as views of Paris or windmills. Using bright colours, Moindre mixes Egyptian, Christian, Hebrew, and pre-Hellenistic styles and symbols. Although it is impossible to identify all the figures with certainty, or the exact nature of the ornaments that embellish them, it can nevertheless be said that the heads of pharaohs, the sphinx, the figure of Moses, with his black beard, and Christ, with a lighter beard, constitute the artist's favourite themes.

Edmund Monsiel (1897–1962) was born in Poland. He went to primary school and several years later ran a small shop in Wożuczyn, a small town in the province of Lublin. When the Germans arrived during the Second World War, they commandeered the shop in 1942. Witnessing an execution in the street was a traumatic experience for him and led him to close himself off from the world. He took to thinking it would soon be his turn to be arrested, so he hid in his brother's loft. By this time he was suffering from autism and auditory and visual hallucinations of a messianic and more generally religious nature. He felt safe in the loft and continued to live there, even though after the war he found work in a sugar processing plant, spending all his free time totally alone and absorbed by the art he had started producing in the 1920s. Monsiel executed some five hundred drawings in pencil, which were discovered in the loft after his death. They almost exclusively represent Christ-like faces, drawn by means of a line which, as it develops, engenders other faces both inside and outside the original figure, and so on ad infinitum. His work shares many features with traditional icons, and indeed it appears Monsiel discovered Byzantine art as a teenager when he used to help his father restore orthodox churches. Pieces of writing — mainly professions of faith, exhortations to piety, or moralising maxims modified to suit him — also appear on the front or back of some of his compositions. Over the years, Monsiel thus seems to have created a kind of parallel world, with new values based on the injunctions of religion, in which he played the central role of Prophet or God's Messenger.

Marc Moret (1943–2021) was born on a farm in Vuadens, in the Swiss canton of Fribourg. Since his parents and grandparents were country folk, he was raised as one too and so he remained, never leaving the family environment. He was a vegetarian and never killed an animal. He looked after his heifers with the greatest tenderness and lived surrounded by his cats. After passing through a phase during which he wrote a lot, he turned to painting, producing brightly coloured abstract pictures, as well as distorted faces and bodies. He then devoted himself essentially to producing three-dimensional collages made of all sorts of materials, without worrying about making something that was beautiful or even merely attractive. Using homemade glue, he assembled various objects found among his mother's things — pieces of broken glass, bits of cloth, buttons — as well as calcified animal bones, tubular tyres, and the hair of the elderly, which he got from the village hairdresser. All these articles were piled up on a wooden support, the accumulations eventually resulting in towering architectural structures that he installed in a room on the first floor of the farm, where he lived alone after the death of his parents. Moret was extremely attached to his creations and would make a daily visit to the first floor, where he would gather himself and contemplate them in memory of his lost ones. His sculptures were nothing short of contemporary reliquaries that were able to establish a connection between the artist, the deceased, and death itself. As with shamans or certain voodoo beliefs, their creator attributed to these works protective, purifying, and even healing powers that accompanied him during his daily rituals.

Michel Nedjar (1947) was born in Soisy-sous-Montmorency, in the Val-d'Oise region of France. His father was a Sephardic Jew from Algeria and his mother an Ashkenazi from Poland. They settled in Paris and both lost several members of their family to Nazi concentration camps. His father was a master tailor and ran a business in the Paris suburbs. At the age of fourteen Nedjar began his own apprenticeship at a tailor's. He had long been fascinated by fabrics in general and made clothes for his sisters' dolls and enjoyed joining his grandmother at her stand at the flea market, where she sold second-hand clothes. He developed a passion for these old garments and their multicultural aura that seemed to release an intoxicating cocktail of sensations involving all his senses. In 1968 he contracted tuberculosis and spent some time in a sanatorium. This experience brought home to him the fact of his own death, and the realisation of his mortality affected him profoundly. The fashion business suddenly seemed a meretricious and futile way of employing his life. He rejected the idea he had formed of his true vocation and began a period of wandering the world, during which he discovered the powerful expressiveness of cultures that seemed better equipped to come to terms with death and more frank in their symbolic representation of it. He was struck by the traditional magic rites and spell-casting dolls he encountered in Mexico. Returning to Paris in 1975, he started making his first fetish dolls out of pieces of cloth and old rags that he would soak in dye baths and then cover with feathers, pieces of string, soil, and animal blood. The effect was a sort of baptism or rite of passage designed to imbue an inert bundle of materials with life. His dolls look like burned corpses, recalling the tragic fate of so many members of his family who ended their lives in concentration camps. Nedjar sometimes describes his work as 'a ritual of being' and very close to those performed by shamans. In 1980 he also began to paint and draw on cast-off supports, which he deliberately prefers to be heavily used and dirty.

Atta Oko Addo, aka **Ataa Oko** (c. 1919–2007) was born in La, Ghana. He was the sixth child in a family that belonged to the Ga ethnic group from the coastal area near Greater Accra, which has a distinct language, religion, and culture. He never went to school, starting work as a fisherman at the age of thirteen before being hired to work on the local cocoa plantations. He then began a three-year apprenticeship in carpentry in 1936, while doing odd jobs in a small cinema, where he lost three fingers cleaning a generator. Between 1945 and 1948 he crafted his first figurative coffins in the tradition typical of his ethnic group. According to the Ga, the deceased preserves his trade or craft and status in the hereafter and funerals have to take this into account, out of proper respect for the ancestors. A few years later Oko was able to build his own little house in La and open his own coffin workshop. In his later years he rarely produced coffins, which required hard physical labour and considerable energy, except for the occasional commission. In 2002, a Swiss ethnologist who was carrying out research in the area asked him to draw from memory the figurative coffins he had built as a carpenter. This is how he came in his eighties to paint what he had formerly fabricated. He put up a little table in front of his house and set to with a will. He did indeed paint his coffins from memory at first, but he actually started to drift away from literal recollection and began to depict other motifs, such as fruit, trees, animals, and fantastical figures. Then he started adding spirits with whom he claimed to be in constant, intimate contact. He pictures them as hybrid, imaginary figures in combat or performing traditional ceremonies.

Michael Pankoks (1894–1983) was born in Nica, Latvia, where his family ran a farm on the Baltic coast. He attended primary school, then continued to study at night school, later taking up a carpentry apprenticeship, although he always kept up his interest in medicine and philosophy. He was called up in the First World War and served as a medical orderly in various hospitals. In the following years, Pankoks dedicated his free time with great enthusiasm to wood and stone sculpture. He was captured during the Second World War and spent time in various concentration camps, particularly Danzig and Dachau. In 1951 he sought refuge first in Austria, then in Switzerland, where he was admitted to the Coire psychiatric clinic, in the canton of Grisons. Arriving with two suitcases filled with little sculptures, he claimed to be an artist and professor of medicine and astronomy. He maintained that he had visions at night during which angels gave him missions to perform and encouraged him to lead a virtuous life. In 1960, at the age of sixty-six, he revived his interest in art and began carving hundreds of little statues out of pieces of wood found among the institute's rubbish. Pankoks attributed a special tutelary power to his works. Wherever he went, he would arrange them around him as if to recreate an imaginary world, or sometimes conceal them in various hiding places as part of a sort of ritual. His effigies, loaded with scientific, religious, or cosmogonic significance, stand like steles or totems offering a hieratic and magical challenge. Destined by war and poverty to a hard life, their author thus invented his own personal mythology using the resources at his disposal.

Laure Pigeon (1882–1965) was born in Paris, France. Her mother, a professional laundress, died when Laure was five, leaving the little girl in the hands of her paternal grandmother, who lived in Brittany. The girl received a strict education. At the age of twenty-nine, against the wishes of her family, she married a dental surgeon and amateur dowser. After twenty-two years of marriage, she discovered her husband was being unfaithful and they separated. She went to live in a boarding house, but found it very hard to recover from what was an extremely traumatic experience for her. There she met a woman who introduced her to spiritualism and she learned to use the astonishing Ouija board to summon up spirits from the hereafter, her efforts producing initial murmurs that broke the silence and loneliness of an environment full of yearnings and beliefs. She claimed to be guided by celestial beings, including her mother Alida, who had, it seems, been a painter in previous lives. Starting in 1935, Laure Pigeon made her first drawings in her small apartment in the Paris region. She hid these from sight but kept them to hand, attributing powers to them that helped her establish contact with the hereafter. These drawings, in blue or black ink, depict abstract figures within a complex web of fine threads. Some can be described as fine graphic needlework from which emerges a face or a figure in profile. The drawings also contain messages and prophecies, but these were noted down under the effect of a trance and the handwriting is uncertain, hesitant, even illegible. Nevertheless, certain first names recur; for example, 'Peter', the Apostle, to whom she was supposed to have been married in one of her previous lives. Her works were discovered in her home after her death.

Giovanni Battista Podestà (1895–1976) was born in the village of Torre Pallavicina, in northern Italy. He was the only son in a peasant family with twelve daughters. His father died when Giovanni was still a child and he suddenly had to leave school and go to work as an assistant stonemason. He was called up at the outbreak of the First World War in 1915 and was sent to the front, where he was captured by the Austro-Hungarians. At the end of the conflict, it soon became clear the land owned by his mother was insufficient to support the family, and Podestà was forced to join the drift away from the countryside. He ended up in Laveno, a town on the shores of Lake Maggiore, where he reluctantly accepted a three-year engagement as a Carabiniere policeman. After his marriage in 1925, he took up a job as a labourer in a ceramics factory, while at the same time beginning to paint and sculpt. When the Second World War broke out, Podestà was enrolled in the territorial service in the Parma area. The experience left even deeper scars than the previous war, and thereafter Podestà spent the vast majority of his free time on his art: multi-coloured sculptures and works in high relief made out of a paste consisting of sawdust, glue, and plaster, which Podestà fashioned with metal wires. His works include sundry cultural, popular, and religious motifs borrowed from the Middle Ages, a period that was an ideological and iconographic benchmark for him. In this way he found an effective means of protesting against the loss of spiritual values in a materialistic industrial society, condemning modern life and idealising the past. In his view, he was only partly the author of his own work, since he regarded his imagination as deriving from a higher power that he sometimes called nature and sometimes God. He wore clothes and accessories he made himself and turned his own body into a medium of expression. Every Good Friday, Podestà would carry his cross to a shrine at the top of a hill, which he climbed on foot. He pursued his artistic endeavours until his wife's death in 1974.

Very little is known about **Catherine de Porada** (1891–1985). She was born in Berlin into a family of intellectuals and grew up surrounded by avant-garde artists. In fact she took lessons in painting and drawing right up until her marriage at the age of twenty. Then, following her divorce several years later, she left Germany for Paris, where she began to take an interest in fashion. She lived in Monaco during and after the Second World War, then moved to Vence to work in Galerie Chave. At that point she started to paint pictures with a symbolist and mystical content, exploring the themes of paradise and reincarnation.
Neuve Invention Collection*

Jane Ruffié (1887–1976) was born in the Haute-Garonne region of France. She completed her high school studies but never entered a profession. She began taking an interest in the occult at the age of eighteen. However, it was the death of her second son, in 1913, that led to her receiving her first messages from spirits. The first of these occurred when her husband was called up; worried for him, she sought help from her dead son, who seems to have predicted that her husband would return home with a wound in his left ankle, which is what duly happened. From that point she lost no opportunity to get in touch with him again. From 1914, she transcribed her 'communications', which she received as automatic writing, in the form of messages, poems, or telegrams. Sometimes words simply appeared just by rubbing a graphite pencil on a piece of paper. These isolated words were then fitted by intuition into complete sentences. Just before the Second World War, Ruffié began for the first time to draw. She was once again guided by her son, whom she suspected must have been a great painter in a previous life, and felt confident that her creativity was suitably underpinned. Her works were at first drawn with her eyes shut, producing a mass of interlocking abstract motifs that created shapes suggesting cocoons that are in the process of metamorphosing. From Ruffié's perspective, her art played a clairvoyant role in her life, providing answers to the questions she asked.

F. Sedlak (?–?). Next to nothing is known about this artist, apart from the fact that he was probably Czech. His drawings, dating from 1924–25, are technically wonderful and were bought in 1985 from a second-hand goods dealer, who was unable to give any information about them. They are certainly permeated by a certain mysticism due to their random, visionary qualities and might be associated with a spiritualist environment. The various titles refer to the Bible, dreams, or death.
Neuve Invention Collection*

Victor Simon (1903–1976) was born in the small commune of Bruay-en-Artois, in the Pas-de-Calais region of France. When he was a child, he witnessed a simulated procession along a Way of the Cross that affected him profoundly, leaving him with a strong religious sensibility. His nights were filled with fantastical visions in which holy temples jostled with sarcophagi. After he had finished school, he went to work in the mines with his father until he found a job in the accounts department, which he left in 1930 to open a bar-tobacconist's. Simon took a serious interest in theology and philosophy and studied Christ's doctrine assiduously, while at the same time attending experimental séances that explored the paranormal. In 1933, he received a message from the hereafter that galvanised him into producing his first monumental canvas, entitled *Resurrection*. Guided by spirits and exploiting his personal experiences, his most profound visions took shape through the act of artistic creation, and a series of divinatory paintings followed. His geometric compositions, often painted using pure colours, contain Christian figures, religious architecture, and ancient Egyptian, Hindu, or Byzantine symbols. Simon's works were accompanied by writings and conferences on spiritualism. In 1947, he became honorary president of the Circle of Experimental and Scientific Spiritualism of Paris. He painted a hundred or so small canvases and around ten large ones between 1933 and 1971 that testify to the community of ideas, beliefs, and practices that were typical of the period.
Neuve Invention Collection*

Palmerino Sorgente (1920–2005) was born in Umbria, Italy. He was called up during the Second World War and immigrated to Canada in 1954 with his wife and children, of which they were to have thirteen altogether. They settled in an Indian reservation at first, before moving into a building in rue Notre-Dame in Montreal. He worked as a janitor, cook, and factory worker. In 1970, an accident at work forced him to take early retirement. As he was housebound, he set up a shop selling religious artefacts on the ground floor of his home, which also served as a workshop and a place to sleep and pray. Sorgente, self-proclaimed 'Pope Palmerino, servant of Jesus', made rosaries decorated with coloured plastic baubles, paintings based on religious images, as well as papal tiaras and headwear. Some of these hats were over a metre high and were made from red adhesive tape and cloth and decorated with sequins and beads. Several of these pieces were lent to the fashion designer Christian Lacroix for one of his fashion shows. Sorgente also used photography so he could take part in person in the role of the pope. He would place his portraits all around his home, creating what were in effect small altars. In one series of images, Sorgente created the fourteen Stations of the Cross, miming Christ's path right up to the Crucifixion. By reinterpreting Catholic imagery in his own way, he sought to convey a divine message of peace and love through his creations, and to encourage piety in those around him. A fire broke out in the building where he lived and worked in December 2000, destroying thirty years of his work and leaving him with serious burns. Discharged from the hospital at eighty-two years of age, the 'miraculously spared' never lost his faith and diligently resumed his work.

Ni Nyoman Tanjung (1930–2020) was born in Banjar Saren Kauh, a village in eastern Bali, Indonesia. Her family were poor peasants and she never learned to read or write, having never gone to school. She spent her time weaving and was particularly fond of dancing and singing. When the island was occupied by the Japanese during the Second World War, she was forced into slave labour. She married in around 1950 and gave birth to four children, three of whom met premature deaths. Following the death of her youngest daughter, she began to behave eccentrically. Further violent, traumatising episodes, such as a series of massacres associated with a coup in 1965, affected her profoundly and worsened her already fragile mental state. She gradually pulled away from the real world, while still managing to meet her daily needs and look after her house. In the mid 1990s she moved into a cottage in a village coconut grove with her husband. Secure in her new dwelling and at the age of seventy, she began to explore her artistic potential. Ni Tanjung started by gathering branches and volcanic stones with a vaguely anthropomorphic shape and painted human faces on them, often adding a torso and two arms. She then arranged these stones so as to create a terraced pyramid structure. This extraordinary construction, which was around ten metres long at its height, is a de-facto altar dedicated to ancestors. She would pay regular visits to place some flowers, leaves, or everyday objects on it as offerings. She would then perform a sort of ritual in which she burned incense, danced, and sang, while making meaningless proclamations. Once she had become bedridden, in 2009, Ni Tanjung found a different outlet for her creative energy. Working in her little windowless room, she would take a piece of chalk and draw figures on scraps of paper and then cut them out and arrange them behind her so she could observe them indirectly using a mirror.

Theodor Wagemann, aka **Theo** (1918–1998), was born in a village near Aachen, in Germany, where his father worked as a stonemason. When he was twelve, he became involved in food smuggling along with other people in the village. One day he and his accomplices were caught by customs officers, who tried to frighten the boys off by firing their guns. Following this incident Theo became withdrawn, retreating into almost total silence and spending more and more time on long walks in the forest. It seems it was also at this time that he started drawing caricatures of clergymen, as well as collecting all sorts of objects found in rubbish bins in the area. During the Second World War, when Hitler introduced his policy of exterminating the mentally ill, Theo escaped the gas chamber thanks to his family doctor, but was subjected to enforced sterilisation. By the time he was sixty-one he was seriously deranged and his family decided to have him committed. He then devoted himself enthusiastically to drawing, using greaseproof paper salvaged from the institution's kitchen and coloured pencils or felt-tip pens given him by his relatives. He made hundreds of drawings, consisting mainly of narrative scenes based on Biblical or political themes, which he would then send to his family or hide under his bed. His works on religious subjects are extremely dense and executed with painstaking attention to detail, often depicting episodes from the Gospels, Jesus's childhood, or events following the Crucifixion. Theo's art expresses an undoubtedly profound faith anchored in the circumstances of his youth and the narrow village environment in which he grew up. The influence of Roman Catholicism is ubiquitously present in his work, as the objects of worship he collected and carefully preserved testify.

We know virtually nothing regarding the life of **Johann Thoma** (1875–1948) except that he was Swiss and lived in Zurich. The predominant feature of his large number of paintings is their esoteric, symbolist flavour in the best tradition of the early twentieth-century Anthroposophists. His work is accompanied by writings in which the author presents his art as follows: 'They express the oscillations and vibrations of the soul of a man who has matured through life's struggles. His creative thoughts have provided him with a reassuring vision. He invites his peers to persevere and to believe in the soul's struggle to perceive the light's power right until the final victory.'
Neuve Invention Collection*

Jeanne Tripier (1869–1944) was born in Paris, France. The daughter of a wine merchant, she spent her childhood in the country with her grandmother, then settled in the Montmartre district of Paris. For several years, she lived with an American, whose son she adopted, and worked in a department store in Boulevard Barbès. At the age of fifty-eight she developed a passion for spiritualism and soothsaying and began exploring her abilities as a medium. And indeed, she soon received her first messages from the hereafter. Under the influence of these spirits, she wrote, drew and made crochet works. Her newfound talents monopolised her to the extent that she gradually stopped going to work. However, Jeanne Tripier was also becoming psychologically unstable, and in 1934 she was admitted to a psychiatric hospital in the Paris region, which did nothing to curb her enthusiasm. She considered all her creations to be supernatural revelations and developed a view of the world that she transcribed in a series of 'messages'. These described her interplanetary journeys, in which she was at times Joan of Arc, at others an 'essential medium' or 'planetary enforcer'; her mission being to prepare the ground for the 'Last Judgment on Earth'. In her writings she frequently added small drawings in black, purple, or blue ink, to which she occasionally added hair dye, nail polish, or medicines. Over the years, these 'snapshots', as she called them, began to cover more and more of the writing until they took over the entire sheet. Her numerous embroideries also take the form of messages, in the same way as clairvoyance tables, lucky charms, or astrological medallions. Through her works, Jeanne Tripier thus attempts to give visible form to the ectoplasm that flows through the universe and in which she so fervently believes. In 1948, four years after her death, more than three hundred drawings, some fifty embroideries, and around two thousand pages of writing were found in a bag and preserved.

Gustave Le Goarant de Tromelin, aka **comte de Tromelin** (1850–1920), was born in Brest, France. In 1868 he obtained his diploma from the naval academy and embarked on an exemplary career, even being awarded the order of Knight of the Legion of Honour. He was a groundbreaking scientist, skilled mathematician, and member of the Academy of Sciences, where he was noted for his distinguished contributions to the study of electricity and magnetism. At the age of fifty-three, the Count of Tromelin retired from the navy, moved to the South of France, and turned to the exploration of the supernatural, having signed a pact with his spirits in which he swore eternal loyalty. As a result, he was convinced that the drawings he started to make responded entirely to their will. He described his first pencil drawings, executed at night, as 'semi-median', where the spirits were fully responsible for most of the works. These works are completely automatic and reveal spectral figures that emerge through the rubbing of the pencil. He subsequently established greater control and experimented with other systems, in which hidden worlds materialise that are inhabited by bizarre figures and creatures. By 1907 the Count of Tromelin was convinced that these divine powers were seeking to entrust him with a mission and teach him a new doctrine, so he published a book entitled *Critique des mystères de l'univers* (Criticism of the Mysteries of the Universe). The reader learns that there are several kinds of spirits — the builders, the giants, floating spirits, and even spirits of love. Not all of them were well intentioned; some even tried to pressure the count into committing suicide, something he was determined to resist.

Virtually all we know of this figure is his first name, **Victor-François** (?–?). He was institutionalised with a diagnosis of 'schizophrenia' and suffering from mystical delusions. Between 1900 and 1915 he made a series of drawings in India ink depicting crucifixions, accompanied by writing recording in particular sentences handed down by courts. Victor-François would also cut pieces of coloured paper that he would stick to the backs of the drawings making them visible through the sheet, thus highlighting the main subject of the composition, such as God's face or body.

August Walla (1936–2001) was born in Klosterneuburg, Austria. Following his father's death he was raised by his mother. He was a solitary child and his schoolmates often made fun of him. From the age of nine he began to suffer from sleeplessness and spent his days filling exercise books with scribbles. He was placed in a special class at school, and, although he completed his education, he failed to find an apprenticeship. By the age of sixteen he was threatening to commit suicide and to burn down his house, so he was sent to a psychiatric hospital. He was later moved to the Maria Gugging hospital, near his hometown, where he was allowed to stay with his mother, with whom he had a morbidly close relationship. In 1986 he was admitted to the House of the Artists (Haus der Künstler), a creative workshop attached to the institution. Having written and drawn since his childhood, August Walla was at last free to devote himself totally to these activities and to fill his whole living environment with words and symbols. Drawing and writing are always intimately interwoven in his compositions, which gather together gods, demons, saints, prophets, and miracle-workers, as well as a number of imaginary deities. He was fascinated by the materiality and plastic nature of words, as he was by every kind of emblem. The sometimes-enigmatic writing and symbols that he adds to his human figures — always depicted frontally in hieratic portentousness — are an integral part of the author's personal mythology. To drive the point home, he frequently inserts himself in his pictures in the form of an all-powerful and at the same time malevolent god. To Walla, his works were like charms with the power to protect him against dangers — particularly spirits, humans, and death.

Maria Wnek (1922–2005) was born into a large family in Olszanka, Poland. After their home was burnt down, the family had to find alternative accommodation and this led to several moves and a disordered life. As a result Wnek received only four years of schooling, on top of which she was naturally diffident and found it hard to mix with other members of the village community. She was already working as a cook in a military barracks as a teenager. She then found an office job and later worked for a dairy company. However, an accident in the factory in 1960 forced her to retire young, and from then on she received a disability pension. She started to travel widely, taking all her possessions with her on every trip. She was mentally fragile and her family frequently sent her to the psychiatric hospital in Kobierzyn, where she was eventually diagnosed with schizophrenia. She began producing art in a community cultural centre at the age of forty. Her faith had always been a bulwark in her life — indeed, she had even made a vow of chastity when she was sixteen — and religion now became the source of her favourite themes. The vast majority of the figures she painted were drawn from the Bible and the history of Christianity, including the Virgin Mary, Christ, and many saints, which she portrayed in an artistically free manner. Many of these works have an explanatory text, often on the back, where she records her view of the world and her moral values. Through her paintings, Wnek takes on the role of God's messenger, warning mankind of rampant moral corruption and a swathe of looming dangers, especially concerning the risk of war and the consequences of the nuclear tests that were common at the time.

Adolf Wölfli (1864–1930) was born in the canton of Bern, in Switzerland. At the age of seven he was abandoned by his father, a stonemason who had become an alcoholic. The boy remained alone with his mother for two years, before being placed in peasant families where he worked as a goatherd and farmhand. Later he became a woodcutter, then a labourer. Wölfli's youth was beset with trials, including unrequited love, an experience that left him profoundly shaken. In 1890, he was arrested for sexually assaulting two children and was imprisoned. On his release, he committed the offence again and, in 1895, diagnosed with schizophrenia, he was admitted to the hospital in Waldau, near Bern, where he remained until his death. At the age of thirty-five, Wölfli started to draw, write, and compose music from morning till night. Extremely agitated by nature, he would calm down when given some chewing tobacco and coloured pencils. His works were collected by a psychiatrist at Waldau, Dr Walter Morgenthaler, who recognised his talent and later published a seminal study of Wölfli's work in 1921 with the intention of presenting the art of a schizophrenic on its own terms and not merely as a symptom of mental illness. Wölfli's output was colossal. It includes 25,000 pages strewn with graphic compositions done with crayons, but also collages, literary creations, and musical scores, which together amount to an extraordinarily rich and complex oeuvre. In a fictional illustrated biography that he put to music, *The Legend of St Adolf*, he tells the story of his imaginary alter ego he calls 'Saint', 'Great-Great-God', 'Genie', and sometimes 'Adolf II'. By reinventing history, geography, music, even religion, Adolf sought a way of coming to terms with creation, space, and eternity itself. During the last two years of his life, he worked tirelessly on a final book entitled *Funeral March*, filling thousands of pages and marking the culmination of his poetic vision.

Henriette Zéphir (1920–2012) was born in Montmaurin, near Toulouse, France. She was brought up by her grandparents until she was eleven and said she had a happy childhood, close to nature. After completing elementary school, her dream of taking up technical drawing at an art school was thwarted by her parents, who did not want her to grow up in what was then an essentially male environment. So she tried to find a way of moving out of the family home, and found the opportunity when she met her future husband in 1940. The couple had planned to settle in Martinique after their wedding, but the boat on which they were traveling was blocked at Casablanca in Morocco. When her husband was drafted, Henriette Zéphir spent two and a half years alone in Morocco before being repatriated to France in around 1945. The couple settled in the Antilles in 1947, but then divorced. Henriette and her two children took up residence first in Nice and subsequently in Castres. Then, in 1961, at the age of forty-one, Henriette felt the presence of her 'Guide', Don Carlos, for the first time. She considered this figure to have been her companion in a previous life and obeyed when ordered by him to fill an exercise book with mysterious signs and symbols for a full seven days. Seeing this as an 'initiatory apprenticeship', Henriette Zéphir continued to follow the spirit's instructions and those of others without demur. Under their influence, she produced several dozen pencil and ballpoint pen works, whose fine, sinuous lines look like guipure lacework. 'Don Carlos' also dictated a prayer and told her to perform 'work on souls' that would ensure that the 'energies' Henriette considered fundamentally beneficial would be widely distributed. She didn't see her work as art, but more a way of recording, giving physical form to these energies through a drawing's lines and colours.

* **Neuve Invention Collection**
Jean Dubuffet originally entitled this collection *Collections Annexes*, renaming it *Neuve Invention* in 1982. It gathers toge ther artists whose social and psychological break with conventional art was less radical than the stance taken by Art Brut, although their works nonetheless lie on the margins of the orthodox art scene.

Selected Bibliography

Aloïse [Corbaz]
BOULANGER, Christophe, LOMBARDI, Sarah, MARINI-JEANNERET, Pascale et al. *Aloïse Corbaz en constellation*. Exh. Cat. Villeneuve d'Ascq: LaM - Lille Métropole Musée d'art moderne, d'art contemporain et d'art brut, 2015.

LOMBARDI, Sarah, MARINI, Pascale. *Aloïse*. Exh. Cat. Lausanne: Collection de l'Art Brut, 2012.

PORRET-FOREL, Jacqueline, MUZELLE, Céline, LOMBARDI, Sarah et al. *Aloïse. Le ricochet solaire*. Exh. Cat. Milan/ Lausanne: 5 Continents Editions/ Collection de l'Art Brut/Musée cantonal des Beaux-Arts, 2012.

PORRET-FOREL, Jacqueline, MUZELLE, Céline, DANCHIN, Laurent et al. *Aloïse: comme un papillon sur elle*. Exh. Cat. Shiga: Haretari-Kumottari, 2009.

PORRET-FOREL, Jacqueline. *Aloïse et le théâtre de l'univers*. Genève: Skira, 1993.

DUBUFFET, Jean. 'Haut art d'Aloïse', *L'Art Brut* 7 (1966), p. 7.

PORRET-FOREL, Jacqueline. 'Aloïse et son théâtre', *L'Art Brut* 7 (1966), p. 23.

Noviadi Angkasapura
PEIRY, Lucienne. *Ecrits d'art brut: graphomanes extravagants*. Paris: Le Seuil, 2020.

ANNE DE HEY! 'Angkasapura', *Hey! Modern Art and Pop Culture* 3, season 2. Paris: Hey! Modern Art and Pop Culture Publishing, 2019, p. 66.

MORRIS, Randall. *Angkasapura*. Exh. Cat. New York: Cavin-Morris Gallery, 2015.

RIGEADE, Pascal. *Outsiders d'Indonésie*. Exh. Cat. Bègles: Musée de la Création Franche, 2015.

Charles Boussion
LESPINASSE, Philippe. 'Charles Boussion, ou le culte des images', *L'Art Brut* 26 (2018), p. 17.

SAUMADE, Pascal. 'Charles "Cako" Boussion', *L'Art Brut* 26 (2018), p. 11.

SENDREY, Gérard. 'Charles "Cako" Boussion', *Création Franche* 19. Bègles: Musée de la Création Franche, 2000, p. 19.

Marie Bouttier
BOCCARD, Anne de. *La place de l'art brut sur le marché de l'art aujourd'hui*. Lyon: Anne de Boccard, 2016.

LUSARDY, Martine, CARDINAL, Roger, THÉVOZ, Michel et al. *Art spirite, médiumnique, visionnaire: messages d'outre-monde*. Exh. Cat. Paris: Halle Saint Pierre/Hoëbeke, 1999.

Fleury-Joseph Crépin
BOULANGER, Christophe, FAUPIN, Savine (ed.). *Lesage, Simon, Crépin: peintre, spirites & guérisseurs*. Exh. Cat. Villeneuve d'Ascq: LaM - Lille Métropole Musée d'art moderne, d'art contemporain et d'art brut, 2019.

BRETON, André. 'Joseph Crépin', *Almanach de l'Art Brut: fac-similé*. Lausanne/Milan: Collection de l'Art Brut/ 5 Continents Editions, 2016, p. 131.

BRETON, André, DUBUFFET, Jean, BOUNOURE, Vincent et al. *Fleury Joseph Crépin 1875–1948*. Exh. Cat. Paris: Idée'Art, 1999.

DUBUFFET, Jean. 'Joseph Crépin', *L'Art Brut* 5 (1965), p.44.

Antonio Dalla Valle
TOSATTI, Bianca, CALICELLI, Cristina, ROSI, Daniela et al. *Antonio Dalla Valle: connessioni*. Exh. Cat. Sospiro: Fondazione Istituto Ospedaliero di Sospiro onlus, 2016.

TOSATTI, Bianca. 'Antonio Dalla Valle', *L'Art Brut* 22 (2007), p. 101.

PONTIGGIA, Paola, TOSATTI, Bianca. *Antonio Dalla Valle*. Parma: Figureblu, 2007.

GOSETTI, Claudia, DALLA TORRE, Paolo. *Antonio Dalla Valle: il ritorno*. Exh. Cat. Mezzana: Comune di Mezzana, 2006.

TOSATTI, Bianca. 'Antonio Dalla Valle', *Ecritures imagées = Schreibbilder = La scrittura come immagine*. Exh. Cat. Bruxelles: Art en Marge, 2004.

Fernand Desmoulin
SI AHMED, Djohar. *Pour une psychanalyse des expériences exceptionnelles: comment penser le paranormal* (revised, expanded and corrected edition). Paris: L'Harmattan, 2014.

GAILLARD, Christophe, BERST, Christian, RAINER, Arnulf. *Fernand Desmoulin:*

leçons des ténèbres. Exh. Cat. Paris: Galerie Christophe Gaillard, 2009.

Lanoux, Jean-Louis, Si Ahmed, Djohar, Decharme, Bruno et al. *Fernand Desmoulin: oeuvres médiumniques (1900–1902)*. Paris: abcd, 2002.

Janko Domsic

Hercule, Lucie. *Inventer Janko Domsic : comment l'absence de sources sur un auteur est-elle utilisée pour construire un discours esthétique et analytique sur son oeuvre et le faire émerger comme une des figures majeures de l'Art Brut?* Paris: Lucie Hercule, 2019.

Berst, Christian. *Janko Domsic: le mécanicien celeste*. Paris: Lelivredart, 2008.

Lanoux, Jean-Louis. 'Pantins et pentacles : l'apocalypse selon Domsic', *abcd: le journal* 2 (2005), [n.p.].

Steiner, Béatrice. 'Barbe bleue, tornade rouge', *abcd: le journal* 2 (2005), [n.p.].

[Domsic, Yanko]. 'Textes de Domsic', *L'Art Brut* 16 (1990), p. 12.

Fitting, Zora. 'Janko Domsic', *L'Art Brut* 16 (1990), p. 5.

Philippe Ducollet Michaëlef

Le Venimeux, Phil. *Vénus putride sainte*, Marseille: Le Dernier Cri, 2015.

Elijah

Cox, Wayne, Poupeye, Veerle, Barnett-Davidson, Monique, *Spiritual Yards : home grounds of Jamaica's intuitives : selections from the Wayne & Marene Cox Collection*, Exh. Cat., [Kingston], National Gallery of Jamaica, 2016.

Sciiader, Eira, Schader, Angela. 'Eli Jah', *Raw Vision* 40 (2002), p. 40.

Schader, Eira, Schader, Angela. 'Eli Jah', *L'Art Brut* 20 (1997), p. 32.

Morris, Randall. *Redemption Songs: The Self-Taught Artists of Jamaica*. Winston-Salem: Winston-Salem State University, 1997.

Minnie Evans

Puchner, Edward M. 'Faith and War: Wilmington, World War II and the Art of Minnie Evans', *Raw Vision* 92 (2016), p. 32.

Coker, Gylbert. 'Elephants Around the Moon: The Art of Minnie Evans', *Raw Vision* 11 (1994), p. 28.

Lovell, Charles. *Minnie Evans: Artist*. Greenville: Wellington B. Gray Gallery/East Carolina University, 1993.

Kahan, Mitchell D. *Heavenly Visions: The Art of Minnie Evans*. Exh. Cat. Raleigh: North Carolina Museum of Art, 1986.

Howell Starr, Nina. 'The Lost World of Minnie Evans', *The Bennington Review* (1969), p. 41.

Jill Galliéni

Berst, Christian, Baudouin, Philippe. *Au-delà : aux confins du visible et de l'invisible*. Exh. Cat. Paris: Christian Berst Art Brut, 2019.

Finaz, Marie. 'Jill Gallieni : tussen poppen, gebeden en dansende zielen', *Out of Art* 21 (2016), p. 40.

Gentil, Antoine. 'Les prières de Jill Galliéni', *Du visible à l'invisible*. Exh. Cat. Paris: Centre d'Etude de l'Expression, 2013.

Monnin, Françoise. 'Jill Galliéni: ouvrages de drame', *Artension* 30 (2006), p. 32.

Madge Gill

Dutton, Sophie (ed.). *Madge Gill by Myrninerest*. London: Rough Trade Books, 2019.

Jeanneret, Marie-Hélène. *Madge Gill*. Lausanne: Ides et Calendes, 2017.

De Novellis, Mark (ed.). *Madge Gill: Medium & Visionary*. Exh. Cat. Twickenham: Orleans House Gallery, 2013.

Bandelier, Gaël. *L'art médiumnique de Madge Gill, Augustin Lesage, Jeanne Tripier : entre protocoles spirites et pratiques artistiques*. Goumoens-le-Jux: Gaël Bandelier, 2008.

Cardinal, Roger. 'Madge Gill', *L'Art Brut* 9 (1973), p. 5.

Jules Godi

Henrion, Françoise, Collin, Brigitte. 'Conversation autour d'un dîner provençal avec Mme Godi', *Bulletin Art en Marge* 31 (1991), p. 11.

Duchein, Paul. 'Jules Godi', *L'Aracine : musée d'art brut*. Neuilly-sur-Marne: L'Aracine, 1988, p. 57.

Fengyi Guo

Güiraldes, Rosario, Hoptman, Laura, Ryor, Kathleen M. et al. *Guo Fengyi: To See from a Distance*. Exh. Cat. New York: The Drawing Center, 2020.

Peiry, Lucienne. 'Guo Fengyi', *L'Art Brut* 23 (2011), p. 7.

Berst, Christian, Zheng, Rong. *'Guo Fengyi: une rhapsodie chinoise*. Exh. Cat. Paris: Lelivredart, 2010.

Guyodo

Braziel, Jana Evans. *Riding with Death: Voudou Art and Urban Ecology in the Streets of Port-au-Prince*. Jackson: University Press of Mississippi, 2017.

Decharme, Bruno. *Art Brut live: abcd collection*. Exh. Cat. Paris: abcd, 2015.

Cuzin, Régine et al. *Haïti, deux siècles de création artistique*. Exh. Cat. Paris: RMN, 2014.

GORDON, Leah. 'The sculptor of grande rue', *Raw Vision* 65 (2008), p. 44.

Werner Hertig
SZEEMANN, Harald (ed.). *Visionäre Schweiz*. Exh. Cat. Aarau: Verlag Sauerländer, 1991.

TROSSMANN, Max. 'Von der Kraft, die aus der Erde kommt', *Luzerner Neuste Nachrichten* 12 (1982), p. 4.

Augustin Lesage
BOULANGER, Christophe, FAUPIN, Savine (ed.). *Lesage, Simon, Crépin: peintre, spirites & guérisseurs*. Exh. Cat. Villeneuve d'Ascq: LaM - Lille Métropole Musée d'art moderne, d'art contemporain et d'art brut, 2019.

NOTTER, Annick, DEROEUX, Didier, THÉVOZ, Michel et al. *Augustin Lesage 1876–1954*. Exh. Cat. Paris: Philippe Sers, 1988.

OSTY, E. [Eugène]. 'Aux confins de la psychologie classique et de la psychologie métapsychique: M. Augustin Lesage, peintre sans avoir appris', *Revue Métapsychique* (January-February 1928).

Raphaël Lonné
DANCHIN, Laurent. *Aux frontières de l'art brut: un parcours dans l'art des marges*. Paris: Lelivredart, 2013.

RASLE, Josette, DELACAMPAGNE, Christian, HERNANDEZ LEON, Juan Miguel. *Raphaël Lonné: Dibujos*. Exh. Cat. Madrid: Circulo de Bellas Artes, 2007.

HAFFNER, Gilbert, RASLE, Josette, RAYNAL, Henri et al. *Deux postiers singuliers: Raphaël Lonné, Pascal Verbena*. Exh. Cat. Paris: Musée de la Poste, 2005.

DUBUFFET, Jean. 'Les dessins médiumniques du Facteur Lonné', *L'Art Brut* 1 (1964), p. 49.

Simone Marye
GOUTAIN, Pauline. *Simone Marye (1890–1961): une oubliée de l'Art Brut* (research paper). Paris: Pauline Goutain, 2010.

DUBUFFET, Jean. 'Simone Marye', *L'Art Brut* 6 (1966), p. 103.

Joseph Moindre
THÉVOZ, Michel. 'L'Orient: réalité et fantasme', *Silex* 13 (1979), p. 96.

DUBUFFET, Jean. 'Moindre l'Egyptologue', *L'Art Brut* 4 (1965), p. 101.

Edmund Monsiel
THÉVOZ, Michel. 'Edmund Monsiel', *L'Art Brut* 11 (1982), p. 52.

BÓL, Katarzyna. 'The Eyes of Edmund Monsiel: The Intensely Detailed Work of a Classic Art Brut Creator', *Raw Vision* 98 (2018), p. 26.

Marc Moret
ROMAN, Pascal. *Art Brut et psychanalyse: une exploration du processus de création*. Lausanne/Gollion: Collection de l'Art Brut/Infolio, 2018.

PEIRY, Lucienne. *Inextricabilia: enchevêtrements magiques: art brut, art sacré, art contemporain, art rituel africain*. Exh. Cat. Paris: La Maison Rouge, 2017.

LESPINASSE, Philippe. 'Les reliquaires acérés de Marc Moret', *Art Brut fribourgeois*. Exh. Cat. Lausanne/Fribourg: Collection de l'Art Brut/La Sarine, 2008, p. 41.

Michel Nedjar
WEISS, Allen S., *Figure against form: the dolls of Michel Nedjar*, Berlin, K. Verlag, 2021.

WEISS, Allen S. 'Michel Nedjar, ou le destin de la poupée', *L'Art Brut* 26 (2018), p. 69.

WEISS, Allen S., BOUHOURS, Jean-Michel, BARBANT, Corinne et al. *Michel Nedjar: introspective*. Exh. Cat. Villeneuve d'Ascq: LaM - Lille Métropole Musée d'art moderne, d'art contemporain et d'art brut, 2017.

CARDINAL, Roger. 'Michel Nedjar', *L'Art Brut* 16 (1990), p. 73.

Ataa Oko
LOMBARDI, Sarah, TSCHUMI, Regula, PEIRY Lucienne, et al., *Ataa Oko Addo*, Biel, edition clandestin, 2021.

PEIRY, Lucienne, TSCHUMI, Regula, LOMBARDI, Sarah et al. *Ataa Oko*. Exh. Cat. Lausanne/Gollion: Collection de l'Art Brut, Infolio, 2010.

TSCHUMI, Regula. *Les trésors enterrés des Ga: l'art des cercueils au Ghana*. Berne: Benteli, 2010.

Michael Pankoks
GINTNERE, Ula, SMITE, Edvarda, SVITINS, Guntis. *Mikelis Pankoks*. Liepaja: Liepajas Vestures un Makslas Muzejs, 1992.

THÉVOZ, Michel. 'Michel Pankoks', *L'Art Brut* 17 (1992), p. 140.

GINTNERE, Ula. *Mikelis Pankoks*. Liepaja: Liepajas Vestures un Makslas Muzejs, 1992.

STUTZER, Beat, SCHERRER, Jakob, THÉVOZ, Michel. *Michael Pankoks*. Exh. Cat. Chur: Bündner Kunstmuseum, 1991.

Laure Pigeon
MAURER, Lise. 'Laure Pigeon, la femme plume', *L'Art Brut* 25 (2014).

LAPORTE, Dominique Gilbert. *Laure ou la prosopopée du ciel*. Genève: Furor, 1982.

DUBUFFET, Jean. 'La double vie de Laure', *L'Art Brut* 6 (1966), p. 69.

Giovanni Battista Podestà

Peiry, Lucienne. 'Podestà: The Middle Ages in the Twentieth Century', *Raw Vision* 45 (2003), p. 43.

Peiry, Lucienne, Thévoz, Michel, Beaud, Paul et al. *Podestà*. Exh. Cat. Lausanne/Fribourg: Collection de l'Art Brut/Musée d'art et d'histoire, 2003.

Peiry, Lucienne. 'Giovanni Battista Podestà', *L'Art Brut* 15 (1987).

Catherine de Porada

Galerie Alphonse Chave. *Les paradis de Catherine de Porada*. Vence: Galerie Alphonse Chave, 1986.

Jane Ruffié

Edelmann, Michèle. 'Jane Ruffié', *L'Art Brut* 9 (1973), p. 51.

F. Sedlak

Thévoz, Michel, Roulin, Geneviève, Peiry, Lucienne et al. *Neuve Invention: collection d'oeuvres apparentées à l'Art Brut*. Lausanne: Collection de l'Art Brut, 1988.

Victor Simon

Boulanger, Christophe, Faupin, Savine (ed.). *Lesage, Simon, Crépin: peintre, spirites & guérisseurs*. Exh. Cat. Villeneuve d'Ascq: LaM - Lille Métropole Musée d'art moderne, d'art contemporain et d'art brut, 2019.

Simon, Victor. *Du moi inconnu au Dieu inconnu*. Paris: Dervy, 1957.

Simon, Victor. *Du sixième sens à la quatrième dimension*. Arras: Société d'éditions du Pas-de-Calais, 1955.

Simon, Victor. *Reviendra-t-il?* Arras: Société d'éditions de presse, 1953.

Palmerino Sorgente

Rousseau, Valérie. *When the Curtain Never Comes Down: Performance Art and the Alter Ego*. Exh. Cat. New York: American Folk Art Museum, 2015.

Rousseau, Valérie. *Vestiges de l'indiscipline: environnements d'art et anarchitectures*. Gatineau: Société du Musée canadien des civilisations, 2007.

Ni Nyoman Tanjung

Djaou, Lucas. *Ni Tanjung: la reine du volcan Agung*. Exh. Cat. Paris: Galerie Patricia Dorfmann, 2020.

Breguet, Georges. 'Ni Tanjung, de l'autel de l'aube aux esprits de la nuit', *L'Art Brut dans le monde*. Exh. Cat. Gollion/Lausanne: Infolio/Collection de l'Art Brut, 2014, p. 48.

Blanche, Patrick. 'A Lonely Passion. For Ni Tanjung, Only Gods Have Meaning', *Raw Vision* 59 (2007), p. 42.

Breguet, Georges. 'Ni Tanjung', *L'Art Brut* 22 (2007), p. 41.

Theo Wagemann (known as Theo)

Küppers, Robert, Schaden, Christoph. 'Theo', *Raw Vision* 44 (2003), p. 30.

Küppers, Robert, Grinten, Franz Joseph van der, Schaden, Christoph et al. *Theo: eine Retrospektive*. Exh. Cat. Bedburg-Hau: Stiftung Museum Schloss Moyland, 2003.

Küppers, Robert. 'Théo', *L'Art Brut* 17 (1992), p. 102.

Johann Thoma

Bertholet, Edouard, Thomas, Maurice. *Guide de l'exposition «Les mystères de l'inspiration»: peintures, dessins, sculptures*. Exh. Cat. Lausanne: Société vaudoise d'Etudes Psychiques, 1932.

Jeanne Tripier

Berglund, Astrid, Herrera Gómez, Sierra, Javier. *Jeanne Tripier: creación y delirio = Jeanne Tripier: creation & delirium*. Exh. Cat. Madrid: La Casa Encendida, 2018.

Maurer, Lise. *Le «remémoirier» de Jeanne Tripier: travaux d'asile*. Ramonville Saint-Agne: Erès, 1999.

Tripier, Jeanne. *Premier cahier: de l'ordre des messages: mai 1935* (afterword by Lise Maurer). Corbières: Harpo &, 1999.

Dubuffet, Jean. 'Messages et clichés de Jeanne Tripier', *L'Art Brut* 8 (1966), p. 5.

Le comte de Tromelin

Dichter, Claudia, Golinski, Hans Günter, Krajewski, Michael et al. *The message: Kunst und Okkultismus = The message: art and occultism*. Exh. Cat. Köln: Verlag der Buchhandlung Walther König, 2007.

Edelmann, Michèle. 'Les dessins «semi-médianiques» du comte de Tromelin', *L'Art Brut* 9 (1973).

Comte de Tromelin. *Les mystères de l'univers: réponse aux "énigmes de l'univers" de Haeckel*. Paris: Bibliothèque Universelle Beaudelot, 1907.

Victor-François

Edelmann, Michèle. 'Victor-François', *L'Art Brut* 9 (1973), p. 121.

August Walla

Feilacher, Johann, Berst, Christian. *August Walla: ecce Walla*. Exh. Cat. Paris: Christian Berst Art Brut, 2015.

Feilacher, Johann (ed.). *Walla!* Salzburg: Residenz Verlag, 2012.

Navratil, Léo. *August Walla: sein Leben und seine Kunst*. Nördlingen: Greno, 1988.

Maria Wnek

Wilk, Sonia. *Maria Wnek: malarka slynna po calym swiecie*. Katowice: Muzeum Slaskie, 2011.

Bihalji-Merin, Oto, Tomasevic, Nebojsa-Bato. *L'art naïf: encyclopédie mondiale*. Belgrade/Lausanne: Edita Jugoslovenska Revisa, 1984.

Krasinska, Ewa. *Wnek*. Krakow: Muzeum etnograficzne w Krakowie, 1983.

Adolf Wölfli

Wölfli, Adolf. *Courte autobiographie* (with CD). Nantes: Lenka lente, 2014.

Zemankova, Terezie (ed.). *Adolf Wölfli: Creator of the Universe*. Exh. Cat. Revnice/Prague: Arbor Vitae/abcd, 2012.

Faupin, Savine, Boulanger, Christophe, Baumann, Daniel et al. *Adolf Wölfli Univers*. Exh. Cat. Villeneuve d'Ascq: LaM - Lille Métropole Musée d'art moderne, d'art contemporain et d'art brut, 2011.

Spoerri, Elka, Baumann, Daniel (ed.). *Adolf Wölfli: Schreiber, Dichter, Zeichner, Componist*. Basel: Wiese, 1996.

Morgenthaler, Walter. *Ein Geisteskranker als Künstler*. Bern/Leipzig: Springer, 1921; reissued Vienna/Berlin: Medusa-Verlag, 1985.

Morgenthaler, Walter. 'Adolf Wölfli' (introduction by Henri-Pol Bouché), *L'Art Brut* 2 (1964).

Ries, Julius von. *Über das Dämonisch-Sinnliche und den Ursprung der ornamentalen Kunst des geisteskranken Adolf Wölfli*. Bern: Paul Haupt, 1946.

Henriette Zéphir

Zanzi, Anic, Lombardi, Sarah, Bouillet, Alain, *Henriette Zéphir*. Exh. Cat. Lausanne: Collection de l'Art Brut, 2017.

Berst, Christian, Bouillet, Alain. *Henriette Zéphir: une femme sous influence*. Exh. Cat. Paris: lelivredart, 2011.

Bouillet, Alain. 'Straight from the Soul: Henriette Zéphir', *Raw Vision* 72 (2011), p. 34.

Dubuffet, Jean. 'Notes au sujet des dessins d'Henriette Zéphir', *L'Art Brut* 14 (1986), p. 71

Photo Credits

All the photographs of the works were taken by collaborators of Atelier de numérisation, Ville de Lausanne: Charlotte Aebischer, Jean-Marie Almonte, Sarah Baehler, Amélie Blanc, Danielle Caputo, Arnaud Conne, Morgane Détraz, Garance Dupuis, Claudine Garcia, Marie Humair, Olivier Laffely, Giuseppe Pocetti, Kevin Seisdedos, Caroline Smyrliadis.

Except for the pages mentioned below:

p. 12: Giovanni Battista Podestà carrying the cross he made, April 1968
Photo: Helen Sager. Archives de la Collection de l'Art Brut, Lausanne

Palmerino Sorgente in his shop in rue Notre-Dame in Montreal,
c. 1980, Quebec (Canada)
Palmerino Sorgente on a leg of his Way of the Cross,
c. 1980, Quebec (Canada)
Unknown photograph. Palmerino Sorgente Collection

Giovanni Battista Podestà
La Croix, n.d., mixed media, 210 x 70 cm
Photo: Claude Bornand. Podestà Alluvion, Laveno Mombello Collection

p. 17: Antonio Dalla Valle, Cremona (Italy), 2005
Photo: Mario Del Curto

p. 18: Marc Moret with his high reliefs stored in a room in his farm, 2003
Photo: Mario Del Curto

pp. 48, 99: Claude Bornand

p. 121: Henri Germond

pp. 138–139: Willy Blanchard

This book has been published in connection with the exhibition *Croyances*, 5e biennale de l'Art Brut, held at the Collection de l'Art Brut, Lausanne, from 17 December 2021 to 1 May 2022.

EXHIBITION

GENERAL COMMISSIONER
Sarah Lombardi
Director, Collection de l'Art Brut

EXHIBITION COMMISSIONER
Anic Zanzi
assisted by Josefina Stewart-Harris

THE BOOK

CONCEPT AND COORDINATION
Anic Zanzi

BIOGRAPHIES
Josefina Stewart-Harris

BIBLIOGRAPHY
Vincent Monod

ICONOGRAPHY
Anic Zanzi and Vincent Monod

ADMINISTRATION
Catherine Borgeaud Papi

Collection de l'Art Brut
Av. des Bergières, 11
CH-1004 Lausanne
www.artbrut.ch

5 CONTINENTS EDITIONS

ART DIRECTION
Annarita De Sanctis

LAYOUT
Camelia Bezzola

EDITORIAL COORDINATION
Elena Carotti
in collaboration with
Lucia Moretti

TRANSLATIONS
Julian Comoy

EDITING
Charles Gute

COLOUR SEPARATION
Pixel Studio, Bresso, Italy

ISBN: 978-88-7439-970-3

5 Continents Editions
Piazza Caiazzo, 1
20124 Milan, Italy
www.fivecontinentseditions.com

Distributed by ACC Art Books throughout the world, excluding Italy. Distributed in Italy and Switzerland by Messaggerie Libri S.p.A.

Printed in Italy in November 2021
by Tecnostampa - Pigini Group Printing Division, Loreto – Trevi, Italy for
5 Continents Editions, Milan

Collection de l'Art Brut thanks:
Georges Breguet, Shari Cavin (Cavin-Morris Gallery), Sophie Dutton, Johann Feilacher (Art Brut KG), Philippe Lespinasse, Jean-David Mermod (Association Aloïse), Paola Pontiggia (La Manica Lunga), Valérie Rousseau, Paul Ruffié, Pascal Saumade (La Pop Galerie), Succession Marc Moret, Succession Giovanni Battista Podestà, Succession Henriette Zéphir.

Expressions of appreciation to
Noviadi Angkasapura, Philippe Ducollet-Michaëlef, Jill Galliéni, Guyodo, and Michel Nedjar.

Expressions of gratitude are extended to the supporting partner: Fondation Jan Michalski, Retraites populaires.

FONDATION JAN MICHALSKI POUR L'ECRITURE ET LA LITTERATURE

Retraites Populaires

Cover: reelaboration of a detail from the work by Philippe Ducollet-Michaëlef published at page 14 of this book